T0293211

Endorsements for Productivity Reimagined

"In *Productivity Reimagined*, author Jacob Stoller draws on both the wisdom of the ages and the most modern ideas of workplace psychology using compelling examples to dispel the myths of what it means to be engaged and productive. He reveals a superior way of thinking that all of us can aspire to and draw on. If you've been stuck for a while now, this is the book to get you on the road to new levels of results."

—Richard Sheridan,
CEO, Chief Storyteller, Menlo
Innovations; author of *Joy, Inc.* **and**
Chief Joy Officer

"*Productivity Reimagined* paints a picture of the incredible outcomes possible when you create environments of caring, collaboration, and continuous improvement. Stoller's latest is an exceptional guide for anyone looking to improve output as well as the lives in their span of care!"

—Bob Chapman,
CEO, Barry-Wehmiller; author of
Everybody Matters: The Extraordinary Power of Caring for Your People Like Family

"*Productivity Reimagined* author Jacob Stoller does a stellar job of connecting the concept and the practices of productivity and identifying the misunderstandings that so often cause productivity initiatives to be counterproductive."

—John Shook,
Senior Advisor, Lean Enterprise
Institute; Chairman, Lean
Global Network

"Stoller provides an exceptional blueprint for companies striving to solve the productivity puzzle and empower their workforce to excel in today's global economy."

—Kerry Siggins,
CEO, StoneAge; author of
The Ownership Mindset

"Imagine a business book that you can't put down! Stoller is engaging, comprehensive, and concise as he draws on a wealth of real-world examples to bring the transformative ideas of Deming and Ohno to a new generation of leaders and practitioners."

—**Kelly Allan,**
Deming Practitioner and Principal,
Kelly Allan Associates, Ltd.

"Whether you're a CEO, manager, or entrepreneur, this book will change how you view productivity and provide the roadmap to achieving it in a way that benefits everyone. Don't miss reading it."

—**Michael Ballé,**
co-founder of Institut Lean France;
author of *The Gold Mine Trilogy*

"Jacob Stoller is a true myth buster as he navigates us through evolved mindsets and practices that show how productivity works in many contexts from the manufacturing shop floor to addressing social justice in a community."

—**Jason Schulist,**
Chief Flourishing Officer, Generative
Local Community Institute

"In *Productivity Reimagined*, Stoller uses excellent examples to expand the vision of what productivity means. I think it will be an important contribution to the discussion about productivity."

—**Orest Fiume,**
retired CFO, Wiremold; co-author of
Real Numbers: Management Accounting in
a Lean Organization

PRODUCTIVITY
REIMAGINED

PRODUCTIVITY REIMAGINED

Shattering Performance Myths to Achieve Sustainable Growth

JACOB STOLLER

WILEY

Copyright © 2025 by Jacob Stoller. All rights reserved.

Published by John Wiley & Sons, Inc., Hoboken, New Jersey.
Published simultaneously in Canada.

No part of this publication may be reproduced, stored in a retrieval system, or transmitted in any form or by any means, electronic, mechanical, photocopying, recording, scanning, or otherwise, except as permitted under Section 107 or 108 of the 1976 United States Copyright Act, without either the prior written permission of the Publisher, or authorization through payment of the appropriate per-copy fee to the Copyright Clearance Center, Inc., 222 Rosewood Drive, Danvers, MA 01923, (978) 750-8400, fax (978) 750-4470, or on the web at www.copyright.com. Requests to the Publisher for permission should be addressed to the Permissions Department, John Wiley & Sons, Inc., 111 River Street, Hoboken, NJ 07030, (201) 748-6011, fax (201) 748-6008, or online at http://www.wiley.com/go/permission.

Trademarks: Wiley and the Wiley logo are trademarks or registered trademarks of John Wiley & Sons, Inc. and/or its affiliates in the United States and other countries and may not be used without written permission. All other trademarks are the property of their respective owners. John Wiley & Sons, Inc. is not associated with any product or vendor mentioned in this book.

Limit of Liability/Disclaimer of Warranty: While the publisher and author have used their best efforts in preparing this book, they make no representations or warranties with respect to the accuracy or completeness of the contents of this book and specifically disclaim any implied warranties of merchantability or fitness for a particular purpose. No warranty may be created or extended by sales representatives or written sales materials. The advice and strategies contained herein may not be suitable for your situation. You should consult with a professional where appropriate. Further, readers should be aware that websites listed in this work may have changed or disappeared between when this work was written and when it is read. Neither the publisher nor authors shall be liable for any loss of profit or any other commercial damages, including but not limited to special, incidental, consequential, or other damages.

For general information on our other products and services or for technical support, please contact our Customer Care Department within the United States at (800) 762-2974, outside the United States at (317) 572-3993 or fax (317) 572-4002.

Wiley also publishes its books in a variety of electronic formats. Some content that appears in print may not be available in electronic formats. For more information about Wiley products, visit our web site at www.wiley.com.

Library of Congress Cataloging-in-Publication Data is Available:

ISBN 9781394244379 (Cloth)
ISBN 9781394244393 (ePDF)
ISBN 9781394244386 (ePub)

Cover Design: Wiley
Cover Image: Courtesy of the Author
Author Photo: Courtesy of the Author

SKY10082131_081624

Contents

Preface

People by nature want to be productive. The urge to work towards something that matters is the force that gets us up in the morning, keeps us going despite obstacles, and compels us to do better than we did last time. When we see the impact of our productivity, it gives us the pride and satisfaction that we've made the world a little bit better.

Companies want their people to be productive as well. Engaged, productive workforces enable companies to overcome barriers and constantly get better at what they do. Productivity growth allows companies to deliver their products and services faster, cheaper, and better; provide better jobs; and contribute to the betterment of their surrounding communities.

There's a disconnect, however, between people's productive inclinations and what actually happens in most companies.

Most people grasp this intuitively. The feeling is that even if they derive considerable enjoyment from their chosen line of work, they are stymied by all the "other stuff" they have to deal with.

The "other stuff" isn't just necessary drudgery like filling out expense reports. It's also the adversarial relationships, fear of speaking out, poor coordination, lack of support, and having to do things just to please the boss.

Disengagement is widespread. In the US, according to Gallup, only 30% of employees reported they were engaged in their work in 2023. Furthermore, 17% reported that they are actively disengaged.[1]

This disconnect causes companies to be much less productive than they should be, and that has severe implications for our economy. The GDP growth that governments report, as will be shown in Chapter 1, is becoming less and less reflective of true productivity growth. In other words, we are in a productivity crisis.

The question is, if people want to be productive and more productivity is needed, what prevents companies from connecting the dots?

The short answer is that the conventional command-and-control management approach tends to divide people and get them working at cross purposes. High productivity, on the other hand, calls for changing this approach to create a workplace culture where all employees participate in improving work processes towards a common purpose.

The command-and-control approach is deeply entrenched, and consequently companies that have achieved this transformation are the exception rather than the rule.

I have had hundreds of conversations over the years with leaders and business experts on why this transition is so difficult to make. On the surface, the conventional methods are reinforced by business school curricula, accounting principles, corporate policy documents, and decades of tradition.

My conversations have revealed that there are deeper reasons. I've learned that there's a widely held belief system that makes it difficult for even the most forward-thinking leaders to abandon the status quo. This belief system, I've concluded, rests on five widely held business myths that fly in the face of reality yet are regarded as immutable fixtures. We will cover these in detail in this book.

They are:

1. **The Myth of Segmented Success**: The productive resources of a company can be organized as a collection of independent components. The whole equals the sum of the parts.
2. **The Myth of the Bottom Line**: The financials tell us everything we need to know about productivity.
3. **The Top-Down Knowledge Myth**: Managers always have the answers and keep workers productive by telling them what to do.
4. **The Myth of Sticks and Carrots**: Workers are most productive when motivated by rewards and threats.
5. **The Myth of Tech Omnipotence**: Technology is the answer to all productivity problems.

The outdated thinking behind these myths has saddled companies with an organizational structure that stymies team productivity and fails to deliver sustainable growth.

ABOUT THIS BOOK

This book shows how overcoming common barriers to productivity can launch companies on a path to sustainable growth. The evidence comes from my conversations with leaders who have countered the traditional rules of top-down command-and-control management to build highly productive continuous improvement cultures in their organizations.

Their companies have achieved excellent financial results while treating and compensating their people well, delivering quality products to their customers, maintaining positive relationships with their communities, and doing their part to conserve our planet. These companies are role models for an approach to business where everybody wins.

The subjects interviewed for this book were influenced by various schools of thought. One is the Lean approach that was pioneered by Toyota. This has been widely promoted and was the subject of my previous book *The Lean CEO*.

Others attribute their success to the principles of W. Edwards Deming, who was a major contributor to Lean methods and an insightful critic of the current school of management.

The people who confront the myths, however, are not limited to those who follow these established methods. You will meet leaders who apply principles of psychology, engineering, and systems theory, and their own personal values to create alternatives to conventional management practices.

A word about remote work. There is wide debate about the individual productivity of knowledge workers who, since the outset of the COVID pandemic, have worked from home. However, as this book demonstrates, it's team productivity that provides the game-changing results that derive from continuous improvement, and that requires the establishment and maintenance of a collaborative work culture. This is why some knowledge companies, several of which are featured in this book, maintain in-person work environments and expect employees to be there at least some of the time.

Another popular news subject is the influence of technology on productivity. Technology is a powerful enabler, but as we discuss in Chapter 7, it often fails to deliver the productivity gains that people expect and is not, despite what many believe, a magic bullet for solving productivity problems.

The book is divided into four parts.

Part One: The Productivity Challenge outlines the productivity problem and the methods for countering it. **Chapter 1: Productivity, Real and Imagined** shows how despite GDP growth and rising stock prices, companies have failed to deliver the productivity growth necessary to raise the standard of living. **Chapter 2: The Productivity Toolkit** provides an overview of the management techniques that a select group of companies have deployed to achieve high productivity through continuous improvement. These methods provide a reference point for the case studies that follow.

Part Two: Shattering the Five Myths addresses each of the five myths through interviews with leaders who have confronted them. **Chapter 3: The Myth of Segmented Success** shows how companies have used a systems approach to dismantle destructive elements of their traditional command-and-control management policies and create work environments of teamwork and high engagement. **Chapter 4: The Myth of the Bottom Line** provides examples of how companies have moved away from reliance on financial reports to reconnect with the productive forces in their organizations. **Chapter 5: The Top-Down Knowledge Myth** explains how companies have enabled workers to initiate improvements using their workplace knowledge. **Chapter 6: The Myth of Sticks and Carrots** describes how companies have built strong work cultures by creating caring work environments where every employee feels safe and appreciated. **Chapter 7: The Myth of Tech Omnipotence** shows how the productive power of technology is often over-estimated, and how companies have used technology to complement the strengths of humans.

In **Part Three: Business Strategies for a Better World**, we look at how leaders are confronting the myths to create a better world. **Chapter 8: Productive Strategies for Preserving our Planet** describes how innovative engineers are countering the myths with a holistic system-based approach to reducing companies' impact on the planet. **Chapter 9: A Prescription for Better Healthcare** shows how healthcare innovators are taking on the myths as they fight to mitigate the current healthcare crisis. **Chapter 10: An Entrepreneurial Approach to Breaking the Poverty Cycle** explains how anti-poverty activists are countering conventional myth-based thinking to enable people to initiate projects that lift their communities out of poverty. In

Chapter 11: Rethinking the Meaning of Disability, we see how an agency is confronting the stereotypes that conventional management imposes on people with disabilities. In **Chapter 12: Joy at Work**, we hear from a company that has crushed the myths in order to create an engaging office environment that instills joy at work.

Part Four: Moving Forward, Chapter 13: We Can Do This! presents the case for moving forward, with an overview of steps that companies have taken to transition their conventional management system to one based on employee engagement and continuous improvement.

People want to be productive. Yet most employees are managed according to an outdated management system that poses countless barriers to productivity.

We have both a problem and an opportunity. It's time to shatter the myths and get down to the business of engaging our workforces to create economic growth that benefits everybody.

Acknowledgments

This book is based on the insights and wisdom of many people who are passionate about their work and generous about sharing their knowledge. Learning from them has been a privilege and a pleasure.

I'd like to start with a special thank you to Orry Fiume, retired CFO of Wiremold, who patiently instructed me on the fine points of defining and measuring productivity, introduced me to other sources, and gave me valuable feedback on the manuscript.

I'm very grateful to a number of people who gave advice and encouragement. Kevin Cahill, CEO, and Kelly Allan, Associate Trustee, of the W. Edwards Deming Institute opened doors for me through introductions and gave advice that helped make Deming's ideas a strong focal point in this book.

Rich Sheridan, CEO of Menlo Innovations, helped frame my thinking long before I began this project, and provided thoughtful input for this book.

Thanks also to Jon Miller and Stan Herschorn, who have been generous with their time and attention as the book developed.

Karl Wadensten, CEO of Vibco, connected me with a number of CEOs early on, and provided input and useful feedback.

John Toussaint, Executive Chairman at Catalysis, has been particularly encouraging and helpful with introductions and insights.

On a personal note, I would like to give special thanks to my family for their ongoing support and encouragement. Thanks to my late father, Claude Stoller, and my mother, Nan Black. Big appreciation to my sisters, Tia and Lisa Stoller, and my brother-in-law, Drew Detsch, who attended to family issues in my stead while I was heads-down writing this book. Thanks to my sons, Mark, Jon, and Ben Stoller, and Mark's partner Carolyn Prouse for their cheerleading as this project unfolded, and to my wonderful wife, Susan, who went the extra mile, giving me feedback and encouragement while keeping the home fires burning.

I owe special thanks to my editors at Wiley, Stacey Rivera and Judith Newlin. It was in my discussions with Judith that the title and outline for *Productivity Reimagined* first took shape, and I am grateful for her expert feedback and ongoing support.

And while we're talking about the book business, a big shout-out to my literary agent John Willig, a true professional who knows the industry inside out, is generous with his time and his knowledge, and kept me on track.

Thanks finally to all the sources who granted me interviews, patiently answered my questions, and provided either direct input or advice:

Bob Chapman, Chairman, and Mary Rudder, Senior Director, Communications, at Barry-Wehmiller; Henry Mintzberg, Professor at McGill University; Bruce Taylor, Founder and President at Enviro-Stewards; Stephen Dixon, Environmental Consultant; Michael Bremer, VP of Awards at the Association for Manufacturing Excellence; Mark Graban, Author and Senior Advisor at Kai Nexus; John Shook, Senior Advisor at the Lean Enterprise Institute; Blair Fix, Author of the blog Economics from the Top Down; Harry Moser, President at Reshoring Initiative; Alexander Wong, Professor at the University of Waterloo; Ben Armstrong, Executive Director, Industrial Performance Center, at MIT; Cliff Ransom, President at Ransom Research; Karen Martin, President at TKMG; Michael Balle, Author and Consultant; Nick Katko, President and Owner at BMA; Joseph E. Swartz, former Administrative Director of Business Transformation for Franciscan St. Francis Alliance of Mishawaka, Indiana; Rich Sheridan, CEO and Chief Joy Officer at Menlo Innovations; Charlie Murphy, Senior VP at Turner Construction; Nick Bauer, CEO at Empire Group; Sam McPherson, Founder at McPherson Business Advisors; Mike Scala, CEO at Western Shelter Systems; Mark Borsari, CEO at Sanderson-MacLeod; Ian Beert, Vice President at Partake Foods; Jim Huntzinger, President and Founder of Lean

Frontiers; Mauricio Miller, Founder at Center for Peer-Driven Change; Randy Kesterson, Executive Advisor; Gary Brooks, Partner at Strategic Development Services; Alex Krutz, Partner at Patriot Industrial Partners; Cheryl Jekiel, independent HR Consultant; Scott Curtis, CEO at Training Within Industry (TWI); Jason Schulist, Founder at Generative Local Community Institute; Stephen Moore, VP of Lean Enterprise and Quality at Parker Hannifin; Bernie Rosauer, President at Wisconsin Compensation Rating Bureau; Carl Livesay, General Manager, Mercury Plastics; Mandeep Kaundal, Director at Results Washington; Larry Coté, President at Lean Advisors; Abe Eshkenazi, CEO at Association of Supply Chain Management; Anders Billeso Beck, Vice President at Universal Robots; Jamie Flinchbaugh, Founder at JFlinch; Patrice Baumann, Chief Integrated Supply Chain Officer at Enersys; Mirka Wilderer, CEO at AqueoUS Vets (AV); Nora Genster, Senior Director of Development at Northwest Center; Gene Boes, CEO at Northwest Center; Paul Nyhan, Public Relations and Editorial Manager at Northwest Center; Pierluigi Tosato, CEO at Bouvard; Steven Haedrich, Owner at New York Label & Box Works; Gary Peterson, Executive VP of Supply Chain and Production at O.C. Tanner Company; Jeffery Varney, Director, Advisory Services at American Productivity & Quality Center (APQC); Ken Snyder, Executive Director at the Shingo Institute; Tom Ehrenfeld, Senior Editor at Lean Enterprise Institute; Sherm Moreland, CEO at Design Group; Greg Guy, CEO at Air Force One; Jason Lippert, CEO at Lippert; Paula Marshall, CEO at Bama Foods; Cheryl Nester Wolfe, CEO at Salem Health; Dan McDonnell, Principal at Gemba Coach LLC; Evan Mitchell, Music Director of the Kingston Symphony; and Kerry Siggins, CEO at StoneAge.

PART
ONE

The Productivity Challenge

1

Productivity, Real and Imagined

On August 19, 2019, the Business Roundtable, a Washington, DC–based association of chief executive officers, issued a statement signed by 181 CEOs of major US corporations titled "Statement on the Purpose of a Corporation." The new document affirmed a "fundamental commitment" to customers, employees, suppliers, and communities.

"Each of our stakeholders is essential," the statement concludes. "We commit to deliver value to all of them, for the future success of our companies, our communities and our country."[1]

This document superseded previous declarations that companies should only advance the interests of shareholders.

While there's evidence that this was little more than a PR gesture,[2] the statement was perhaps the most significant acknowledgment by corporate leaders that our economy is not delivering on the dream of shared prosperity.

We have always believed that our system of free enterprise generates a rising tide that lifts all boats. Accordingly, businesses grow by providing goods and services that customers choose to buy. That growth leads to more and better jobs and higher profits that are reinvested to grow the business further. Companies then ensure their long-term viability by helping their suppliers succeed, supporting their surrounding communities, and treating our planet with respect. Positive outcomes for all stakeholders flow naturally from this virtuous cycle.

The Business Roundtable statement reflects a widely held sentiment that this virtuous cycle is what the public should expect from a growing economy. However, what we're seeing is very different – a kind of growth that is creating economic inequality, marginalizing communities, and rocketing us towards a climate catastrophe.

This book argues that there is a better way, and that the key is a bold new approach to productivity. In the pages ahead, you will read about companies that have thrived by turning productivity into a competitive advantage and, in the process, have helped their employees, customers, and communities thrive as well.

First, let's take a look at how productivity is defined and measured. Then we'll consider how truly meaningful productivity growth has actually been absent in much of the economic growth that we've seen.

WHAT IS PRODUCTIVITY?

The Bureau of Labor Statistics (BLS) is the federal government agency that tracks employment-related statistics in the US. In conjunction with the Bureau of Economic Analysis (BEA), which calculates and tracks the GDP, BLS gathers, analyzes, and reports on labor economics and statistics in the private and public sectors.

BLS defines productivity in three instructional videos on its website.[3] The first, *What is Productivity?* features Beth, an entrepreneur who makes and sells birdhouses. By improving her production methods and her skills, the video shows, Beth can increase the number of birdhouses she can make in an hour, thereby increasing her productivity.

"Productivity is a measure of economic performance that indicates how efficiently inputs are converted into output," says the narrator. "Growth in productivity is measured by dividing the change in output over time to the change in inputs over time."

$$Productivity\ Growth = \frac{Change\ in\ Output}{Change\ in\ Inputs}$$

By increasing her productivity, the video tells us, Beth can improve her standard of living, enabling her to either make more money, or work shorter hours. The key here is that Beth improves the business by finding ways to become more efficient, and higher productivity is the outcome. Productivity growth, therefore, is the kind of growth that allows businesses, and by extension society, to become more prosperous.

"The standard of living for the country as a whole depends on improvement in overall productivity," says the narrator. "Historically, productivity growth has led to higher wages for workers and higher profits for businesses."

The video, however, doesn't take into account expenses other than labor and materials. In the second video, *Ingredients for Total Factor Productivity*, Clementine, the owner of a small bakery, brings some additional costs into the equation. These include energy, equipment, capital, and outside services such as bookkeeping. The result is a ratio called Total Factor Productivity (TFP).

$$Total\ Factor\ Productivity\ Growth = \frac{Change\ in\ Output}{Change\ in\ Combined\ Inputs}$$

Notable here is that Clementine has included what are called fixed costs, which do not vary with the amount of output being produced. The carrying costs for a new oven, for example, are now included as inputs. This can get very tricky, as we will see in Chapter 4.

However, the goal is still the same: to continually increase the output in relation to the input by producing more efficiently. "Gains in Total Factor Productivity indicate productivity growth in output that is not a result of using more inputs," says the narrator. "It is a measure of production efficiency."

We are then told how improving TFP is the productive force that drives the US economy forward. "Understanding total productivity growth for the US economy helps us understand how the nation can produce more without using more resources," says the narrator. "These advances in efficiency help keep the US competitive."

A third video, *Understanding Unit Labor Costs*, takes us to a sandwich shop where dozens of employees engage in various food preparation activities. If the staff work diligently and improve their skills, they will increase their output, improving the company's profits and its capacity to pay workers and provide benefits.

$$Labor\ Productivity\ Growth = \frac{Change\ in\ Output}{Hours\ Worked}$$

The ratio, however, is not a measure of how efficient the sandwich shop is – the costs with respect to Total Factor Productivity still apply. Furthermore, while a more capable staff can help, Labor Productivity Growth can be affected by factors that have nothing to do with the capabilities or diligence of the workers, such as variations in sales volume or disruptions due to equipment failure. As we will see, this point is often overlooked.

MAKING THE NUMBERS USEFUL

The productivity metrics described in the videos are some of the most commonly used ratios for tracking the performance of a business. The main idea here is that these numbers can be useful in guiding decisions about how to improve profitability in order to finance further growth.

In real-world scenarios, however, there are many complicating factors that can make these ratios either difficult to calculate or, in some cases, misleading. Two of these are worth noting at this point.

The first one is quality. Let's say Beth decides to accelerate production for the spring season when birdhouses are in most demand. Faster is better according to the equation, but what if working faster has created some quality problems? These may be very difficult for Beth to detect and may not become visible until months after the product was sold. By the time the complaints start coming in, it could be too late for Beth to save her reputation. So that apparent productivity growth might come with strings attached. This problem will come up repeatedly in the pages ahead.

Another factor is the influence of changing prices on the productivity ratio. If material costs have gone up for Beth, that output over input ratio is going to decline, showing lower productivity. Furthermore, a competitor might enter the picture, forcing Beth to reduce her prices, and reducing the productivity number. A key aspect of tracking productivity accurately in order to improve it, therefore, is the ability to isolate it from price fluctuations. We'll discuss this in detail in Chapter 4.

PRODUCTIVE OR NONPRODUCTIVE GROWTH?

The suggestion on the BLS website that overall improvements in the general standard of living can be attributed to businesses like Beth's is certainly appealing. But is the link real or imagined?

Let's look at how productivity is measured at a national level. Essentially, as its website explains, BEA starts with the GDP, and applies weighing formulas that compensate for inflation and other variations. National productivity statistics, therefore, are dependent on how the GDP is derived and calculated. In fact, many economists and journalists simply use the GDP as the standard for determining labor productivity.

The assumption that a rising GDP truly reflects the accumulated result of businesses producing faster, better, or cheaper without adding resources, however, is highly questionable. The problem is that many of the contributors to GDP growth have nothing to do with productivity as defined by the BLS.

"Economists take income and call it productivity, and that's the idea behind the GDP. But if that assumption is wrong, then everything falls apart," says Blair Fix, a political economist and author of the blog "Economics from the Top Down."

Let's look at the ways in which that assumption breaks down.

Moving the Goal Posts

Changes made over the years in methods for calculating the GDP have made economic growth appear stronger than it actually is. "The Bureau of Economic Analysis (BEA) has changed its methods multiple times over the years," says Fix, "and it's always biased towards higher growth. One example is changing how it calculates the base year for prices. In the 1990s it changed over to a method for that called chain weighting, which ended up showing higher growth. Then there are what are called imputations. The classic example of that is that if I own a home, I don't add to the GDP by paying rent. And so, in response to that, BEA imputes the price I paid myself for rent, and that goes into the GDP. There are a whole bunch of those."

In a study titled "Imputing Away the Ladder," authors Jacob Assa and Ingrid Harvold Kvangraven conclude that revisions to the System of National Accounts (SNA), which is used to derive the GDP, "have had the effect of boosting the GDP of the West relative to the rest of the world."[4]

A key contributor to this has been the addition of the Finance, Insurance and Real Estate sectors (FIRE), as the study explains:

"In 1993 and then again in 2008, there were reforms to the SNA that led to significant changes of the location of the so-called production boundary, which determines what is included in GDP and what is not. Many economic activities – financial intermediation, research and development and the production of weapons – were previously excluded from GDP as either non-productive or as constituting productive inputs to other outputs (hence deducted as intermediate consumption). The inclusion of these economic sectors in the production boundary since 1993 and 2008 has added disproportionately to the GDP of developed countries, which have in recent decades specialised in these activities and moved away from traditional pillars of development such as manufacturing and infrastructure-related services."[5]

Under the new rules, the US continued to look rosy even as it hollowed out its manufacturing sector, while China, with its much smaller financial sector proportionally, looked less so, even as it amassed a growing trade surplus with the US.

The Rise of Financialism

The inclusion of banking activity not only biased the GDP to show higher growth, but in some cases included inputs that were harmful to the economy. For example, a new concept called financial intermediary services indirectly measured (FISIM) was added to the SNA in 1993. Accordingly, the high-risk loans that led to the crash of 2008 were judged to be contributing high value to the economy.

"In banking, spreads increase when risk rises," explains *Financial Times* journalist David Pilling in his book *The Growth Delusion*. "If a banker judges you quite unlikely to repay a loan, she will raise the interest rate to reflect the higher risk of default. So, from an accounting point of view, the riskier the portfolio of loans the greater the contribution to growth. Put another way, the more catastrophically irresponsible bankers are, the more we judge them to be helping the economy to grow."[6]

This change in focus has also caused banks to relinquish their traditional role of lending to businesses, causing their influence on real productivity growth to decline. "Back in the early 1980s, when financialization began to gain steam, commercial banks in the United States provided almost as much in loans to industrial and commercial enterprises as they did in real estate and consumer loans; that ratio stood at 80 percent," wrote *Financial Times* journalist Rana Foroohar in her book *Makers and Takers.* "By the end of the 1990s, the ratio fell to 52 percent, and by 2005, it was only 28 percent. Lending to small business has fallen particularly sharply, as has the number of start-up firms themselves."[7]

The Rent Effect

Another contributor to the gap between productivity growth and GDP growth is the growing market power of companies to charge what economists call rents, or markups in excess of what they would earn from growing their productivity in competitive markets. One study showed that markups for publicly traded companies in the US had nearly tripled between 1980 and 2014.[8] Another found that 80% of the equity value of public companies is attributed to the ability of these companies to extract rents.[9]

"Thus, at best, rents are unhelpful to growth and efficiency, at worst, harmful," wrote Nobel Prize–winning economist Joseph Stiglitz. "They can be harmful because they distort the economy, because they 'crowd out' the kind of 'good' economic activity that is the basis of true wealth creation."[10]

Noninclusive Growth

The changes in SNA practices have also placed more emphasis on investment income as a proportion of the GDP.

"The majority of Americans share in economic growth through the wages they receive for their labor, rather than through investment income," wrote Jay Shambaugh and Ryan Nunn in the *Harvard Business Review.* "Unfortunately, many of these workers have fared poorly in recent decades. Since the early 1970s, the hourly inflation-adjusted wages received by the typical worker have barely risen, growing only 0.2% per year. In other words, though the economy has been growing, the primary way most people benefit from that growth has almost completely stalled."[11]

Accordingly, much of the GDP growth does not reflect a rise in the standard of living for the average citizen.

"It isn't the amount of money that a society has in circulation, whether dollars, euros, beads, or wampum," wrote Nick Hanauer and Eric Beinhocker in their paper "Capitalism Redefined." "Rather, it is the availability of the things that create well-being—like antibiotics, air conditioning, safe food, the ability to travel, and even frivolous things like video games. It is the availability of these 'solutions' to human problems—things that make life better on a relative basis—that makes us prosperous."[12]

DIRE WARNINGS

In June 1980, TV journalist Lloyd Dobyns made a sober prediction. "Unless we solve the problem of productivity," he said, "our children will be the first generation in the history of the United States to live worse than their parents."[13]

The remark came at the close of a two-hour documentary titled *If Japan Can Then Why Can't We?* It was reported to be one of the most widely watched documentaries in television history. The program was aired amidst growing concern about the rising dominance of Japanese manufacturing and the corresponding failure of US companies to keep pace with rising global standards.

A number of events during the 1970s accelerated the crisis. In 1973, the OPEC embargo effectively signaled the end of the cheap energy era that had fueled America's industrial juggernaut. The national debt had soared during the Vietnam War, and when the vets came home, unemployment soared to 8%.

To make matters worse, the post–World War II boom that had propelled America's unparalleled growth had begun to slow. Inflation began to spiral out of control, and the American standard of living started to decline. At the same time, the stock market declined steadily. The Big

Four American automotive producers continued to lose ground, and by the end of the decade, Chrysler had declared bankruptcy, and Ford and General Motors were losing money.

What Japan had done, the show demonstrated, was outproduce American companies by more than a two-to-one ratio with far less equipment, technology, natural resources, and expertise. The big difference was that Japanese companies were using superior management practices to create far more value added per worker than the American factories. And they were doing it with the active participation of millions of employees who were committed to an "all-hands-on-deck" effort to improve productivity.

Furthermore, the Japanese automakers were producing products of higher quality than what Americans were used to. The ongoing joke at the time was that you could drive a Toyota or a Honda down the highway and not hear the wind whistling around the doors. The cars also needed fewer trips to the repair shop and retained a higher resale value.

The concluding 12 minutes of the program featured an interview with Dr. William Edwards Deming, who at the time was virtually unknown in the US but was a household name in Japan. As a leading authority on statistical quality control, Deming had been sent by the US government to assist in Japan's post–World War II reconstruction.

Deming's work in Japan had begun with a series of lectures to electronics manufacturers. He wasn't, however, simply putting forward statistical equations and methods, nor was he presenting quality as a siloed discipline for quality inspectors. For Deming, this was about building a participatory culture around quality, which he saw as inseparable from productivity.

The events were so successful that a Japanese business group, the Union of Japanese Scientists and Engineers (JUSE), began to sponsor his lectures. Deming returned numerous times, and his lectures and seminars drew thousands of participants. Inspired by his methods and those of his colleague Joseph Juran, JUSE created a quality standard called "Total Quality Control," which became the basis of a national quality movement in Japan.

Hundreds of companies joined JUSE and began to pursue excellence using the TQC standard, and millions of people joined ad hoc work groups to make incremental improvements in their workplaces. Efforts ranged from pursuing productivity targets, savings in energy, or reducing defects and rework. In 1951, JUSE honored Deming by creating a prize in his name for companies that achieved excellence in TQC. Hundreds of companies engaged in comprehensive long-term improvement projects to win this highly coveted prize.

During the documentary, Dobyns asked Deming what Japan's secret was. Deming said there was no secret. "I think people here expect miracles," he said. "American management thinks they can just copy from Japan – but they don't know what to copy!"[14]

What was needed, Deming said, was a complete rethinking of how corporations were run. "There's no one coming out of a school of business that ever heard of the answers that I'm giving your questions – or probably even thought of the questions," he told Dobyns.[15]

PRODUCTIVITY GETS SIDELINED

Concerns about the failure of US companies on the global stage led to a Congressional investigation on the productivity crisis. The resulting report, titled "The Productivity Slowdown: Causes and Policy Responses," was published by the Congressional Budget Office (CBO) in 1981, and framed the problem as a major crisis. "Many Americans feel that the US economy performed dismally during the 1970s," reads the introduction, "and that the outlook for the future is not much better."[16]

Deming's revelations, and a widespread fear of Japan's growing dominance, spurred a flurry of activity that culminated in what is known as the quality movement. Companies invested in their quality departments, and many of Deming's statistical methods became standard practice.

In the late 1980s, methods used in Japan were introduced in the US by Shingijutsu – a consulting organization made up of former leaders at Toyota-affiliated companies. Toyota had been actively sharing its methods with its suppliers, essentially letting the cat out of the bag. These methods, which included just-in-time (JIT) and other concepts, became collectively known as "Lean." Today, Lean methods are widely used in companies throughout the world, including in many companies you will meet later on in this book.

Toyota has also become the role model of continuous improvement that many companies aspire to. There are dozens of books about Toyota and its leadership philosophy, and the company's methods are widely proliferated through courses, seminars, and industry events. Toyota also shares its methods widely through its affiliate not-for-profit educational organization, the Toyota Production System Support Center (TSSC).

Through the ensuing quality movement, organizations made significant improvements. Workplaces became safer, defects decreased, and production lines became less wasteful. Just-in-time, the practice of ordering materials in smaller batches to reduce the costs and disruptions of handling inventory, became standard practice in supply chains. And many of these improved quality management practices were codified in international ISO standards that cover not only industrial efficiency, but environmentally sustainable practices in virtually every industry.

However, the true productive power of the methods Deming and Toyota had put forward was seldom realized. In the following sections, we'll look at why.

A DIFFERENT FOCUS

Perhaps the most influential proponent of modern command-and-control management was Alfred Sloan Jr., the iconic CEO of General Motors. His 1963 book, *My Years at General Motors*, is still regarded by many as the definitive work describing the structure of the American corporation. The key to GM's success, Sloan wrote, was allowing his divisions – Chevrolet, Buick, Cadillac – the flexibility of pursuing their markets while exercising centralized control. "How could we exercise permanent control over the whole corporation in a way consistent with the decentralized scheme of organization?" he wrote.[17]

Control was all about controlling the purse strings. "Silent Sloan," as he became known as, was very much a "behind the scenes" manager who depended on financial reports for his decisions. This was in stark contrast to the approach of Japanese companies that would soon be grabbing market share away from GM.

Toyota's leaders, by contrast, were keen observers of shop floor productivity, as documented in *Welcome Problems, Find Success* by Kiyoshi "Nate" Furuta. As the top HR executive at Toyota, Furuta was at the table when Toyota made some of its most important strategic decisions.

"Toyota Japan used a single manufacturing KPI: productivity," he wrote. "Other factors – such as quality, safety, and employee morale – were determined to be drivers that boosted labor productivity."[18]

Senior management meetings at Toyota, he wrote, were all about productivity. "On a monthly basis, we discussed productivity improvement towards the annual target at executive meetings at a host plant (rotated every month).... Plant management checked progress on labor productivity and its drivers, such as quality, safety, run ratio of assembly, or daily equipment uptime based on a daily plant productivity indicator."[19]

Managers were also held accountable for return on assets (ROA). "I believe that when processes or operations are improved, a good business result will follow," Furuta wrote. "But business management also requires forecasting and making decisions based on unforeseen events: What will demand be? How much should we invest? How much cash should we have?"[20]

"To fulfill customer need, we have to install capacity, and when we do so, we incur risk and we also bring into the equation some complexity in terms of how we think about profitability and productivity," notes John Shook, Senior Advisor at the Lean Enterprise Institute, who wrote the Foreword for Furuta's book. Toyota's results, financial and otherwise, have been nothing short of phenomenal. Toyota continued to grow its productivity even through the 2008 meltdown that precipitated GM's insolvency. "This single KPI at Toyota Japan spurred amazing results: productivity increased at 3–5% a year for almost a half century, even during times of recession, or when Toyota was relinquishing production volume to overseas plants."[21]

The key difference is that while GM's executives were sitting in boardrooms discussing reported results and then using those to surmise what the company's problems were (some refer to this as managing through the rearview mirror), Toyota's executives were focused on shop floor events, constantly on the lookout for subtle signals from the workforce. This emphasis on frontline activity exposed them to the conditions that were driving the performance of the company, allowing them to exercise far greater foresight in their decisions.

A MISSED OPPORTUNITY

In 1984, GM and Toyota entered into a unique joint venture. GM was keen to learn the secrets of Toyota's phenomenal productivity, while

Toyota was planning to build factories in the US and wanted to gain an understanding how it could implement its Toyota Production System in a North American work environment.

The resulting enterprise was called New United Motor Manufacturing Inc. (NUMMI). Through the partnership, a shuttered GM plant in Fremont, California, was revived. This had been GM's worst performing plant, characterized by poor morale, a plethora of quality problems, and a toxic relationship between workers and management.

Nate Furuta, the executive who negotiated the labor agreement with United Automotive Workers (UAW), commented on the atmosphere preceding the agreement. "Employee grievances numbered in the thousands, and stories were rampant that workers intentionally sabotaged processes and products. Fremont under GM was the exact opposite of mutual trust."[22]

Because much of the original workforce was hired, the experiment provided a true apples-to-apples comparison between the Toyota Production System and GM's traditional command-and-control methods.

The venture proved to be a phenomenal success. Workers embraced the Toyota Production System, learned the methods, and experienced respect that they never saw in the previous plant. "Workers preferred the NUMMI system to the old combative one at GM," Furuta wrote. "Many told us they enjoyed coming to work for the first time in their lives."[23]

In the first four years of the partnership, the plant rose from the worst-performing GM plant in North America to the best. The success was documented in the groundbreaking book *The Machine That Changed the World* by Jim Womack and Daniel Jones. Many hoped that the overwhelming evidence of this superior management system would revolutionize management practices in the US.

That, however, never happened. GM pulled out of the venture as part of the restructuring from its 2008 bankruptcy, and the NUMMI experiment was discontinued in 2010 by mutual agreement between Toyota and GM. Both parties had benefited from the experiment. Toyota had gained insights on how the Toyota Production System can work in a diverse unionized environment outside of Japan. GM had gained competencies in Toyota methods such as *kanban* and 5S. But GM senior management, it appears, never appreciated the importance of the culture that was so central to Toyota's success.

FURTHER BARRIERS TO PRODUCTIVITY

Around the time Deming was gaining a following in the US, another thinker was attracting wide attention. Milton Friedman, an economist credited with founding what's known as the Chicago school of economics, emerged as a champion of shareholders. Pointing to the decade-long decline in the stock market, Friedman blamed a phenomenon he called the agency problem – the idea that corporate management often acts in its own interests instead of those of the shareholder.

Friedman believed that there was a conflict of interest between owners and managers of a firm. Owners want to maximize profits, he argued, while managers might be inclined to give precedence to their own career or personal interests. Friedman and his followers proposed that this problem could be minimized by aligning managers' interests with those of the owners through compensation incentives and contracts that link their pay to the firm's financial performance.

To achieve this alignment, public corporations began to award bonuses to their senior executives for increasing the share price of the company's stock. A profession of Wall Street analysts emerged, whose job was to make short-term estimates for various metrics, such as earnings per share, which would drive stock price. CEOs and CFOs began to issue "guidance" on what numbers to expect.

Consequently, shareholder value became the rallying cry of the Wall Street investment community, and CEOs began to manage not for the long term, but to maximize quarterly results in order to meet shareholder expectations. One of the most harmful practices in this approach is the implementation of layoffs to boost share prices. It's well known that if a company announces an impending layoff, share prices will almost automatically increase, regardless of the circumstances, the amount invested in those employees, or the long-term implications for the company.

Shareholder expectations, however, are driven not by operational reality, but by heuristics and rules of thumb that Wall Street analysts use to assess businesses. In 2005, three Duke University researchers, John R. Graham, Campbell R. Harvey, and Shiva Rajgopal, conducted a survey of 401 financial executives titled "The Economic Implications of Corporate Financial Reporting." In it, the authors concluded that for most managers, meeting shareholder expectations re earnings per share (EPS) numbers takes precedence over investments in the long-term viability of the company. "The majority of firms view earnings, especially EPS, as the key metric for outsiders, even more so than cash flows," reported the authors. "Because of the severe market reaction to missing an earnings target, we find that firms are willing to sacrifice economic value in order to meet a short-run earnings target. The preference for smooth earnings is so strong that 78% of the surveyed executives would give up economic value in exchange for smooth earnings."[24]

Short-termism is further amplified by companies spending their cash on dividends and share buybacks rather than investing in developing their businesses. "If you chart the rise in money spent on share buybacks and the fall in corporate spending on productive investments like R&D, the two lines make a perfect X," writes Foroohar. "The former has been going up since the 1980s, with S&P 500 firms now spending $1 trillion a year on buybacks and dividends – equal to more than 95 percent of their net earnings – rather than investing that money back in research, product development, or anything that could contribute to long-term company growth."[25]

In other words, many large companies, including ones committed to the Business Roundtable declaration, are far more interested in boosting short-term share price than in creating long-term value through investments in productivity growth.

THE PRODUCTIVITY CRISIS

As mentioned earlier, TV journalist Lloyd Dobyns had warned in 1980 that unless the productivity problem was solved, the next generation would be poorer than their parents. It's now clear that his prediction has come to pass, as the *New York Times* reported in 2022:

> "Americans born between 1981 and 1996, the most educated and most diverse generation in U.S. history, were once considered harbingers of economic progress and promise. But now, even well into their careers, most of them lag behind the financial and familial strides of previous generations."[26]

The symptoms of an economy that's leaving more and more people behind are everywhere. A large segment of the population, many of whom once held well-paid jobs, are now living from paycheck to paycheck. Society has become increasingly angry and polarized. And, for the first time in history, life expectancy has begun to decline.

Much of the public discussion about economic inequality centers around the role that government policy has played in the crisis. This conversation is beyond the scope of this book, but has been covered by many leading authors, several of whom are cited in this chapter. Suffice to say, productivity is not the entire answer to the crisis, but is certainly a part of it.

What businesses need to come to terms with is that growth without productivity is ultimately not sustainable, and given the pressures of global economics, political instability, social unrest, and climate change, companies unable to compete based on productivity could soon find their survival in jeopardy. Several factors can help companies become more productive. Technology is perhaps the most widely discussed – developments in areas such as collaborative robotics, Internet of Things (IoT) connectivity, and AI-powered ChatBots are widely hoped to alleviate the worker shortage in a number of industries.

Governments can also play an important role. By providing strong education and healthcare systems, for example, governments can ensure that companies will be able to recruit well-educated and healthy workforces. By providing incentives and constructive trade policies, governments can make it worthwhile for companies to make long-term investments in increasing their productivity. By creating and enforcing fair competition laws, governments can help ensure a level playing field for emerging companies.

Companies can't control what governments do, however, nor can they shape the next technological trend. They can, however, control how they manage.

This book is about how companies can change how they manage in order to continually improve the output they are able to produce from a given set of inputs. This will give them a durable competitive advantage based on productivity that doesn't depend on factors beyond their control.

IT'S ABOUT PEOPLE AND PROCESS

The phenomenal success of Toyota and other companies that have followed the continuous improvement path is not the result of technology, materials, designs, or getting people to work harder. It is about relentless

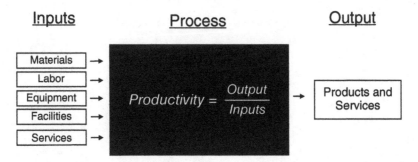

Figure 1.1   Process is how companies convert inputs to output.

improvement of processes – the means by which all inputs are combined to maximize productivity.

Processes, however, are difficult for most people to grasp – to outsiders, they appear as black boxes that magically convert inputs into output. Similarly, they are invisible to executives who rely on conventional management reports to explain their operations.

Understanding processes, and how improving them can yield breakthrough gains in productivity, requires a special kind of laser vision that can only be attained through a radical change in focus and a heightened level of communication between frontline employees and senior management. In the next chapter, we'll look at some of the tools and methods that companies are using to achieve this.

2

The Productivity Toolkit

As W. Edwards Deming told television viewers in 1980, the "miracle" that turned Japan around was not achieved by adopting a few production tricks, but through a radically different approach to management that defied anything that business graduates had learned in school.

The work of managers, according to this alternative approach, was not in their traditional command-and-control role, but in enabling a collaborative work environment where every employee was expected to take an active role in improving work processes.

To appreciate the scope of this, let's look at a hypothetical comparison. Imagine two companies that operate in the same region and compete with each other. It doesn't matter what sector they're in. But let's assume that they are the same size and have access to similar resources.

Company A follows traditional top-down management practices. Leaders determine how the work is to be done and give orders to their staff accordingly. Individuals, functional groups, and departments are treated as independent entities under centralized control. Pay and promotion are determined by individual performance according to a set of predetermined criteria. Employees are ranked and encouraged to compete with each other.

Company B is managed as an interactive system where people and functional teams depend on each other. Supervisors aren't expected to have all the answers, and they rely on frontline workers to share their workplace knowledge and take an active role in improving their work processes. All employees know they are participants in a team culture pursuing common goals, and solve problems together to move the company forward.

Ninety-five percent of companies fit into the "Company A" mold. That's what is taught in business schools and reinforced in the business press, by management consultants, and by decades of tradition.

However, there is ample evidence, as we will show in the chapters that follow, that in a head-to-head competition, Company B will outperform Company A by a significant margin. This is not because Company B builds its brand by being nice to people or by winning awards. It's because it establishes productivity as a competitive advantage, enabling it to outperform its competition according to hard-core business numbers such as profitability, efficiency, speed, customer satisfaction, and employee retention.

Transforming companies to become like Company B is what this book is about. The work that must be done, as you will see from the case studies, entails creating a company-wide culture of teamwork, mutual trust, accountability, and dedication to a common purpose.

The journey also involves mastering a set of conceptual tools and heuristics that companies use to improve their processes. These are widely used and frequently referred to in the case study examples in the remaining chapters of this book. This chapter's purpose, therefore, is to provide a rough overview of these tools for context purposes.

These tools, it should be noted, are interrelated, and designed to work in conjunction with each other.

This chapter draws from two overlapping sources of knowledge – the principles taught by Deming and his followers, and Lean principles based on the Toyota Production System, which Deming had a profound influence on.

A word of warning. If you're new to these concepts, please be advised that this is not a "how to" guide, nor does it treat these concepts comprehensively. These methods require significant expertise and practice to implement, and readers interested in moving forward should expect to engage in an extensive learning journey through books, courses, seminars, mentors, and visits to companies that practice these methods.

Toyota's remarkable rise during the latter half of the 20th century provides a useful model for explaining what is possible with these methods. The methods should not, however, be seen as inherently Japanese, but as techniques developed in the East and the West that have been successfully adopted by organizations throughout the world.

Let's look at how it all began.

RISING FROM THE ASHES

In the period immediately following World War II, the outlook didn't appear promising for the Toyota Motor Corporation. Much of Japan's industrial infrastructure had been systematically destroyed by allied bombing, forcing many manufacturers to suspend operations.

In spite of the dire circumstances, Kiichiro Toyoda, Toyota's founding CEO, urged his employees to move onward. "Catch up with America in 3 years," he said, "or the automobile industry in Japan will not survive."[1]

Even before the war, the company had been fighting an uphill battle. Compared with the US, Japan had no raw materials, little engineering expertise, and a relatively small domestic market. Furthermore, according to manufacturing experts, Japan had a major productivity problem – it was estimated that American workers were ten times as productive as Japanese workers.

Thus, meeting the productivity challenge became the major focus for a young Toyota engineer named Taiichi Ohno. Ohno had experimented with production methods at Toyoda Loom Works – the precursor of Toyota that was sold to create the new company.

When considering the productivity question, Ohno didn't blame the workers – instead, he looked at the conditions that might be linked to low productivity.

"Could an American really exert ten times more physical effort?" he later reflected. "Surely, Japanese people were wasting something. If we could eliminate the waste, productivity should rise by a factor of ten. This idea marked the start of the present Toyota Production System (TPS)."[2]

Reducing waste, consequently, became the strategy for narrowing the perceived productivity gap. Ohno's definition of waste, however, was much broader than the way the word is commonly used. Ohno used the Japanese term *muda*, which connotes any outlay or expense that doesn't directly contribute to the value that the customer will receive.

For example, if an assembly-line worker is installing a side mirror on a car, this work adds value because the car increases in utility as a result of that addition. Accordingly, installing the mirror is value-adding work. If, however, that same worker has to walk across the plant in search of a screwdriver, this effort is considered waste because the car-in-process sits idle, waiting for the worker to continue the value-adding work.

In this, Ohno took inspiration from Henry Ford, who understood the costs and frustrations around wasted motion, and had built the processes at his famous Highland Park factory to minimize walking, stooping over, and other extraneous activity.

TPS also made a distinction between waste and necessary non-value-added (NVA) activity. For example, filling out a report regarding the use of a toxic substance might be required by law and therefore a necessary non-value activity, while having to search for a solvent in a storeroom is a preventable waste of time and should be a target for elimination.

By that definition, work done by management is also considered necessary non-value-added because, while somebody has to run the company from a legal and financial perspective, that work does not contribute directly to customer value, and should therefore be minimized wherever possible.

Waste defined this way can be seen in any line of business. If a nurse has to go back to the nursing station to fill out paperwork while the patient waits to be cared for, that's considered waste. If a bank teller has to consult a manager about a transaction while the customer waits, that's waste. If construction workers are standing around on a jobsite waiting for a truck to arrive, that's waste. Eliminating this kind of waste is an endless journey that is highly dependent on input from the frontline workers who live in these processes day by day.

Accordingly, TPS established managers as enablers who helped frontline workers improve their processes in order to minimize waste. Frontline employees were also deeply respected because they are the people producing the value that the customer is willing to pay for.

IDEAL PRODUCTION CONDITIONS

TPS is guided by the pursuit of an ideal condition called flow, which Henry Ford had honed at the Highland Park plant. When flow is achieved, a workpiece moves through the production process at a steady pace, with all processes and subprocesses arranged so that there is no delay between completion of a process and commencement of the next. Accordingly, the workpiece moving through production doesn't have to "wait" for a process to initiate at any point in the production sequence – it arrives at the moment the next stage of processing is ready to receive it. Note that flow is an ideal condition that will be pursued, but never completely achieved.

The flow concept applies to nonmanufacturing environments as well. In healthcare, patient flow means that an emergency room patient might progress through admitting, triage, examination, and discharge without having to wait between stages. For an insurance claim, a file might progress through the various stages of approval with no waiting in between.

The key, from an economic standpoint, is that by identifying and eliminating removable waste, it is possible to improve flow without adding additional resources.

Toyota extended the mandate to create flow beyond production to the company's suppliers and distributors. When shipping to customers, for example, the best scenario from a flow perspective is to ship product as it comes off the line rather than maintaining inventories and then shipping in large batches. In addition, Toyota established a practice of ordering materials and components in smaller quantities so that they would arrive on an as-needed basis. This removes the waste associated with storing, managing, and accessing inventory.

The practice of producing "what's needed, when it's needed, in the amount needed" became known as just-in-time (JIT). Early on, it was established as one of the pillars of the Toyota Production System. The practice was so widely known that JIT became the accepted buzzword for the "Japanese" approach to manufacturing.

Inherent in JIT is that the entire system is demand driven in that the rhythm of production is determined by the rate of customer demand. Accordingly, Ohno and his colleagues designed a system that delivered signals to produce in the reverse of the conventional mass production approach.

Traditionally, production is initiated from the start of the process, and the work is "pushed" through the system. The demand-driven process, by contrast, initiates the signal from the customer end of the production chain – essentially, the customer "pulls" production from the company.

The pull approach is similar to the way a vending machine works. The customer presses buttons to select a product and the product slides into a tray, and is immediately replaced as another slides into place. Once the machine is running low on a particular product, a signal is sent to the supplier to restock the machine.

Ohno and his colleagues created a low-tech card-based system, which became known as *kanban*, to relay these demand signals up the production line. Accordingly, each step in the process produces "on demand" in response to a signal from the next step in the production chain. Today, electronic *kanban* systems are widely used, but many still swear by the simplicity of Ohno's 75-year-old approach. Appreciation for the simple reliability of low-tech systems is one of the recurring themes in the Lean movement.

CONTEXT

One of the central ideas that Deming promoted was that the organization must be understood as a system that's directed towards a specified aim. Consequently, it's the job of management to establish and clearly communicate the aim, and to ensure that all activities are aligned with that pursuit.

Deming described the system according to the diagram shown in Figure 2.1. A key feature here is the feedback loop that includes the customer – without the customer, there can be no purpose and no system.

The flow diagram makes it clear how all of the activities related to the development, production, and distribution of products or services function as a system. As Deming explains, the diagram was widely used in Japan as its companies moved forward with their quality initiatives. "The flow diagram...was the spark that in 1950 and onward turned Japan around," Deming wrote. "This simple flow diagram was on the blackboard at every conference with top management in 1950 and onward."[3]

Another approach to the systemic flow diagram, called Value Stream Mapping, (VSM), was introduced by authors John Shook and

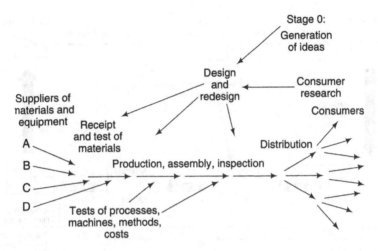

Figure 2.1 Flow diagram used by Deming.

Source: W. Edwards Deming,. The New Economics for Industry, Government, Education., Cambridge, MA: Massachusetts Institute of Technology Center for Advanced Engineering Study, 1994, p. 58, fig. 6.

Mike Rother in their 1984 book *Learning to See*, and is widely practiced. Here, the emphasis is on creating an end-to-end view of how production flows through its various stages.

VSM includes a number of refinements that make it suitable as a strategic tool for improving processes at any level in an organization. In Figure 2.2, the production steps move from left to right, and the information, either from customer orders or *kanban* demand signals, moves from right to left.

Timeline indications reveal how much time is spent in value and non-value activities. It's clear in this diagram that, relatively speaking, a very small proportion of the time a workpiece spends in the plant is being utilized for value-adding activity. This could be due to bottlenecks, transportation of the workpiece, poor coordination, or some other cause, any which would be attacked aggressively for elimination in a Lean environment.

In any case, this example shows that the flow efficiency – that is, the proportion of value-adding work – is very low. And while the scenario shown might seem shockingly inefficient, it is by no means atypical. Furthermore, a person schooled in Lean methods would see a diagram like this as a treasure trove of opportunities to improve, making the company

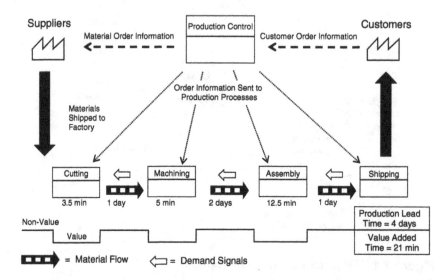

Figure 2.2 Simplified value stream map describing current state.
Source: Adapted from Jacob Stoller, The Lean CEO: Leading the Way to World Class Excellence, New York, NY: McGraw-Hill, 2015, p. 34, Fig 2-1.

more efficient and more profitable. This is where the productivity-enhancing power of continuous improvement really kicks in.

The idea of flow efficiency, however, is completely foreign to most companies. The way efficiency is traditionally tracked is by assessing and optimizing the efficiency of each functional component in the production process. The underlying assumption is that the performance of a production system is the sum total of the performance of all of its components. (We will look at this false assumption in detail in Chapter 3.)

Lean companies often use VSM to bring cross-functional teams together to improve work processes. The key here is that they consider the entire process from end to end. In the above example, representatives from cutting, welding, assembly, and shipping might form a team to find ways to improve the flow efficiency. In traditional organizations, those people would be unlikely to ever interact.

The people that form these teams aren't just managers or executives, but also frontline employees who work in the processes on a day-by-day basis. Such workers, in a Lean environment, are respected for having the most accurate view of how the processes work, and what their defects might be. In fact, the success of these initiatives often depends on the knowledge that only frontline workers can bring to the processes.

Traditionally, a VSM team will work in a conference room, mapping out the production steps with Post-it Notes and colored marking pens. The team might start by systematically looking at the journey through the production process, often walking the production line together from shipping all the way back through the first production stage.

The team then compiles detailed lists of all the steps involved at each stage, including all of the communication that takes place with other processes. Every step is identified as value adding, necessary waste, or unnecessary waste. In the case of the above diagram, there would be considerable emphasis on what happens between the processes, because this is where the vast majority of the waste is taking place.

The key to looking for waste or problems is to uncover conditions that interfere with flow. Often, there are issues that involve more than one functional area. For example, assembly might be having problems because it is receiving defective workpieces from machining, and this could cause delays and disruptions to flow. Communications problems between functional areas are also common.

Once the VSM team has identified the most prominent opportunities for improvement, a Future State Map is created, which shows what the end-to-end process could look like if those problems or sources of waste were eliminated. Using that, the team identifies a list of potential projects to bring the value stream closer to that future state.

VSM is widely used outside of manufacturing.

As Figure 2.3 shows, the value stream doesn't necessarily involve the physical fabrication of a product – it could involve a file, a financial transaction, or, in the case of healthcare, a patient moving through the system.

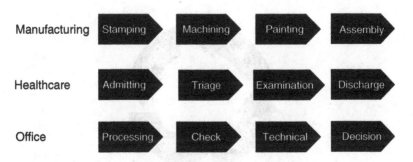

Figure 2.3 How value streams vary in different industries.

MAKING IMPROVEMENTS

As we will show in the case studies that follow, the key to optimizing processes is wide workforce participation in identifying and removing process deficiencies. The everyday practice of continually making processes better is often called *kaizen*, roughly translated from the Japanese as continuous improvement.

Kaizen got a boost in 1950 when Deming introduced a simple but powerful methodology, the Plan-Do-Study-Act (PDSA) cycle for learning, solving problems, and organizing improvement projects, in his training sessions in Japan. Deming called this "a flow diagram for learning and improvement of a product or a process."[4] He attributed its origin to his mentor Walter Shewhart, who was a scientist at Bell Laboratories. The cycle is alternatively called Plan-Do-Check-Act (PDCA).

Essentially, PDSA is a framework for investigating problems and then planning and testing solutions in a methodical and verifiable way. The big idea here is that PDSA enforces a scientific discipline that preempts the human tendency to jump to conclusions.

As shown in Figure 2.4, PDSA is usually illustrated as a circle to signify that the progress continues as people strive to make the process better and better.

The steps are:

1. **Plan:** Develop a plan for designing, testing, studying, and potentially implementing an improvement to an existing process. Establish a clear aim and criteria for evaluating results.
2. **Do:** Implement a trial of the plan.

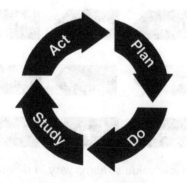

Figure 2.4   Plan-Do-Study-Act (PDSA) cycle.

3. **Study:** Measure and analyze the results to determine if aim and criteria have been met. Consider what has been learned.
4. **Act:** If the aim and criteria have been met, adopt the change. If not, either abandon it, adjust it, or run it through the PDSA cycle again.

Much of the work in this involves careful planning. An executive at Toyota once commented that Toyota spends 80% of the time planning and 20% executing, while traditionally managed companies do the reverse of that.

"Step 1 is the foundation of the whole cycle," Deming wrote. "A hasty start may be ineffective, costly, and frustrating. People have a weakness to short circuit this step."[5]

Toyota also developed a variant on the PDSA cycle called the eight-step Problem–Solving Process, or the Toyota Business Practice (TBP). The emphasis here is on investigating and correcting conditions leading to delays, defects, waste, or safety issues. It is also widely used for post-mortems to ensure that everybody learns as much as possible from a bad decision or an adverse event.

The plans are customarily presented on a large A3-sized sheet of paper and are usually referred to as A3s.

The eight steps are:

1. Clarify the problem: collect and analyze data to fully understand a condition that doesn't meet standards.
2. Break down the problem into manageable subproblems, and define scope of solution.
3. Set a numerical target for improvement that can be verified with test results.
4. Analyze the root cause of the problem using the available data.
5. Develop countermeasure(s) that will resolve the situation by correcting the root cause.
6. Implement countermeasure(s) according to plan.
7. Evaluate the results.
8. If criteria are met, revise standards to accommodate countermeasure. If not, repeat the cycle.

Note the emphasis on planning – the first five steps are dedicated to it. This is quite a contrast to the "go with your gut" attitude that's so popular in conventional management.

STATISTICAL LITERACY

As we saw above, Deming stressed the importance of following a scientific approach in order to change work processes without falling into the trap of jumping to conclusions. In addition to following the PDSA cycle, he also advocated that anybody in the workplace who is involved in changing a process should have an understanding of the statistical influences on workplace occurrences.

Deming explained that there are two types of variation that can influence a process: common cause and special cause. Common cause variation results from all combined factors that influence a process, while special cause variation is attributable to a specific unexpected influence. When it comes to reducing this variation, each of these requires a different course of action.

What surprises most people is that only 5% of variations are special cause, while 95% are common cause. This misunderstanding leads people to jump to the conclusion that a special cause is to blame whenever they see a deviation in a process. This often leads to interventions that make a process worse rather than better.

To avoid this, Deming insisted that before proposing a solution to an unwanted variation, the initiator collect and plot relevant data on a graph or control chart, and then use simple rules to determine the type and severity of the variation.

The Statistical Process Control (SPC) charts that Deming introduced are widely used in continuous improvement environments, as well as other visual tools used to record, analyze, and display statistical results.

STANDARDIZED WORK

An important prerequisite to changing a process for the better is having an established understanding of the process's current state. Consequently, companies that practice continuous improvement maintain written standards for all workplace processes.

"There can be no improvement where there are no standards," wrote Masaaki Imai, one of the early pioneers who brought Japanese methods to the West.[6]

Work standards at Toyota were typically displayed, often in hand-written form, at each workstation. They included a list of steps in the process, the allotted time for each step, and a list of all of the materials and equipment that were required. Today, standard forms are available online for documenting these standards.

Job and task descriptions, of course, aren't particular to continuous improvement environments. The difference is that here, the standards aren't imposed in top-down fashion, but are developed and maintained with worker involvement. Workers, therefore, own those standards, and take pride in maintaining them.

One of the most popular formats for work standards originates from Training Within Industry (TWI), the highly successful training model developed in the US to train temporary workers during World War II. TWI had recognized the importance of creating an environment where workers take ownership of their work processes, making it highly appropriate for use in continuous improvement environments.

DEVELOPING AN EYE FOR WASTE

Waste, according to the broad definition used in TPS, can be found any-where in an organization. In order to keep everybody on the lookout for it, Ohno described seven categories of waste. An eighth was added later to include unused talent due to not utilizing valuable input from employees. The Eight Wastes are:

1. Overproduction: Producing more than required by the next downstream process, or the customer. Ohno saw this as the "cardinal sin" of waste because essentially it forces all the other wastes.
2. Waiting: Workers standing idle awaiting the next step.
3. Transportation: Excessive movement of workpieces, parts, or equipment.
4. Overprocessing: More than the necessary amount of work being done on the workpiece, perhaps due to poor process design or defective tools.
5. Inventory: More finished goods, works in process, parts, or raw materials than required by customer demand.

6. Movement: Unnecessary movements by workers, including bending, straining, and walking to procure tools or parts.
7. Defects: Fabrication of defective workpieces that will get shipped to customers or require rework in the plant.
8. Unused talent. This is sometimes called the worst waste, because it cuts out the most powerful weapon for improving processes – people.

The Eight Wastes as a conceptual tool has proven to be remarkably adaptable to workplaces outside of manufacturing, as shown in Figure 2.5.

An important feature of waste defined in this way is that it does not manifest as line items management reports – instead, it shows up in hundreds or even thousands of small incremental problems, many of which are visible only to people in the workplace. Furthermore, environments change, so new wastes crop up every day.

Consequently, the campaign to reduce waste can only be successful if the entire workforce engages in it. Much of the work of management, therefore, is creating a work environment where frontline workers have the freedom and autonomy to contribute to these efforts.

GETTING IT RIGHT THE FIRST TIME

Sakichi Toyoda's patented loom that was the basis of Toyoda Loom Works, the predecessor of Toyota, had a unique feature. When a thread broke during the weaving process, the loom would stop automatically, preventing any more work on a defective piece of cloth. The feature was later characterized as "autonomation," that is, automation with a human touch.

Industry	Waste	Description
Healthcare	Movement	Nurse walking to retrieve supplies or equipment
Financial Services	Over-Processing	Redundant forms, unnecessary processing steps
Construction	Waiting	Workers standing idle awaiting instructions
Retail	Inventory	Excess stock cluttering aisles

Figure 2.5 Examples of waste in different industries.

When his son Kiichiro founded what was to become the Toyota of today, autonomation, or *jidoka*, became one of the foundations of the company's management approach. Accordingly, if a defect or a safety threat is discovered during production that cannot be corrected on the spot, production halts immediately.

At Toyota and in most Lean environments, every workstation has an alarm, called the *andon*. When an anomaly is first detected, the worker uses the *andon* to alert a supervisor, and if the problem is not resolved immediately, the *andon* is used again to deliver a signal to the line to halt production.

This is radically different from the quality control processes in most companies, where stopping a line might be a fireable offense. In that case, quality is usually monitored by inspectors at the end of the production line, who refer defective products for either rework or disposal. When analyzed from a value stream perspective, dealing with quality problems after the fact is phenomenally wasteful.

Getting the *jidoka* concept embedded into every process takes enormous discipline but removes many of the hidden costs of rework and recalls, and helps improve quality overall. The point is that quality problems are often symptoms of defective processes, and improving these processes at the source often yields not only better quality, but less waste, shorter lead times, and lower costs – in other words, higher productivity.

Results from this approach repudiate the common rule of thumb that speed, quality, and costs are mutually exclusive. In fact, pursuing quality in this holistic way is a key economic driver for companies that practice continuous improvement. It's not surprising, therefore, that *jidoka* and just-in-time were established by Toyota as the pillars of TPS.

CREATING ORDER

Continuous improvement places considerable emphasis on maintaining order in the workplace. There are several reasons for this. First of all, in many lines of business, such as manufacturing, construction, and healthcare, disorderly work environments pose safety hazards.

Messy work environments also make it difficult to see waste and substandard conditions. If parts of an assembly are in disarray, for example, it's difficult to see if something is missing or defective. If a service organization's files are disorderly, it can be difficult to investigate a customer complaint.

Finally, neglect of the workplace environment sends a subtle message that the work doesn't really matter and dampens the worker engagement that is essential to a continuous improvement environment.

Maintaining orderly workspaces throughout the organization, therefore, is a top priority in organizations that practice continuous improvement. An approach known as "5S" is used to organize company-wide activities to accomplish this. The 5S words are:

- **Sort:** Declutter the workspace by removing unnecessary items and either disposing of them or storing them remotely. In manufacturing, this could mean the tools no longer used or unneeded materials. In an office work area, it could be deleting redundant files or drafts of documents.
- **Straighten:** Arrange all items used in the work process so that they are logically placed, easy to reach, and readily visible. A key here is that if something is missing or out of place, it will be immediately obvious.
- **Shine:** Clean the workplace and equipment of dirt and debris. A "shined" workspace should be safe and pleasant to work in.
- **Standardize:** Establish standardized procedures for repeating the sort, straighten, and shine steps on a regular basis, including schedules, responsibilities, and visual aids such as photos or charts.
- **Sustain:** Establish a culture in which all employees practice 5S without even thinking about it.

Organizations customarily schedule periodic 5S events in which all employees participate. The material benefits of 5S come from creating a workplace that is free from distractions and conducive to productive work. The cultural aspect, however, is equally important. 5S helps instill a continuous improvement culture by building teamwork across functional divisions, promoting trust and respect, and helping establish a discipline of solving problems and reducing waste.

For those reasons, 5S is often used in early stages of a continuous improvement transformation.

THE "WHY" BEHIND THE METHODS

The methods I've listed are powerful enablers for creating a continuous improvement transformation, but they are only tools. Most organizations, unfortunately, adopt them superficially for tactical purposes such as cost cutting. This might result in some short-term gains, but without a continuous improvement culture to support them, they are not sustainable, and the tools typically fall into disuse.

The thinking behind the methods, therefore, is vitally important. The case studies ahead will reveal some of that thinking. Deming also addressed it extensively in *The New Economics*, which he was still revising at the end of his life. The book argues that a company should be a system where everybody – employees, customers, investors, communities – wins. It also reflects a set of values around education, fairness, and human dignity.

The book introduces Deming's System of Profound Knowledge® (SoPK), a set of four interactive components that he described as a "theory for transformation."[7] Applied together, the components support a mutually supportive business environment where people think and learn together in pursuing a common goal of achieving the aim of the organization. While there is a technical side to them, the components are basically about creating a productive work environment based on learning, teamwork, and mutual trust.

The four components are:

- **Appreciation for a system:** Understanding how people, processes, and technology interact as components of a complex adaptive system directed towards a stated aim of the organization and staying in business
- **Knowledge of variation:** Appreciating and anticipating the influence of common-cause and special-cause variation on the outcome of a process or initiative, and knowing how to measure and respond to variation
- **Theory of knowledge:** Understanding the workings of knowledge mechanisms such as operational definitions, control charts, and the PDSA cycle, and reflecting on how we can truly know what we think we know

- **Knowledge of psychology:** Understanding and respecting the dynamics of human reactions and interactions in the workplace, including the vital importance of creating an atmosphere where people aren't afraid to admit mistakes and point out problems

"This book is for people who are living under the tyranny of the prevailing style of management," Deming wrote in the preface. "The huge long-range losses caused by this style of management have led us into decline. Most people imagine that the present style of management has always existed, and is a fixture. Actually, it is a modern invention – a prison created by the way in which people interact. This interaction afflicts all aspects of our lives – government, industry, education, healthcare."[8]

THE PRODUCTIVITY EDGE

The methods outlined above have been proven to produce game-changing productivity improvements that can become a company's source of competitive advantage.

But there's a catch. If these methods are used just as standalone productivity tools, as they are in most cases, they lead to limited, unsustainable gains. The productivity advantage can only come from the holistic company-wide use of these tools in a supporting role for pursuing the Company B model.

The remainder of this book is dedicated to shattering the myths that perpetuate the prevailing style of management that Deming so passionately criticized.

Onward!

PART TWO

Shattering the Five Myths

3

The Myth of Segmented Success

Myth: The productive resources of a company can be organized as a collection of independent components. The whole equals the sum of the parts

Rich Sheridan, CEO of Ann Arbor–based custom software developer Menlo Innovations, recently welcomed his granddaughter to his office. Because of the company's philosophy that minimizes hierarchy, his work area had none of the trappings of his CEO status. Sheridan was surprised at how a young child perceived this.

"We had a lot of our family in town for my middle daughter's wedding," says Sheridan. "We had just moved our office, so everybody wanted to see it. So my eight-year-old granddaughter, for whom the age of reason is just kicking in, asked me, 'Where do you sit, Pop-Pop?'"

Sheridan took her over to a table in the middle of the open office area. "This is where I sit, and here's my computer," he said.

His granddaughter looked puzzled, and then asked, "Where's your name? Don't you have your name somewhere?"

Sheridan was amazed. "I thought 'wow,' she already has it in her head that as CEO, I should have corner office with a placard that showed how important I am. And you know, I felt a little embarrassed. She was somehow implying that I can't be much of a CEO if I don't have a placard with my name on it. And she's only eight!"

Rich Sheridan, however, is no ordinary CEO. According to his leadership philosophy, success depends on team productivity as opposed to the accumulated efforts of individuals. The office layout at Menlo, therefore, is designed to support a team environment where people can enjoy collaborating. What better way to model that culture than to show that he is a teammate like everybody else?

That way of thinking, however, doesn't reflect the mental models that dominate the way we think about businesses.

THE IMAGES THAT GOVERN US

Our human mind couldn't make sense of the world without using conceptual tools and images to simplify what we see. Accordingly, our understanding of how companies work, and what a CEO's desk should look like, is strongly influenced by conditioning we acquire at a very young age.

"Our ordinary conceptual system, in terms of which we both think and act, is fundamentally metaphorical in nature," wrote cognitive scientists George Lakoff and Mark Johnson in their groundbreaking 1980 book, *Metaphors We Live By.* "The concepts that govern our thought are not just matters of the intellect. They also govern our everyday functioning, down to the most mundane details. Our concepts structure what we perceive, how we get around in the world, and how we relate to other people."[1]

The problem with these mental tools is that they can mislead us. As authors Debra Smith and Chad Smith explain in their 2014 book

Demand Driven Performance: Using Smart Metrics, conventional management theory is based on scientific logic from another era. "From the late seventeenth century until the early twentieth, the Laws of Motion and other linear, mechanical principles discovered by Isaac Newton dominated the understanding of science and filtered down into every aspect of the Western world," they wrote. "This view of reality penetrated our educational system, our culture, our language, our organizations, and our management practices so completely that it becomes taken for granted. The result has been that interdependence and interconnectedness were deemed less and less important and essentially ignored."[2]

This embedded way of thinking causes companies to focus on its components while disregarding the larger systemic factors that could influence a company. It's assumed, for example, that each stage in a manufacturing environment can be managed as a subsystem, and that an efficiency improvement in any of these stages will filter down to an overall efficiency improvement for the company.

This belief is reinforced by goals, targets, and compensation schemes that reward managers for the performance of their particular subsystems. In manufacturing, the head of a stamping or machining department might get a bonus for achieving a utilization target – that is, running the equipment as close to 100% of the time as possible. In an insurance company, there might be separate targets for number of claims processed, customer service calls handled, or sales.

The science that this approach originates from, however, has moved on since Newton. In the early 20th century, new paradigms revolutionized the way scientists view the physical world. This new way of thinking led to the development of complex adaptive systems (CAS) theory, a field that emerged in the 1940s. In contrast with Newton's tidy mechanistic explanation, CAS depicts environments that are far less predictable and centralized, and far more vulnerable to instability.

Deming stressed the importance of CAS in understanding the day-by-day occurrences in companies, and the implications for management. As we saw in Chapter 2, his System of Profound Knowledge® (SoPK) reflected the overlapping components of systems, statistics, theory of knowledge, and psychology, allowing managers to move away from the traditional subsystem approach to management to a more holistic approach that acknowledges and responds to influences on the entire system.

What was needed, Deming showed, was a fundamentally different way of managing that would enable a company to operate as an interdependent system. "A system is a network of interdependent components that work together to try to accomplish the aim of the system," he wrote in his 1992 book *The New Economics*.[3]

Deming was highly critical of conventional management theory. His harshest criticism was of the pyramid-shaped top-down management structure. The pyramid org chart, Deming explained, is not only unhelpful, but destroys the kind of systemic interaction that is required to for companies to rise to their potential.

"The pyramid only shows responsibilities for reporting, who reports to whom," he wrote. "It shows the chain of command and accountability. A pyramid does not describe the system of production. It does not tell anybody how his work fits into the work of other people in the company. If a pyramid conveys any message at all, it is that anybody should first and foremost try to satisfy his boss (get a good rating). The customer is not in the pyramid. A pyramid, as an organization chart, thus destroys the system if ever one was intended."[4]

Deming believed that in contrast with the command-and-control school of management, leaders must manage the interdependencies of the system through clear communication of the purpose and the role of each employee in pursuing that. "It is management's job to direct the efforts of all components toward the aim of the system," he wrote.[5]

Furthermore, he warned that organizations must heed the dangers of segmentation of purpose, where individuals seek their own gain to the detriment of others. "Everyone must understand the danger and the loss to the whole organization from a team that seeks to become a selfish, independent profit center."[6]

Self-serving practices, Deming demonstrated, often stem from misuse of one of the most firmly entrenched pillars of conventional management – Management by Objectives (MBO), the process of measuring, rating, and ranking employees according to numerical goals.

"In MBO, as practiced, the company's objective is parceled out to the various components or divisions," Deming wrote. "The usual assumption in practice is that if every component or division accomplishes its share, the whole company will accomplish the objective. The assumption is not in general valid: the components are most always interdependent."[7]

Consequently, one of the key milestones for companies following Deming's approach is the removal of MBO incentives that stand in the way of company-wide collaboration.

YOU EAT WHAT YOU KILL

Perhaps the granddaddy of rating and ranking systems is the time-worn practice of judging and compensating corporate salespeople based on the dollar value of the business that they bring in. Sales reps are generally compensated on a combination of base salary and commissions based on their sales numbers. Declarations like "There's no limit to how much money you can make" are widely touted, and when times are good, sales reps are celebrated as heroes and in some companies, flown to annual "achievers' club" events at high-end resorts.

The flip side is that if you don't make your quota, you're fired. This is harsh, but as they say, that's business, and to this day, few organizations question it. But the system isn't just tough on salespeople. If, for example, a sales rep, desperate to make quota, sells machinery to a company that doesn't have the staff to support it, that "deal" might weigh heavily on the service department and turn into a money-losing proposition.

TAKING ON SALES MANAGEMENT 101

In 2009, the conventional sales compensation scheme clearly wasn't working at Air Force One, one of the largest HVAC service companies in Ohio. Revenue and headcount growth had stagnated, and the newly minted CEO, Greg Guy, who had taken over from his father, Bill, feared that he didn't have what it took to run the company.

Guy invested in more staff and more training to grow the business, and the effort appeared to be paying off. However, he began to see signs that all was not well with his sales team. Reps and managers frequently fought over commissions, some staffers were withholding sales leads, and the general manager was fired for collecting commissions on sales that had been made by his subordinates.

While all this was going on, Guy read Daniel Pink's *Drive: The Surprising Truth About What Motivates Us* and was profoundly shaken.

The whole idea of sales commissions, Pink argued, was not a good way to motivate salespeople.

To explore alternatives, Guy attended a seminar in 2013 given by Kelly Allan, a Deming disciple. "After spending time with Kelly and attending his three-day seminar, I ran a PDSA in our Cincinnati office where we removed all sales commissions from that sales team," says Guy. "Basically, we took everybody's sales commission that they were earning and added it to their base salary."

The change, however, was not arbitrary. As Allan explains, a fundamental change like this has to be planned and executed carefully. "We never go in with guns blazing in terms of getting rid of commissions and performance reviews because those things are so deeply embedded in the Western belief system," says Allan. "People sometimes go back after a seminar and take people off commission, and sales go up, but then they hit a plateau. Guy was able to pull this off because he kept studying the Deming principles and understood how the existing system was working and where the defects were."

For example, Guy understood the highly interdependent relationships between the sales force and the service delivery organization. "The problem with targets and goals is that they're typically set without any understanding of what the capability is," says Allan. "Sales is out there making promises to customers, but the capability in the system may not be able to keep up with that. So now it comes down to 'we've got to work overtime. We've got to have more people. We've got add more equipment.' But what they should be doing is looking at the entire system and finding out how to get more octane from every one of those assets that they have."

That systemic approach turned out to be a game-changer. "What this did is take away any structural hurdles to collaboration between the different siloed sales groups," says Guy. "And the outcome was fascinating. All of a sudden, collaboration, team spirit, and sales productivity increased dramatically. We were selling better deals to better clients that were healthier for the overall enterprise."

The initiative was soon adopted company wide. "Over time, we went from our Cincinnati office to our Cleveland office to our Akron office to our Toledo office and to our Columbus office," says Guy. "And within about an 18-month window, the entire business was commission free, and we've been that way ever since."

The change has also proved to be sustainable – the firm grew over 300% between 2020 and 2023, fueled by organic growth and by acquisitions financed from the cash generated by organic growth.

CORPORATE DYSFUNCTION

Sales reps are subject to much derision, but it should be clear from the above example that the most objectional qualities of sales reps – pushiness, untruthfulness, and a tendency to disappear after the deal is done – are usually not due to character flaws of the sales rep, but to the nature of the system in which they work. Nobody's job security should depend on bringing in a bad deal that is going to harm the customer, the company, or both.

Conversely, sales reps who are motivated to create win-win relationships between their company and their customers can be powerful change agents that help companies understand and adopt new productivity-enhancing technologies. However, reps proposing innovative solutions often find that their prospective customers are subject to segmented thinking. And for the sales rep, this will manifest as corporate inertia.

Let's look at a hypothetical example. Rebecca, a technology sales rep, has approached a large retail bank that has a customer service problem: too many calls are clogging up its call centers. Costs are mounting, wait times are long, employees are quitting in droves, and customers are disgruntled.

Suppose that Rebecca's company, ABC Technologies, has released an AI-based software product that could reduce the bank's customer calls by 35% by clarifying the information on the bank's website, perhaps with the help of hyperlinks, audio, video, and other tools. Assume that this could save the bank millions a year and improve customer satisfaction as well.

Rebecca has made a presentation to the bank featuring a successful case study at a comparable bank. It included a live demo and data showing how the AI model had trained itself on millions of customer service calls, and then developed, through a machine learning model, instructional materials added to the bank's website that were demonstrated to reduce incoming call volume. Rebecca was able to show that if the bank were to adopt this technology, the cost of the system would be repaid within the first twelve months. A no-brainer, right?

Wrong. Even though the benefits are clear for the bank, the levers of powers are segmented in a way that could make even a slam-dunk business case a tough sell. The solution Rebecca was proposing involves making changes that fall within the jealously guarded territory of marketing. The benefits of fewer calls to the call centers, on the other hand, accrue to customer service.

Furthermore, a successful call prevention solution that was instigated by customer service might make marketing look bad – it might imply that marketing hadn't done a good job of informing customers about the bank's services.

The problem is that these organizations have different budgets and different incentives. Their VPs might even be competing for a promotion.

Ideally, of course, customer service and marketing should work together as a team to reduce the frustration of customers and employees. That level of collaboration, however, would require a fundamental realignment of incentives, and a departure from the conventional segmented view of the business. Unfortunately (as we will see in Chapter 4), senior managers tend to see their companies not as a system of value-creating activities, but through a financial lens that disregards the problems that poor coordination of functional areas creates.

QUALITY IS A TEAM SPORT

Paula Marshall is CEO of Tulsa-based Bama Foods, a family-owned business that provides frozen baked goods to commercial food companies. Today, Marshall is the only active CEO who has worked personally with Deming.

"I had just taken over the company for my family," says Marshall, "and we were dealing with some quality issues at the time. I was very fortunate to be dragged to one of Dr. Deming's seminars by my friends at McDonald's, which was our biggest customer. It was an eye-opening experience."

Marshall was one of the only CEOs in the audience, and after the first session, Deming invited Marshall to be part of a study group that met on a regular basis. Deming took a special interest in Marshall's work and began to ask probing questions about how Marshall was managing people.

Bama had recently implemented an incentive-based pay system developed at considerable cost by a high-profile management consulting firm. "It was not unlike the programs that a lot of companies have in corporate America," says Marshall. "It had detailed appraisal criteria for coming up with a numerical rating for each employee, and everything was broken down in silos according to functional responsibilities. Then there were guidelines for using the rating scale so that the ratings stayed within specific boundaries."

The program, however, wasn't working as intended. "The ratings weren't averaging out within the guidelines," says Marshall, "and I often had to override the system because I didn't feel right about paying somebody less than they'd made the year before. So, in the end, we were doing all this work, but I wasn't really paying people any differently than I had before."

Deming counseled Marshall to cancel the program, but Marshall was hesitant. "I had to admit that it wasn't doing anything to improve the performance of the company," says Marshall, "but I'd spent a lot of money on it and was reluctant to give it up."

The company experimented with various adjustments, including changing from a seven- to a ten-point scale, but ultimately, nobody was satisfied with the system. Then, on a conference call with Dr. Deming, they agreed to scrap it.

"It was probably one of the most hated systems in the company," says Marshall, "because nobody liked their rating, nobody liked their boss for giving them that rating, and the bosses weren't happy anyway. So everybody was ready for something different. And so, I said, 'What if we just didn't have anything?'"

The following year, the company developed a new employee review process that was not tied to compensation. Instead of numerical ratings, the conversation was about career goals and removing barriers.

"Since we stopped fiddling around with numbers, those conversations have become a lot more positive," says Marshall.

With the divisive process of rating and ranking out of the picture, the company began, with Deming's guidance, to create a culture where each employee is defined not by rank or silo, but by how they contribute to the system that defines the company. With the barriers removed, team productivity increased significantly.

"According to Dr. Deming's guidance, we don't have any more functional silos, no rating and ranking, and no management by objectives," says Marshall. "Instead of putting everybody in a box in terms of the organizational structure, we work on everybody's role within the system. Instead of somebody saying, 'I'm the VP of this and I have these functional reports," it's more "here's my piece of the system, and here's what we do to continuously improve the system.'"

Projects to improve performance are initiated and managed by cross-functional "pit teams" that use the PDSA process. "Now, instead of a functional director standing up there telling you what to do, everyone gets together in your team and figures out how to best support improvements that the company is trying to make," says Marshall. Employee approval now stands at between 80 and 85%.

While pleased with Bama's transformation, Marshall finds it discouraging that so few companies have followed a similar path. "I believe, and a lot of employee surveys corroborate this, that there's never been a larger number of disengaged workers than there are right now," says Marshall. " I feel bad when I go to speak to other companies, and I see the level of disengagement and dissatisfaction, and that people feel that there's no way out until they retire."

Marshall is frequently asked what her secrets are. "When I go and talk to other companies, they ask, 'How can we become more like you?'" says Marshall. "And the first thing I says is, 'You have to take out your incentive-based compensation system.' And right away, the CEO of the company will walk out, because that's not something they want to hear. And honestly, Dr. Deming spent his entire career trying to end those practices because they don't engage people, they're very off-putting, and they create a lot of team member dissatisfaction. And ultimately, they don't help the company at all."

Citing survey data that the vast majority of employees regard their employers negatively, Marshall is concerned about the impact that many corporations are having on society.

"People are so disengaged," says Marshall, "and it's all in how we treat them. When you hear that a private company is being sold to a public company or a big private equity company, I just look at the faces of the people who work there. They're often getting ready to leave and go somewhere else, because they just don't want to be part of a corporate structure. So we're very focused on staying private."

A TEAM APPROACH TO INNOVATION

Managing a team of knowledge workers whose creative output is central to their identity is a special challenge for any organization. The default mode of operation is that workers closely guard their knowledge, often fearing that sharing too much of it might endanger their job security. This makes it difficult for the kind of knowledge sharing and collaboration that made Air Force One and Bama so successful.

One firm that committed to creating an open and collaborative environment for creative workers is the architectural design firm Design Group, based in Columbus, Ohio, and Pittsburgh, Pennsylvania. The firm specializes in public and private facilities such as hospitals, schools, libraries, cultural centers, and office projects. The company has won numerous awards and designed a number of LEED-compliant projects.

Design Group has followed the Deming philosophy for 25 years. Sherm Moreland, the Design Group CEO, believes that architects, by designing the spaces that in many respects define how people live and work together, have a major influence on people's lives. Joy at work, to quote a phrase that Deming frequently used, comes from appreciating the huge responsibility architects have, and fulfilling it.

"Whether it's the built environment or the space between buildings, it's all for people," says Moreland. "Your existence on this planet is going to be inside or outside, and that space more than likely has been thought of by someone. So there is some greater responsibility around what it is that we do to elevate people."

The concept of elevating people with good design is part of a five-point vision that the company developed under Moreland's leadership:

- Civic responsibility
- Healthy communities
- Lifelong learning
- Sustainable architecture
- Design that elevates

These values are critical in healthcare, Moreland explains, where people are sick and workers are stressed. "The satisfaction that healthcare architects get is you get to design spaces that have to be at their best when people are at their worst," says Moreland, "and if that doesn't get you jumping out of bed and running to work in the morning, excited about what you do and the importance of it, then I don't know what will."

Channeling the joy and satisfaction that comes from working towards a purpose larger than oneself is a driving force in the firm. What's essential, Moreland explains, is that the firm and the individual are growing together. How that mutual growth is progressing is a central question he pursues when he has his annual conversation with his employees. "We use the analogy of the two ladders, which was introduced to us by our consultant, Kelly Allan," says Moreland. "This illustrates how the individual and company have to be growing together. It's a symbiotic relationship."

The firm began working with Allan in 2000, two years after Moreland had joined the firm. Early on, Allan helped the firm establish the Plan-Do-Study-Act (PDSA) cycle (described in Chapter 2) as a company-wide standard for problem solving.

In 2008, the company abandoned the traditional performance review. "Deming really was a way for me to make sense of all these things in a way that went beyond what I just knew in my gut were not right, which was rating, ranking, and measuring people," says Moreland. "When I first started at Design Group, you would sit down for your annual review, people were ranked in various categories on a one-to-five scale. So we wound up talking about all the wrong things. I was instrumental in helping to throw out that rating and ranking system and turn it into what we call the annual conversation."

The annual conversation today is much more two-sided and explores ways in which the employee and the firm can grow together. "I've adopted a practice when I sit with people in our annual review where I say, 'Think about a day when you sat down and got your cup of coffee, and then you looked up and you said, 'Oh my gosh, it's 6 p.m. – where did the day go?' We really need to find out what was special to this employee, and how we can create more of that," Moreland continues. "We really try to understand how we can not only remove barriers but put back the joy in the work and the joy in craftsmanship."

To reinforce the team culture, Allan introduced Deming's famous Red Bead experiment – a roleplaying game where each "willing worker" dips a paddle into a bin and retrieves a combination of white and red beads. The stated objective, the participant is told, is to pick as few red beads as possible, and participants are rated accordingly. The catch is that the paddle selects the beads randomly, so the participant can't influence the result. The exercise illustrates the frustration workers experience from being judged and evaluated based on events they have no control over. "We did the Red Bead experiment during one of our company-wide training days," says Moreland. "That was a real eye-opener for everybody."

Another was the Red Squares game, which stresses the idea that nobody wins unless all participants win. That idea can be difficult to instill in architecture and other creative endeavors where expertise is seen as one's career insurance. Therefore, there is a high level of trust necessary to encourage people to share their knowledge openly. As Moreland explains, if you keep everything to yourself, you lose in the long run because you don't grow.

"If you want to be a team of one, there's a limit to growth, personally, professionally, and corporately," says Moreland, "so we try to coach around how not to think that way. For those who really want to advance, we use the concept of capacity. If you're a team of one, you can only work on two or three projects, and you've reached your capacity, and your opportunity for growth is stymied. But if you train others how to do what you do, and you're overseeing that, and then you're taking on bigger and better projects with more sophisticated clients and maybe perhaps more interesting, you're growing your capacity and now you're working on 20 projects. But you're really managing four people, because you've built a system dependent on teamwork and knowledge sharing. But at the early stage, you've got to drive out that fear of people stealing your best thinking."

This was a tough lesson to learn in 2008 when anxiety about job security was at its peak. "In architecture, you don't really get into your stride until later on in your career," says Moreland. "When I was in mid-career, one of my senior colleagues, in a very heartwarming moment, told me, 'You know, when times were tough, I was put in this leadership position over a team of people, whereas I wanted to keep all the work for myself, because I was afraid that if I ran out of work, you could get rid of me.' So I had to get comfortable with the fact that this was absolutely the wrong thinking. And I had to share what I knew and get things done, which would free me up to then go find more work, which was what the company needed."

Another fear that has to be driven out is the fear of revealing what you don't know. Architectural firms like Design Group select multidisciplinary teams to run projects. If you're the only interior designer or the only spec writer on the team, the project depends very much on your expertise. Team members, therefore, have to be unafraid to ask for help when they need it.

"The idea of Deming's training on the job is really baked into almost every internal interaction between a senior person and a junior person," says Moreland. "And that's a two-way street. The senior person has to ask the junior person 'Do you know how to do what I'm asking you to do?' And the junior person has to be unafraid to raise their hand and say, 'I don't. I've never done this task before. Can you explain what you want from this so I know that I am doing it right?' That is an approach that we've had a lot of success with."

Shunning a junior person looking for help is not tolerated. "There are two things that nobody will ever tell you at Design Group," says Moreland. "They won't say, 'That's not my job,' and they won't tell you, 'I don't have time to explain that to you.'"

Overcoming fear of failure is another important priority. "When it comes to fear of failure, I try to lead from example," says Moreland. "I have initiated a lot of things that failed. And I tell our staff, 'If you want to look at failure, I've had plenty of it – just look through the list.' But we've had lots of successes too. And you have to try things and not be afraid."

Openness is also key in a profession where bad communication can throw a wrench into a large project. "We believe in bringing all parties together – owner, architect, builder, subcontractor, you name it – to say how we will work better together," says Moreland. "We ran a study twice and the data is clear. There are seven points of risk in a project, and communication is at the top of the list every time. If communication isn't good, you're at risk of not having a good outcome. So communication is key."

Communication is also a key differentiator for the firm. "I have a planning background, and we've adopted a methodology for teaching planning within our company," says Moreland. "And we then use that as a competitive advantage to be able to articulate to our clients why our approach results in higher-quality solutions."

However, the competence of Design Group personnel at participating in constructive dialogue is not limited to following the planning approach – they get lots of practice in any PDSA exercises that take place internally.

"We use the PDSA model quite a bit," says Moreland. "If somebody has some ideas and wants to challenge a question or create an improvement, we ask them to design a PDSA study." The person is expected to define the purpose and scope of the study, the expected duration, and the desired outcome.

A critical element of the PDSA approach is the emphasis on communication. Anybody involved with the work affected by the PDSA should understand precisely what the objectives are. Accordingly, everybody at Design Group has to be an expert at communicating in areas such as evaluation of data, problem-solving, and the dynamics of organizational change.

PDSA is therefore much more than a conceptual tool – it provides a framework for employee interaction that helps build a culture of teamwork and trust in an organization. Rather than judging people for being right or wrong, PDSA provides a framework for learning together, which in turn is essential to the firm and the staff member growing side by side at Design Group.

Many of the firm's established practices are created with PDSA. One of these is a set of guidelines setting a quality standard for a set of drawings. "If we had infinite time and money to do our work, we could make a perfect set of drawings," says Moreland. "But we have fees, schedules, and time limits. So we became very intrigued with the idea of creating a what we called the biddable set – a set of drawings that was just enough so that the contractor would understand the owner's conditions of satisfaction, and could build it to a level of quality that was expected by the owner, but not with too much detail that would jeopardize project profitability. So we ran a PDSA on the biddable set, and we still use that today."

The process that the firm underwent underlines the need for a common point of reference when people are working together on multiple projects. "When you're working on a lot of projects at once, coordination becomes the key to customer satisfaction, to team member satisfaction, and to the ability to make profit," says Allan, who worked with the firm on this project. "So people have to share operational definitions, for example, which is part of the theory of knowledge."

Creating a "biddable set" using PDSA is an example of how people work and learn together. "So, if my operational definitions are not the same," says Allan, "I will have different architects and designers, perhaps, drawing to different levels of detail. Some of them are going to draw to more detail than is required. Some may not be drawing enough detail."

Getting the definition right isn't just a matter of optimizing the workflow within the firm – too much detail can make plans difficult to work with, while not enough can lead to mistakes, rework, and frequent iterations. Either of these outcomes can be costly for the customer, the contractor, and the firm.

Another PDSA involved staffing. "A PDSA we ran recently, which we called 'New Ways of Work,' was about how to handle smaller projects," says Moreland. "We're used to doing $100 million projects, which we are able to staff with six or seven people," says Moreland, "so we needed to get a better understanding of how we staff a smaller project with two people. How do you train those people so that they feel confident, have joy in work, and can feel as good about what they're doing just as much as a big job? And so, we've used these PDSAs as leadership products what might happen."

The firm's established culture of mutual supportive teamwork makes the firm unique in its ability to communicate with customers and solve problems with them in a collaborative way. This alleviates the biggest risk in construction – communication.

"I think Design Group's competitive advantage is understanding why the manner in which we work is different and better than our competition," says Moreland. "Being able to visually document and articulate our systems and processes to our clients, and being unafraid to share that learning internally as we train other members of the Design Group team helps us differentiate ourselves in the market and demonstrate our value to our clients."

SILOED THINKING ON THE GLOBAL STAGE

The same fragmented thinking that causes managers to disregard interdependencies within their organizations also impacts how they design and manage their supply chains. For North American companies, the strategy has been to keep what's regarded as the high-value planning and design work at home and offshore the rest. The idea is that design and production can be optimized independently of each other.

"Most people don't do their product design at the same time as their process design," says Jim Huntzinger, president and founder of Lean Frontiers, a company that organizes events promoting Lean methodology. "They tend to do that using segmented silos."

This segmentation of processes means that many inefficiencies in the supply chain are ignored. "If you're doing your design in North America and your parts are coming from Asia, you're not going to be able to create flow because you're holding these massive amounts of inventory in your supply chain," says Huntzinger. "And then, if you want to fine-tune your processes, you're stuck with a very slow iterative process between design and production."

The siloed approach also creates dependencies that can have disastrous consequences. As we saw in 2020 at the outset of the COVID pandemic, overdependency on a small number of medical equipment suppliers based in Asia left even some of the richest countries in the world unable to supply their emergency healthcare responders with the most basic tools to combat the virus, exacting an enormous human toll.

The situation was entirely preventable, says Abe Eshkenazi, CEO of the Association of Supply Chain Management, the largest nonprofit association for supply chain.

"When the pandemic hit, it became clear that we were living in sort of a bubble," says Eshkenazi. "We assumed that supply chains can be resilient and responsive no matter what type of disruption we're dealing with. And we clearly found out that we were not prepared for any type or every type of disruption, especially in the frequency and the duration that we experienced."

The problem was the same segmented thinking that stymies productivity within companies. "I think that historically, people have tended to do things that are departmental or functional with the assumption that if everybody else does their job, we'll all arrive at the same place at the same time," says Eshkenazi. "I think that fallacy has been highlighted in a number of examples. The mature supply chains have a very integrated activity not only in terms of eliminating those silos, but ensuring the quality of information that is shared across the enterprise. It needs to be seen as one enterprise – not a series of different functions within an organization."

Manufacturing, for example, can no longer be managed independently of the supply chain, but must be seen as a component of it. "In terms of the supply chain, you need to have the appropriate partners at the table developing the strategies in front of the production, not after," says Eshkenazi. "That's how you create true visibility and transparency within your supply chain, so that you can anticipate potential bottlenecks and address those upfront as opposed to dealing with them as an outcome."

The thinking that led to the recent supply chain debacle, however, is nothing new. Failure to see supply chains as the complex adaptive systems they are has also led many companies to misread the financial implications of outsourcing production to China and other countries where the cost of labor is relatively low.

One person who has studied this is Harry Moser, president and founder of Reshoring Initiative®, a nonprofit dedicated to bringing manufacturing jobs back to the US. In addition to advocating for government policy changes, the organization educates companies on strategies for manufacturing and sourcing within US.

"Productivity in a country is determined by ratio of value add over labor hours," says Moser. "In the US over the last 40 years, we went from making everything here to sourcing maybe half of the components in Asia at a 30 to 40 percent lower price compared with making them here."

Price alone, however, doesn't reveal the true cost of purchasing components from offshore providers. "When companies source offshore, they measure the cost using FOB price, but not the total cost of ownership of those components," says Moser. "That approach often undervalues the actual cost by 20 to 30 percent. That means that the cost of making the final product looks much lower than it is, and productivity appears to go up. So therefore, it's very likely that 20 years ago when we still had pretty good, measured productivity growth going on, it was due to an overstatement of value add."

To remedy this, Moser advocates using total cost of ownership (TCO) rather than just price as a cost measure for offshored components. Reshoring Initiative provides a free online calculator that helps companies reveal "hidden" offshoring costs such as shipping, inventory, risk mitigation, and production delays. The analysis typically shows that the TCO is 20 to 30% higher than the purchase price of the imported product.

This more realistic analysis narrows the perceived price advantage of offshoring. "The Ex Works price (EXW) of a product sourced from China averages about 72 percent of the US price, while the Total Cost of Ownership (TCO) averages about 95 percent of the US TCO," says Moser.

The point is, seeing supply chain components as isolated elements makes them vulnerable to chaotic influences, and leads to short-sighted financial decisions. Whether we've learned from the crisis of 2020 remains to be seen.

PRODUCTIVITY ON THE PODIUM

The 2023 docudrama *Maestro* begins with an early-morning phone call. Leonard Bernstein, then a 25-year-old unknown, was being summoned to fill in for ailing conductor Bruno Walter. That evening, Bernstein led the New York Philharmonic to a triumphant performance that made front-page headlines in the *New York Times*.

A point the film chose to emphasize was that Bernstein had done this with no rehearsal. Rehearsals, however, are what conducting is all about, explains Evan Mitchell, music director of the Kingston Symphony, who has conducted major orchestras across Canada. Furthermore, the art of conducting is largely about the ability to make those rehearsals as productive as possible.

"Once you get to the performance, all that's left is to facilitate and let the magic happen," says Mitchell. "I like to think of performances as a sort of celebratory accumulation of the work that we've done. If throughout the rehearsal process you have provided the appropriate vision, inspiration, and motivation, and you have given the players the space to lift themselves up and showcase their own artistry, that sets up the best-case scenario for success for the performance. But that same magic happens by virtue of the committed artistry of a group of people who are in the moment."

Bernstein's job as assistant conductor was to study the scores and serve as understudy. As the story goes, he reviewed the program in detail with Walter before the performance, marking his own score with all the instructions that Walter had given the orchestra.

While Bernstein went on to become a great conductor and was extraordinarily gifted in understanding the music and conveying that understanding, the success of that performance undoubtedly owed much to the work Walter had done in the rehearsals. And orchestras of New York Philharmonic caliber, Mitchell notes, are capable of performing without a conductor.

Conductors, therefore, are not superheroes who create brilliant performances out of thin air. The best are consummate musicians with highly developed knowledge of the works they are performing, and also skilled managers who can create a cohesive performance with 50 or 60 musicians under incredible time constraints.

"The nature of what orchestral musicians have to do in terms of working together is very precise," says Mitchell. "If you think about the degree to which there has to be unity and conformity, it's literally milliseconds before even a layperson can notice that the ensemble's not together. And so the level of focus, determination, and drive is very high, and has all the accoutrements of a high-stress job of that nature."

Deming, himself an amateur musician and composer, would have concurred. In his talks to business leaders, he often used the orchestra as an example of an interdependent system where all players work together towards a common aim. He wrote the following in *The New Economics*:

> "An example of a system, well optimized, is a good orchestra. The players are not there to play solos as prima donnas, each one trying to catch the ear of the listener. They are there to support each other.... The conductor, as manager, begets cooperation between the players, as a system, each player to support the others."[8]

Preparing an orchestra for a performance, consequently, is a highly team-intensive effort. It's also a race against the clock in which preparation can make all the difference. "The rehearsal process is an incredibly precious resource," says Mitchell. "There are all sorts of things that we can do before the rehearsal. If you're able to do something beforehand that takes you half an hour, but it saves you 90 seconds in rehearsal, that's actually a good exchange."

Before the first rehearsal, Mitchell invests hours penciling in indications on each individual part such as "play shorter," "play longer," "bring this out," and the like. "This is something I'd recommend to any conductor," says Mitchell. "With 50 or 60 parts, this takes an outrageous amount of time. But that way, you can leapfrog some of the iterations in the rehearsal process. That might only add up to five minutes, but that five minutes can be the difference between an excellent performance and one that is truly transcendent."

Getting the orchestra ready for that magical performance requires a delicate balance between showing strong leadership on one hand and allowing the performers to exercise their artistic judgment. This is something that conducting courses don't teach.

"I had a truly excellent musical education, but what they don't really teach you is how to deal with people," says Mitchell. "A symphony orchestra has all the social dynamics you see in the office with some added quirks – you're dealing with people who are very intense, are very creative, and have very big personalities."

The people part of the equation is a balancing act of providing a strong vision while giving players the freedom to deploy their artistic skills to implement it. This resembles the abilities of the business leaders you met earlier in this chapter.

"I like to think about the big picture," says Mitchell. "I like to empower players. I think one of the greatest skills that I have acquired over the course of my career is the knowledge and the capability to discern between the points in which I am very much needed as a leader to show, for example, precisely what the tempo is and lay that down. But the flip side of that coin is to be able to let players just play, and to communicate to them that I am giving them the freedom and the flexibility to exercise their artistic judgment. People respond to that and play better, in my estimation, so that's my personal philosophy."

TAKEAWAYS FROM THE MYTH OF SEGMENTED SUCCESS

- Conventional management practices are based on an outdated view of the world that emphasizes reductionism and predictability, and ignores the influence of complexity and interdependencies.
- Operating a company so that interdependencies are reflected in management practices and understood by all employees enables wide engagement in improving quality and productivity.
- To create a strong team environment, managers need to remove barriers such as siloed incentive plans and clearly communicate the aim of the organization.
- Recent lessons from supply chain disruptions during the COVID epidemic show how segmentation extends beyond the walls of the company, and how closer collaboration with supply chain partners can prevent such disruptions.

As we've seen, the Myth of Segmented Success is deeply entrenched in companies through policies, job descriptions, incentive plans, and years of tradition. What makes it especially difficult to shake its influence is that it works in conjunction with the four other deeply entrenched myths that we will explore in this book. Let's start with finance.

4

The Myth of the Bottom Line

Myth: The financials tell us everything we need to know about productivity

When confronting complexity, it feels reassuring to look at a single metric that purports to explain everything. As we saw in Chapter 1, people tend to look at the GDP as the sole indicator of economic progress, not because the figure is accurate, but because it is intuitively graspable and there's nothing else to grasp.

In business, the bottom line plays a similar role, giving insiders and outsiders alike what appears to be a definitive rating of the health of a company in a single, easy to digest number. Reliance on it is so ubiquitous that it is seen not as the construct that it is, but as a figure that is validated by proven scientific principles.

That science however, as we saw in Chapter 3, has been outdated in many respects for over a century. When we look at organizations through the lens of complex adaptive systems (CAS) theory, it becomes clear that excessive reliance on traditional accounting systems leaves management blind to forces that deter productivity, and often leads to counter-productive behavior.

In the next section, we look at how a CFO, whose company was confronting early shock waves from the emerging global economy, found a better way to look at the numbers.

WHAT THE NUMBERS WEREN'T SAYING

In the early 1980s, Orest (Orry) Fiume, a CPA and the chief financial officer of the Wiremold Company, an electrical components manufacturer based in West Hartford, Connecticut, enrolled in a part-time master's degree program at the Hartford branch of Rensselaer Polytechnic Institute. The course catered to full-time professionals, so the sessions took place in evenings and on weekends. All of his classmates were employed in various industries, and most of the instructors were adjunct professors with day jobs.

"This was a very different atmosphere from my undergraduate days," recalls Fiume. "These people were all working in industry, so we were having lots of real-world discussions about the problems we were all grappling with."

Productivity was one of the issues of the day, and the subject of one of the courses that Fiume took. As a practicing CFO in an industry that was increasingly threatened by overseas competition, the issue was particularly concerning. Even though Wiremold was doing well, Fiume felt that it was his duty to help his leadership avoid the mistakes that had recently sunk some of America's most respected manufacturers.

The readings for the course were not from a textbook, but from case studies and papers by leading thinkers in the accounting field. One of them was a 1977 paper called "How to Measure Productivity at the Firm Level," published by the American Productivity Center (APC), a not-for-profit that had been founded that year by business professor C. Jackson Grayson. (The organization was later to be renamed the American Productivity and Quality Center, or APQC.)

Grayson was well connected in Washington – he had served as chairman of the Price Commission in the Nixon administration, and as an advisor to President Reagan. APC was founded as a reaction to the productivity crisis, which Grayson didn't trust governments to address.

Fiume felt that the paper identified a significant gap in the tools accountants had at their disposal. The big idea behind it is that to understand and control profitability, it's necessary to create a clear separation between two of its components: productivity and price recovery, the latter being the influence of changes in the cost of purchases, such as materials, on the selling price. If the cost of materials increases and the selling price increases accordingly, the cost recovery is zero. Cost recovery can also be negative if the company is unable to raise the price to absorb that cost, or positive if it is able to increase the selling price by more than that added cost.

"The accounting profession measures everything in dollars," says Fiume, "so it's a mathematical product of a quantity of something times the unit price of that thing. But once you separate those two, you can make a critical distinction between productivity and price recovery, and each of their effects on profitability. These are two different concepts and need to be managed differently."

That separation allows a much more focused inquiry when comparing the profit generated by a process at two respective points in time. If the profit increased, for example, this might be due to higher productivity – that is, the process using its deployed resources more efficiently.

On the other hand, it could be due to price changes on either the input or output side of the equation. Fluctuations in material prices or labor rates, or energy costs, for example, affect profitability but not productivity. The same is true with a rise or drop in the selling price of a product. Price recovery can affect profitability either negatively (if, for example, material costs go up and the company is not able to recover that in the selling price), or positively (material costs go down and the company doesn't lower the selling price of the product).

Having this knowledge helps organizations focus on where they can affect profitability. "Very few people in any organization can affect the purchase or selling price of anything," says Fiume, "but everybody in the organization affects resource utilization. So, in looking at price recovery and productivity separately, you can see what's driving the dollars. In addition, you can measure both separately for each category of resources used: materials, labor, energy, capital, etc."

This approach brings the challenge of productivity out into the open. The point is that in some scenarios, productivity is the only variable that the company has control over. "The way you create productivity gains is by using less input per unit of output," says Fiume. "You cannot create a productivity improvement without having physical change. That's the only way you can change the relationship between the quantities consumed and the output."

In November 1981, Fiume wrote a memo to the Wiremold management team outlining his system for measuring productivity. With examples using actual numbers, Fiume showed how to isolate a productivity improvement or decline from price influences. He also showed how important trends, such as a decline in productivity, could be hidden in the financial reports.

A RADICAL NEW APPROACH

Wiremold continued to grow in sales and profitability during the early 1980s, and Fiume's colleagues on the senior management team showed little interest in his observations. However, by 1985, growth had slowed, and noticing the number of new electrical products that were being certified by UL, they realized that it was only a matter of time before their sector would be hit by foreign competition. Then, in 1988, the numbers started to decline.

In response, the company decided to enter the growing market that specialized in power protection products for electronic environments. This led to conversations with companies about potential acquisitions. One of these was Brooks Manufacturing, a Philadelphia-based manufacturer of surge protectors that was owned by founder Joe Brooks and his son Gary. The conversations went well, and Brooks was acquired by Wiremold in 1988.

Gary Brooks, it turned out, was to profoundly influence Wiremold's ultimate direction. He was on the board of the Philadelphia Area Council for Excellence (PACE), which was a sponsor of W. Edwards Deming's renowned four-day workshops. Encouraged by his conversations with Brooks, Fiume took the course, and was so impressed with Deming that he convinced the rest of the executive team to take the course as well. The NBC documentary *If Japan Can Then Why Can't We?* was shown to all employees.

The learnings from Deming encouraged the management team to commit to a company-wide "Total Quality" program. In 1989, Fiume signed up for a workshop on *kaizen* led by Masaaki Imai, one of the original pioneers who brought Japanese manufacturing methods to the West. The workshop presented, in Fiume's view, the "how" behind Deming's philosophy, and Fiume prepared a presentation for the team showing how these *kaizen* methods reinforced what Deming was teaching.

The workshop included two days in a classroom and three days of hands-on training in a local factory. Fiume convinced the team to nominate Wiremold as the example factory for the workshop. That offer was accepted, and for three days, two veteran Lean practitioners, Yoshiki Iwata and Chihiro Nakao, led an improvement effort on the Wiremold factory floor, and the company got its first exposure to Japanese manufacturing methods.

EARLY EXPERIMENTS

Inspired by these events, the company pressed forward with an implementation of just-in-time (JIT), which was the term used, rather loosely, to describe the Lean principles they had witnessed in the workshops. However, the efforts were at best haphazard. Ordering materials in smaller quantities led to shortages and producing in smaller batches to reduce inventory meant machines had to be set up more frequently for different products, and long setup times were causing delays and higher costs.

"We made every mistake in the book," says Fiume. "We were implementing just-in-time, which meant reducing inventories, but at the same time we were installing a new Manufacturing Resource Planning (MRP) IT system without realizing that the two were completely incompatible."

The company's finances, in the meantime, had continued to worsen. Over the period from 1987 to 1990, operating income declined by 82%, bringing the company into dangerous territory.

Fiume wanted to use financial information to provide better guidance to the rest of the team but found that the traditional GAAP-based reporting systems weren't providing any clarity regarding what was driving margins downward. At the core of this was standard cost accounting – the practice of assigning allocated costs to each product manufactured and sold, and then attempting to account for discrepancies, or variances, when the allocated standard costs don't match the actual cost numbers. Where there were declines (i.e., "unfavorable variances"), the numbers gave him no clue of how to trace them to their origin because they were the aggregate of an entire month's production, three shifts per day.

   In addition to the lack of clarity, there could be a productivity decline even though there might not be unfavorable variances. The spreadsheet on the left in Figure 4.1 shows a standard cost report comparing two production years for a product.

   In the second year, the Standard Cost P&L shows the standard number of labor hours was increased by 10% because a process step had to be added to rectify a quality problem. This moving of the goal posts, however, is obscured in a standard cost accounting financial report, which shows the labor efficiency to be 100% because it met the standard. However, productivity had actually declined by 10% because it took 10% more time to produce the same item.

   Another common misleader is the way GAAP accounting includes inventory as an asset. "One of the rules in accounting is called the matching principle," says Fiume. "This says that I want to match my cost of producing something and my revenues from selling it in the same time period. If I make something today, but I don't sell it today, that means I have no revenue, and I have to now defer, under the matching principle – I have

Standard Cost P&L		
	This Year	Last Year
Net Sales	100,000.00	90,000.00
Cost of Sales:		
Standard Cost	48,000.00	45,000.00
Purchase Price Variance	–3,000.00	10,000.00
Material Usage Variance	–2,000.00	5,000.00
Labor Efficiency Variance	7,000.00	–8,000.00
Labor Rate Variance	–2,000.00	9,000.00
Overhead Volume Variance	2,000.00	2,000.00
Overhead Spending Variance	–2,000.00	8,000.00
Overhead Efficiency Variance	16,000.00	–17,000.00
Total Cost of Sales	64,000.00	54,000.00
Gross Profit	36,000.00	36,000.00
Gross Profit %	36%	40%

Plain Language P&L			
	This Year	Last Year	% Change
Net Sales	100000	90000	11.1
Cost of Sales:			
Purchases	25300	34900	
Inventory Material:			
Increase / Decrease	6000	–6000	
Total Material Costs	31300	28900	8.3
Processing Costs:			
Factory Wages	11000	11500	–4.3
Factory Salaries	2100	2000	5.0
Factory Benefits	7000	5000	40.0
Services and Supplies	2200	2500	–12.0
Equipment Depreciation	2000	1900	5.3
Scrap	2000	4000	–50.0
Total Processing Costs	26300	26900	–2.2
Occupancy Costs:			
Building Depreciation	200	200	0.00
Building Services	2200	2000	10.00
Total Occupancy Costs	2400	2200	9.1
Total Manufacturing Costs	59800	57800	3.5
Inventory-labor, Overhead			
Increase / Decrease	4000	–4000	
Cost of Sales	63800	53800	18.6
Gross Profit	36200	36200	0.0
Gross Profit %	36%	40%	

Figure 4.1   Standard Cost P&L compared to Plain Language P&L.
Source: Adapted from Jean E. Cunningham, Orest J. Fiume., Real Numbers: Management Accounting in a Lean Organization., Cambridge, MA.: Lean Enterprise Institute, 2019, Loc 1526, Fig 6-1 and Loc 1585, Fig. 6-2.

to defer the cost of making that into the future when I do sell it. And the way you do that is you capitalize those costs, and we call it inventory." The problem is that only the material component is a physical asset. The rest, labor and overhead, is a deferred operating cost. Thus, when we build inventory, we take current operating cost and put it on the balance sheet in the account called "inventory." Conversely, when we reduce inventory, we take that deferred cost and add it to current operating costs.

To help clarify what was really happening, Fiume developed an alternative presentation that was later to be called the Plain Language P&L, which is shown on the right of Figure 4.1. A comparison of the two shows how a gain in productivity can be falsely indicated as a loss in a Standard Cost Report.

In this case, the company improved productivity while at the same time reducing inventory that was tying up space and generating a monthly expense. While the depletion of that inventory made the company healthier from a financial perspective by generating cash, the costs that had been capitalized in prior periods would have been removed from the balance sheet and charged to current operations, hiding the benefits of inventory reduction.

Here we see in broad daylight the divide between what's really happening on the shop floor – the place where wealth is created – and what the financial numbers are telling us. On the financials, inventory is a good thing – an asset that can absorb our expenses and make the balance sheet look healthy. But that positive aspect of inventory assumes that the products in inventory will eventually be sold. That, as we've seen in many meltdowns, should never be taken for granted.

Even in the best of scenarios, inventory creates a number of physical problems in production which translate into costs. Stored inventory takes up valuable space. It often clutters operations, increasing the time it takes to move materials into production areas. And as it sits, it often becomes obsolete. Unfortunately, many of these costs don't show up clearly in the standard cost financials.

The situation can be worse than misleading. In some companies, people take advantage of the arbitrary nature of standard costs to game the system to their own advantage. Overhead, for example, gets assigned based on a predetermined standard, and that can be the subject of interdepartmental warfare in companies over how it is allocated. Therefore, the system creates conflict among employees who should, in the company's best interests, be supporting each other to maximize productivity.

ACCOUNTING FOR SHOP FLOOR REALITY

In response to these problems, Fiume began to collect and track financial information based on real time inlays and outlays. Drawing on his earlier experience with measuring productivity, he realized that he was going to have to look beyond the financial statements to get what he needed. Much of this information was difficult to come by, but after some persistence in identifying information sources and experimentation with different ways of presenting the information, he was able to produce the Plain Language P&L on a regular basis.

The report was, by intention, accessible to all who were in a position to influence the results. The information not only explained the numbers to people with no financial background but revealed many influences on the bottom line that had been previously hidden. Furthermore, it gave managers the tools they needed to make wiser decisions about resources.

"As people began to understand productivity and price recovery, we started having people budget quantities and prices separately," says Fiume. "So, the question became 'What resources do we need to create the amount of output that we expect to sell? And then, what are we going to pay for those resources?' When you do that, you can get a much more detailed understanding of what's driving the business from a financial standpoint."

That activity proved to be timely. In 1991, Wiremold's CEO retired, and the board decided to hire a replacement who could champion the transformation of the company according to its new vision. Fiume was on the hiring committee, and the goal was clear – find someone who really understands how to move the company forward in its journey of transformation.

In September 1991, Art Byrne joined the company as CEO. Byrne had cut his teeth as a group president at Danaher, a consolidated manufacturing company that had been the first North American plant to engage Shingijutsu, a Japanese consulting company formed by former Toyota managers, including the aforementioned Iwata and Nakao. Byrne had a deep understanding of the fundamental differences between the traditional ways of managing a factory and the methods that had been so successful in Japan.

In his first presentation to his new management team, Byrne made it clear that productivity was key to the company's success. His first slide, Fiume recalls, displayed the equation shown here.

Productivity = Wealth

Byrne also understood that standard cost accounting was not compatible with the razor-sharp focus on productivity that he was committing the company to – one of his first acts was to discuss with Fiume that he wanted the company to no longer use standard cost accounting.

Fiume immediately produced one of his Plain Language P&Ls and asked what Byrne thought. "That works," he said. And so, actual costs, presented in clear English, rather than standard costs became the new financial reporting for the company.

Another step Byrne took was to revise the organizational structure into value streams, one for each product family. Each was led by a value stream manager who focused on the following metrics:

- Customer service percentage (percent orders shipped on time)
- Productivity (sales divided by full time equivalent employees - (FTEs))
- Quality (percent reduction in defects)
- Inventory turns (cost of sales divided by value of inventory)
- Visual control (determined by 5S and other metrics)

The rest is history. During Byrne's decade-long tenure, Wiremold grew its productivity by 14% per year for the next decade and increased its valuation from $30 million to $770 million. One of the reasons these achievements were possible was because managers were freed from the artificial metrics of accounting, and thus able to pursue shop floor metrics that signified increases in productivity. Consequently, instead of meeting their allocation targets and quibbling over variances, his managers stayed focused on reducing the number of defects, shortening lead times, removing unnecessary steps from processes, and reducing costly inventory. In other words, managers were spending their time improving the physical processes that create the value that customers pay for.

The story became the subject of many Lean books, including *Lean Thinking* by James Womack and Daniel Jones. Many of the leaders at Wiremold went on to lead continuous improvement journeys in other companies.

THE DISCONNECT BETWEEN TRADITIONAL ACCOUNTING AND PRODUCTIVITY

At the time when Wiremold began working with Plain Language P&Ls, some accounting experts were connecting the dots between the widely discussed productivity crisis and accounting systems.

In their 1988 book *American Business: A Two-Minute Warning*, APC founder C. Jackson Grayson and co-author Carla O'Dell warned of an impending crisis caused by lack of productivity in US companies. One of the culprits, they argued, was that accounting systems don't give managers the information they need to improve productivity:

> "Organizations urgently need global and widely understood measures of productivity that consider all the factors of production (labor, capital, materials, and energy) and link directly with their financial planning, budgeting, and management incentive systems. Unfortunately, the accounting profession, as outside auditors, has no interest in creating accepted principles for productivity reporting."

Management accountant Thomas Johnson was even more pointed in his seminal book *Relevance Regained*:

> "American businesses fall short of what is required to compete in today's customer-focused economy primarily because top managers use information from accounting systems to shape and control the actions of company personnel. If American business is ever to restore its lost competitive edge, companies must eschew the use of top-down accounting information to control operations. They must empower workers, and managers, to listen to and respond to the voice of the customers they serve and the voice of the processes in which they work."

Everybody knows how this story ended. Over the ensuing decades, business leaders generally ignored the warnings, and the US ceded its manufacturing leadership, which had once been a source of national pride, to China.

ASSESSING COSTS WITH REAL NUMBERS

Fiume's Plain Language P&L evolved, along with the work of other like-minded CFO's, into a field called Lean accounting, which has resulted in the retraining of thousands of accountants and other practitioners. In 2003, Fiume collaborated with Jean Cunningham, another Lean-minded CFO, to create their book *Real Numbers: Management Accounting in a Lean Organization*, which serves as a guidebook for Lean accounting.

Fiume dislikes the term Lean accounting, however, for the simple reason that his approach wasn't developed as an alternative to GAAP to manage the financial aspects of Lean – it was to get a true cost picture of production that he wasn't able to get from conventional GAAP accounting reports. (Recall that Fiume's experiments with the approach began long before he had any direct involvement with Lean.)

As the title indicates, the big idea behind *Real Numbers* is that it's possible to create monthly accounting reports based entirely on actual inlays and outlays, and without numbers derived through accounting algorithms. The fact that this alternative approach is fully GAAP compliant makes it a suitable (and legal) replacement for the standard cost driven reports that are commonly used.

Referring to the comparison of the two approaches in Figure 4.1, the first line (revenue) and the last line (net income) are identical in both reports, meaning they use the same accounting principles. What is different are all the lines in between – these explain the company's financial results in a straightforward manner that can be easily understood by people with no accounting background. They also provide transparency to the company's activity, revealing the true numbers rather than numbers buried in standard cost allocations.

Fiume had initially used spreadsheets to manage these numbers and compare them with their traditional reports. This made everyone comfortable (including its auditors and banks) with the fact that he wasn't defying GAAP rules. Eventually, in addition to eliminating the standard cost elements of the company's computer systems, he integrated the Plain Language P&L into its basic financial reporting systems.

The new approach removed the arcane process by which the performance of functional areas is assessed. Essentially, accounting sets standards based on forecasts, and then, at the end of a reporting period, compares the actuals with the standards. Differences are labeled as variances, and often the manager of the process is called upon to explain the variance.

Figure 4.2 shows how the various events unfold. Some weeks after the end of a reporting period, process owners are asked to explain their variances. Maybe there was a machinery malfunction, an unexpected nonstandard order, employee turnover, or an increase in material costs.

This approach is not only unhelpful to a manager who's striving to improve productivity, but actually a hindrance. First of all, it forces managers to look weeks into the past to explain variances, which is typically a waste of time. Secondly, it conceals much of the information that managers need to make improvements.

Finally, the approach creates discord. A manager's performance numbers are bundled together with that manager's share of building depreciation, taxes, insurance, and other indirect costs that the manager has no control over. Share of these costs is governed by management decisions that are often contentious.

"Using allocated costs, managers are tempted to make operating results look good by changing allocation methods," wrote Fiume and Cunningham. "Looking at results that are based on costs incurred by, and thereby assigned to, an operation, increases accountability. The way to improve results is by eliminating waste, not shifting blame."

Another important feature of the Plain Language P&L is that unlike the Standard Cost Report, it clearly separates the costs associated with inventory at the time they are incurred. This puts an end to practice of hiding these costs and then allowing them to negatively impact the current income statement when the inventory is liquidated.

Separately reporting costs incurred when inventory is created removes the false incentive to generate excessive inventory that ultimately costs

Figure 4.2 Conventional accounting cycle.

the company money in terms of depreciation, storage, and the cluttering of production areas. It also frees operations management to maintain their focus on improving inventory turns.

Perhaps the most important lesson from Real Numbers, however, is that it's a mistake to rely solely on financial numbers. As Fiume discovered in his experience at Wiremold, productivity is based on physical events, and therefore, can't be assessed independently of those. "Along with these columns of dollar figures, non-financial measurements are also needed to track the physical factors of a business, because improving productivity requires physical change," wrote Fiume and Cunningham.

Bringing these nonfinancial metrics – defects, inventory turnover, on-time delivery, pieces produced – into the executive decision-making process can be a key accelerator of productivity, as we will see in the following examples.

OPERATIONS AS A STRATEGIC ADVANTAGE

The importance of aligning corporate strategy with operational metrics, as opposed to the strictly financial metrics that guide most companies, is key to driving long-term value through continuous improvement. One of the best examples of this approach is Parker Hannifin, a manufacturer of motion and control technologies that employs over 60,000 worldwide. The company has been on a Lean journey since 2001 when then CEO Don Washkewicz oversaw its introduction.

The company distinguishes itself by its "Win Strategy," of which continuous improvement is a major pillar.

"*Kaizen* and continuous improvement activities are a key component of that Win Strategy," says Stephen Moore, VP of Lean Enterprise and Quality at Parker. "Our CEOs have made that clear in their conversations with the investment community."

Senior executives at Parker aren't just spectators of continuous improvement, however. Over the years, the program has expanded beyond the shop floor into the company's office environments. "Starting around 2006, we really started focusing very extensively on non-manufacturing transformations," says Moore. "And we do those not only at the corporate level, but in all of our divisions as well. We've run *kaizen* events in finance, HR, legal, tax, and IT. These events are geared toward solving a particular problem that they have. I think the culture at Parker, even beyond manufacturing, is really one around continuous improvement and problem solving. We provide our team members with extensive training, from basic problem solving up to Six Sigma Black Belts."

This unified approach provides enormous clarity about the direction of the company. "When we focus in our value streams, whether that's manufacturing or not, we're really looking at two major metrics," says Moore, "overall lead time, or the time it takes to bring that product to the customer, and productivity."

The metrics are essentially a tool to support improvement at the team level. "We want the metrics to be something that teams can really influence," says Moore. "I can use the system to see high level metrics for the entire company, like sales per employee, but when you get down to the value stream level, those metrics don't do much for us. So we want to start looking at questions like, 'How many pieces did we produce per labor hour?' We get down to the individual teams themselves. Those are the metrics that a team can impact."

CONTINUOUS IMPROVEMENT ON A GLOBAL SCALE

Another large corporation using operational metrics to drive continuous improvement is Enersys, a global battery manufacturer based in Reading, Pennsylvania. At Enersys, operations is seen as a source of strategic advantage in a global environment that is constantly changing. The company pursues operational excellence through the EnerSys Operating System (EOS), a strategic framework for developing enterprise excellence in order to improve the company's competitive position.

"In some companies, operations is seen as a black box," says Patrice Baumann, chief integrated supply chain officer in charge of global operations at Enersys. "We see the full complexity of what the market needs and what it takes to be able to make the basic operations of the company successful. It is a lot about agility."

Increasing productivity through operational improvements, Baumann explains, has the potential to either grow capacity without investing more money or reduce costs such as overtime. "The good thing about that way of cost and productivity improvements is that you can gain in capacity, or you can also gain cost flexing," says Baumann. "You can either produce 10 or 20% more with the same resources, or you can spend 5 or 10% less because you no longer need the overtime expense of running your machines on the weekend."

EOS includes a system called Managing Daily Improvements (MDI) where workplace staff on the shop floor track their progress based on a set of KPIs. This allows his team to manage overall progress and as well, to replicate the most successful practices in the company's different plants.

"With our MDI process, we pursue standardized KPIs across all the plants," says Baumann. "So, we have seven standardized KPIs and that allows us to create visual charts that help us do benchmarking between the plants. That way, I can see who the best ones are, and then go and see how they do it."

While the reporting framework is very structured, plants have some flexibility. "We let the plants select the KPIs that work best for them," says Baumann. "Quality, for example, can be a lot of different KPIs. It can be reducing the number of defective parts per million. It can be the scrap rate. It can be the rework rate. It can be the first past yield. It depends on the area. The main idea is that you select that KPI, and then make sure you can get down to the root cause of problems and get the countermeasures to fix them."

Ultimately, the emphasis is on developing people so that they can improve their processes and in turn, improve the bottom line. "We start by making sure we get the right thinking to our people so that they can see waste and find ways to reduce it," says Baumann. "At the end, you may be able to quantify those costs, but if we just go looking for cost reductions, we're not going to grab all the opportunities we have. So I always say, start with the people."

THE POWER OF VELOCITY

One of the hallmarks of highly successful Lean companies has been the pursuit of aspirational goals that stretch the capabilities and the imagination of everybody involved in the value streams. These are not targets in the conventional sense, where the boss says, "Make this number or else." Instead, they are team initiatives where a leader or coach says, "Let's all work together and see if we can cut our lead time in half." George Koenigsaecker, an early adopter of Lean in North America, often spoke of "doubling the good and halving the bad."

What's surprising is just how successful these stretch initiatives can be. They not only produce game-changing results, but engage workers as they contribute their ideas in a team effort to achieve those results. People in Lean organizations often speak of being at war with bad processes!

Dan McDonnell, a consultant who has led large-scale value stream transformations at major manufacturers like GE and Trane (formerly Ingersoll Rand), emphasizes this when he works with senior executive teams. "People freak out when we talk about cutting a timeline in half," says McDonnell. "They think it's more realistic to look for a 5% or a 7% improvement. But that really amounts to what I call calibrating the problem – people can just find ways to tweak the numbers to show that improvement. But there's no possible way to double the good or halve the bad without a reinvention of the process. So you're forcing your teams to think outside of the box. And that can be at a workstation level or an enterprise level."

To illustrate, McDonnell draws a point A and point B on opposite ends of a whiteboard and then draws a line, representing a timeline, joining the two. The space in between, he explains, represents the processes required to get from point A to point B. "The process could be anything," says McDonnell. "It could be in a hospital, a bank, or a factory."

Then, underneath that, he draws a similar timeline that moves point B to the middle, cutting the timeline in half. He then repeats that, cutting the timeline in half again. Then he goes back to the original and asks the participants what occurs between the two points. With a little prompting, executives start to name examples. There are production steps of course, but also issues such as quality problems, safety problems, inventory, waiting, costs, and rework.

"Usually, we end up with a list of ten or twelve things," he says. "Then I ask, what do you think would happen to quality if we shortened the timeline? Is it better or worse?"

A key concept behind this is that, as we saw in the Deming chain reaction, improving quality, cost, or speed is not a zero-sum game. Participants get an intuitive sense of this during the exercise, and this is where the light comes on.

"What they realize at this point is that a lot of the cycle time in the original timeline is consumed with waste, quality issues, and things like that," says McDonnell. "So if we truly honestly reduce the cycle time, then the only way we're able to do that is to eliminate all those issues."

The inquiry continues as the participants speculate on the effect of shortening the timeline on safety, costs, rework, and other non-value issues, and gradually, the participants begin to appreciate the power of shortening the timeline, as Taiichi Ohno had so famously illustrated.

The message is that in a large company, regardless of line of business, the master production metric is time, that is, the speed at which a workpiece progresses through the value stream. "Velocity is a powerful weapon," says McDonnell. "It's not just velocity itself – if you truly get to be that much faster, your quality is better, your safety is better, your deliveries are better – everything's better. I think that's why Taiichi Ohno said what he did sixty years ago."

The context for all this is that Lean is ultimately a growth strategy, not a cost-cutting strategy. "I'm a big productivity driver," says McDonnell. "A lot of places that we've done the work over many, many years, we've seen significantly differentiated productivity that way and, in all regards, not just labor, but all spends. But I believe that ultimately, it's about growth, not about cutting costs. If you're doing it right, you're gaining share, which by the way, is going to give you a lot of leverage on the P&L around growing operating margins. So without even considering the productivity gains that you're going to see, I'm going to get significant margin gain just by being able to grow at a differentiated rate to my competition."

All this, McDonnell explains, depends on culture. As we saw in Chapter 1, the problems that have to be solved to make significant gains in productivity are numerous and granular, so you can't cut a timeline in half without the full engagement and cooperation of all employees.

"If you interviewed a hundred people at large and asked, 'Who owns safety?' they'd all say, 'I do' or 'we do' without a single thought," says McDonnell. "But if you went out and grabbed another hundred people at random and asked them who owns quality, you'd hear things like 'the quality engineer,' 'the line inspector,' 'the line quality manager,' etc. Almost never will you hear 'I do this.'"

When working with executives, McDonnell continues to press the issue. "When I'm working with a team that's trying to drive all this,

I ask them, 'What if we came back here in five years and asked that same question, and 100% of people said "I own quality" without hesitating. What do you think would have happened to quality over that period?' My point is that with respect for people, everybody owns the process, and team members are respected even by a vice president as colleagues. I think that's one of the magic bullets of Toyota – they've created a broad deep sense of true ownership of both the process itself, the way everyone interacts together, and the results that go to customers."

PRACTICES ENTRENCHED IN IT SYSTEMS

One of the developments that has cemented the use of traditional GAAP accounting is the automation of accounting processes through Enterprise Resource Planning (ERP) systems. Often, the systems companies select are chosen by finance people who have little understanding of the data requirements in operations.

"Accounting and finance probably benefits from ERP systems by having an easier month-end close, but operations tends to suffer, because they already had a system, but now they have to adapt the systems they already had to a new system," says Randy Kesterson, a management consultant based in Charlotte, North Carolina, who provides strategic advice to senior executives. "And a lot of times, that doesn't work out very well. I see evidence everywhere I go of finance-led ERP implementations, where operations was the tail of the dog. It should be the reverse. Operations is where the value is created. Apologies to my friends in accounting and finance, but you're keeping score while operations is playing the game."

Because of the way ERP systems are designed, companies often have to customize their system or use manual workarounds in order to extract the kind of information used in the Lean accounting Plain Language P&L. This process is often unreliable.

"I've been around long enough to know not to trust the data in an ERP system if I'm going to make a major decision," says Kesterson. "I was working with a group recently where they were trusting the data from the system for a three-month build plan, and I suspected that the data was flawed. So we did some manual digging and within 30 minutes found several problems that would prevent us from shipping in the next three months but would not have been found in the system. There were parts with no source codes, parts with no lead times, but these things weren't being flagged. But as these people saw it, the system had been working fine – they clearly didn't have the experience of being burned by flawed (or missing) data."

This problem gets extremely difficult when companies have multiple operations in different locations. "When the needs of operations are treated as secondary or tertiary to those of accounting and finance, it can make it very difficult to effectively and efficiently run the business," says Kesterson. "For example, I observed (after the fact) that a client with more than a dozen manufacturing sites around the world had selected an ERP system designed for continuous flow manufacturing when some of the sites were using batch or discrete manufacturing approaches. It's like having five children, each with a different vision prescription, and giving them all the same eyeglasses. Will it work? For some better than others!"

THINKING LONG-TERM

The continuous improvement approach has implications for investors, and that needs to be clearly communicated if a transformation is going to succeed. Pierluigi Tosato, CEO of the European baked goods producer Bouvard, has a well-established reputation for applying continuous improvement in the food and beverage sector. "In the investment community, I'm known as a *kaizen* guy," says Tosato.

Tosato's strategy is to avoid getting caught in the quarter-by-quarter cycle and establish a culture for long term sustainable improvement. "I can improve the short term by cuts, but that can damage the company in the long term," says Tosato. "This is why we should not do it. On the other side, there's a lot of inefficiency in companies that are experiencing losses that you should focus on. I'm taking out the waste, but I'm not cutting costs in the old way, because this is old school. It's easy that way to fix things short term, but you might damage the company. That is not my goal."

What this requires is shareholders adjusting their expectations. "*Kaizen* is slower," says Tosato. "Unlike cost cutting, you need more time to change the culture inside the company. You do this bottom up, not top down. So you involve the people, involve the blue collars. That takes time. And you need to be able to explain to your shareholders that if you start with *kaizen*, the good news is that we are not going to ask them for money. The bad news, you ask for time." In Europe, he notes, investors are more willing to look at the longer term, compared with US investors.

Perhaps the most convincing testament to the value of non-financial metrics is Toyota's approach to productivity, as explained in Chapter 1 according to Kiyoshi "Nate" Furuta in his book *Welcome Problems, Find Success*. While the company carefully tracked its financial numbers, it recognized that they only tell part of the story.

Toyota Japan's single KPI, as mentioned, was determined largely by non-financial metrics such as quality, safety, and employee morale. Improvements in these areas are not immediately visible in the financials, yet they are factors that companies can control, whereas many others – costs of materials, shortages, market fluctuations – are subject to external conditions. Toyota's relentless focus on productivity proved to be incredibly durable – the company grew its productivity reliably year after year in spite of varying external influences.

A NOVEL INVESTMENT APPROACH

Cliff Ransom is president of Ransom Research Inc., an investment equity research firm that focuses on publicly traded companies committed to Lean methodology. Over the years, Ransom has evaluated and tracked a portfolio of companies that he believes are excellent long-term investments based on their Lean practices. Parker Hannifin is one of the companies on his Super Achievers list.

Like Fiume, Ransom doesn't believe in standard cost estimates – his approach is to dig deeper to understand the company's operations. "Wall Street tends to focus on the income statement, where almost every GAAP accounting number is an estimate," says Ransom. Many of the metrics Ransom tracks are the nonfinancial indicators that are driving the success of companies like Parker Hannifin. Much of his emphasis is on how a company treats its employees.

"When I'm looking at a company, I start with safety," says Ransom. "If you don't have safety, you can't have engaged employees. I don't care how you motivate them or reward them – if they feel unsafe, and they're worried about going home without an arm, they're not going to work well – they're not going to listen to you. But most companies don't even measure safety effectively. They only collect recordables, not Near Misses, much less Risk Forecasting."

Ransom has seven categories for evaluating companies' long-term growth prospects – they must be Consistent, Repeatable, Improvable, Integratable, Scalable, Sustainable, and Predictable (CRIISSP). "Very few companies can get 8 or 9% organic growth for a sustained period," says Ransom. "But if they get to seven or eight, they fall into my CRIISSP acronym. Each of those seven words adds about a point or a point and a half to that organic growth number."

How they spend their cash is also important. "My preference is for free cash flow to be spent on supporting and expanding existing businesses, R&D, new product development, exploration of ancillary, contiguous, or related markets, broadening geographical reach, and widening or deepening feet on the street," says Ransom.

Ransom believes that the common practice of stock buybacks diverts funds that could be used to improve the business. "To me, large stock buybacks are a sign from management that it does not see that it has the ability to expand its existing business," says Ransom. "I ask CEOs, 'If developing your own business is not a priority, why should I or my clients invest in your company?'"

THE FUTURE OF ACCOUNTING

The success of Lean companies has had little impact on the training of accountants. In 2024, graduates still believe that the bottom line tells them everything they need to know.

"Accountants are trained to think like they can understand everything through the numbers or a spreadsheet," says Nick Katko, president and owner of BMA, a consulting firm that helps companies adopt Lean accounting. "That applies to any operation – not just manufacturing operations. There's a lot of variability, and there are a lot of problems every day. That's what accountants don't understand."

Consequently, productivity is often discussed in boardrooms with little understanding of what drives it let alone how to improve it. "Productivity is increasing output with the same resources," says Katko. "That's a performance measurement, but it's not accounting in the sense that people usually see it. When you use the word accounting, everybody starts thinking debits, credits, and financial statements. So you can't measure productivity from just looking at the financial statements."

A major sticking point appears to be that discovering variability and problems requires leaders to connect with people on the front lines – something that graduates, for the most part, don't even realize is a requirement.

"You can't teach people with no experience the craft of managing people because the craft is experience based," says Henry Mintzberg, a Cleghorn Professor of Management Studies at McGill University in Montreal, and the author of numerous books that criticize conventional management training and practice. "What MBA students learn is the analysis of managing, which is a small part of it. So people graduate assuming that management is all about technique and analysis and numbers and measures, and that distorts things. And the evidence of the performance of MBAs as CEOs is not good."

On the other hand, analyzing a business from an operational standpoint isn't rocket science. "I don't think that analyzing a business is that complicated," says Katko. "If you're a for-profit business, you've got to provide more value in order to sell more. And inside any business, if you want to manage costs, you'd better manage operations in order to improve productivity. It doesn't work top down where you dictate that expenses have to go down 5% next quarter."

THE OUTSIDE VIEW

The majority of people learn about productivity based on what they read in the popular press. Unfortunately, the media invariably base their reports on the views of economists, who paint a very misleading picture of what productivity is.

"The problem with economists is that they can't tell the difference between productive and destructive productivity," says Mintzberg. "Because to determine productivity, economists measure the ratio of productive outputs to labor inputs. And when that looks good, they declare an economy to be productive. But they're assuming that this is the result of workers being trained, that they're using the right machinery, and so on. This is no doubt the case for some of productivity, but not all of it. For example, if you're the CEO of a manufacturing company determined to become the most productive company around, here's what you do – fire everybody in the factory and ship from stock. Sales will continue while working hours go down. Any economist will tell you that's productive and great for the company, until, of course, it runs out of stock. And that's what a lot of executives are doing, and it shows up in the economists' statistics as productive."

Conventional GAAP accounting is also used for financialization, that is, the representation of an organization as a portfolio of financial assets. This oversimplification doesn't only mislead; it provides a precept for corporate practices – such as laying off employees to boost share prices – that most people find reprehensible. It also leads corporations and private equity firms to acquire businesses where they have little or no expertise, often with disastrous results. But when people decry these practices, few cite the fact that conventional accounting methods don't reveal any alternatives, let alone an understanding of why these practices might be unsustainable.

THE MYTH OF THE BOTTOM LINE TAKEAWAYS

- Reliance on financial reports as the ultimate authority on an organization's productivity is often misleading, and causes managers to initiate actions that are counterproductive.
- Managers can gain forward-looking insights on their productivity by following direct production costs as well as nonfinancial metrics such as safety, employee engagement, inventory, and lead times.
- Lean accounting methods developed by Orest Fiume and others provide a GAAP-compliant alternative to conventional methods, allowing clear visibility of the numbers affecting the organization's productivity.

This alternative approach to accounting requires gathering data that can only be collected by interacting with people on the front lines. Many managers, however, believe that part of their role is to have all the answers. In the next chapter, we'll see just how wrong that belief is, and how some innovative leaders are countering it.

5

The Top-Down Knowledge Myth

Myth: Managers always have the answers and keep workers productive by telling them what to do

In his highly influential 1911 book *Principles of Scientific Management*, Frederic Winslow Taylor related a story about how he had directed a worker, whom he called Schmidt, to nearly quadruple his output, measured in tons per day of pig iron loaded onto a truck. Taylor's method was to assign a supervisor to direct Schmidt's exact movements, and to increase Schmidt's pay for meeting that target by 60%.

Central to Taylor's method was his assertion that by observing the movements of Schmidt and other laborers, he could determine the most efficient way of doing the work, which he called the "one best way," and then instruct workers accordingly.

The directions were very precise. When the supervisor told Schmidt to "walk," he was to walk. When he told him to pick up a "pig" (piece of pig iron), he was to pick up a pig. When he told him to sit down, he was to sit down.

Taylor honed his approach at Bethlehem Steel, where he was head of engineering. The publication of *Principles of Scientific Management* made him an overnight phenomenon. Soon he was lecturing all over the world, and lauded in both business and academic communities.

The impact was enormous. Thousands of stopwatch-bearing "efficiency experts" were hired to conduct time-and-motion studies and instruct workers, based not on workplace knowledge but on "scientific" principles. The approach was adopted first in manufacturing and then in other sectors, either through direct practice or its influence on management training.

Productivity grew remarkably during the first half of the 20th century, powered by exponential improvements in the capacity, speed, and efficiency of production machinery. Taylorism was seen as an important contributor to this period of unparalleled growth.

The practice of creating and maintaining job standards to ensure consistency in the way employees carry out their work is certainly an enabler of high productivity. However, the notion that a manager or efficiency expert can determine that best way with no input from the workforce proved to be fatally flawed. In his 1982 book *Out of Crisis*, Deming, citing the decline of America's industrial competitiveness, warned that the managers who had assumed they knew all the answers were clueless about why they were performing so poorly in comparison with their Japanese peers:

> "The supposition is prevalent the world over that there would be no problems in production or in service if only our production workers would do their jobs in the way they were taught. Pleasant dreams. The workers are handicapped by the system, and the system belongs to management."[1]

In a nutshell, workplaces are far more complex, interdependent, and subject to random variation than conventional management theory indicates. The upshot is that workplace problems don't manifest as clearly defined line items in a management report – they are granular, numerous, and often only visible upon close examination in the workplace.

Deming's message, therefore, was that American companies would not be able to dig themselves out of the hole they were in unless they engaged not just the hands, but the brains of their entire workforce in company-wide campaigns of continuous improvement, as Toyota and other Japanese companies had so convincingly demonstrated.

The good news was workers could be counted on to rise to the occasion. The bad news was that for the most part, management would have none of it.

CHALLENGES TO THE OLD WAY

During the early 20th century, a number of theorists began to challenge the top-down paradigm that defined American management. One of the most prominent was Douglas MacGregor, a professor at Sloan School of Management at MIT and disciple of Abraham Maslow. In 1960, in his seminal work *The Human Side of Enterprise,* McGregor outlined two contrasting styles of management: theory X, which is the traditional command-and-control approach, and theory Y, which represents a less rigid and more collaborative approach.

McGregor argued that organizations would perform better if they integrated theory Y principles into their management style. Many of these principles are acknowledged by today's managers, but integrating them into the traditional hierarchical pyramid is challenging, because that pyramid is essentially held together by theory X thinking. Theory X is the simplest way of approaching the relationships between managers and those who report to them, and therefore tends to be the default. If there is an argument between taking a theory X or theory Y approach, theory X will invariably win.

A number of thinkers, however, began to ask, "How can we change our management structures to accommodate this more realistic view of human productivity?" This question has turned into a focus of the Shingo Institute, a program of the Huntsman School of Business at Utah State University, and home of the Shingo Prize™.

"Shigeo Shingo, who wrote 17 books, talked a lot about the work of Douglas McGregor, and used the terminology of Theory X and Theory Y companies," says Ken Snyder, the Shingo Institute's executive director. "He believed that the Theory X approach – command and control – which is the way organizations have been run for decades, is not the way they should be run. So he wrote about Theory Y a lot, which was his way of describing the best practices at the time of Japanese businesses. He believed that people need to be respected in what they do, not only by being in charge of their own work, but being responsible for doing it correctly. So there was a good controversy about that going back to the 1970s."

Snyder, who began studying the topic when he was in graduate school, cited the principal barrier – Theory X tends to overwhelm Theory Y. "Theory X precludes Theory Y unless you change the fundamental ways of running the organization," says Snyder. "All these aspects of it – command and control, only the boss knows best – you've got to throw that out the window and rebuild it in a different way."

Snyder cites Toyota, which had engaged Shingo as a consultant. "This is what Toyota has done," Snyder says. "There are a lot of great organizations that have figured out that it's not all about the bosses controlling everything; it is about engaging the people in a common purpose that all team members buy into. And, to a large extent, people can use their agency and govern themselves to do great work. And as a whole, they can do a lot more than the bosses alone can do with the robots that they bring along with them."

The approach, however, has been slow to pick up. "The biggest hurdle we see is the mindset of leaders," says Snyder. "Leaders need to change to where they are respectful of their people and willing to listen to them. They need to think of their people as their most important asset, and see that their job is to give their people the resources they need to give them to do their job. So you create a culture of respect."

Culture, however, is viewed as a nontangible soft target compared with financialization and short-term profit seeking. Often relegated to the HR department, culture is rarely seen as central to productivity, even when the evidence is overwhelming.

Snyder's favorite example of this dogged disregard for culture is the demise of New United Motor Manufacturing Inc. (NUMMI), the famous joint venture between Toyota and General Motors that was described in Chapter 1.

"What did GM learn from Toyota?" asks Snyder. "They walked away with *kanban* and a bunch of other Lean tools. But they never learned the culture side of it. So the whole thing was killed from a lack of investment."

Snyder is confounded by the seeming inability of American managers to adopt new ways. One of most widely discussed contributors to this is the influence of Wall Street, which invariably sets a short-term agenda that precludes any long-term investment in culture.

"The main actors that reinforce Theory X practice are Wall Street," says Snyder. "They value quarterly results and to give one example, they think that whenever there's a temporary downturn, that you need to adjust your workforce accordingly. But when you do that, you destroy the culture within the organization that you've spent so much time and effort building."

In the long run, Snyder explains, the destruction of the culture eventually leads to the company being worthless.

Of course, there are situations where the work disappears and layoffs or redeployments are necessary, Snyder acknowledges – at issue is a knee-jerk reaction that has become a firmly entrenched pillar of management culture.

"We've got this idea of command-and-control that we hold so dear that we have to keep supporting it and keep enacting it," says Snyder. "We've got all these examples of a better way. Why don't we learn that better way?"

VALUING EMPLOYEES PAYS OFF

The COVID pandemic that began in 2020 placed enormous stress on companies' revenues, and in response companies resorted to layoffs in astounding numbers – an estimated 20 million Americans had filed for unemployment benefits during the first weeks of the pandemic.

The staggering impact that this had on workers and their families has been widely publicized and discussed. What is less well known is the loss of experience and expertise that companies were faced with when they engaged in widespread layoffs. Financial decision-makers, this shows, are so far removed from the productive forces in their organizations that they have no idea of the true value that workers are capable of providing. Consequently, they see workers as merely a dispensable cost that should be alleviated wherever possible.

Snyder cites DENSO – an auto parts manufacturer that was spun off from Toyota and now supplies to all OEMs – which faced a crisis during the pandemic because they didn't have the chips to continue production, and neither did their OEM partners. So they held off on all the orders, but instead of laying off their workers, as their competitors had done, they kept them on and implemented many of the process improvements that they had been working on. They also did a lot of proactive maintenance on their machinery and facilities.

"Because they knew that the market would come back as soon as the supply chain issues got resolved, they realized it was a temporary problem," says Snyder. "They said, 'Let's not lay off our workforce and risk losing all of this built-up knowledge and training that we have in all of these wonderful people that work for us. Let's keep them ready. When the orders came back, DENSO hit the road running, while their competitors who had laid off their workers, were unable to deliver. DENSO's contracts, which had previously been split 50/50 with competitors, grew to 100% of the available business, while DENSO's competitors took months to catch up. And so DENSO more than made up for whatever it lost by carrying their workforce for a few months."

This was not a scenario that Wall Street could relate to. "Was Wall Street happy? Maybe not," says Snyder, "but who cares? Maybe some Wall Street people who think long term. Was the business strengthened? Yes. Were customers happy? Yes, because they could respond when others quit. But this shows a whole different kind of a mindset than what we see in most companies."

As companies eventually caught up, they began to complain about phenomena publicized as "the great resignation" and "quiet quitting." The idea is that workers have lost their motivation, and don't want to work. Not discussed is that corporations lost the trust of the workforce during the pandemic and workers are revolting against the "money only" stance of management.

"You're not going to get people engaged because the shareholders and top executives might get more money," says Snyder. "What motivates people is a purpose. And if they buy into the purpose of the organization, they'll put their heart and soul into it if you give them a chance. They'll be thinking, 'How can we make this organization better and better and better?' But I don't know anybody who wants to go to work for a company that is all about making more money for just the shareholders and the leaders."

CREATING AN ENDURING CULTURE

The Shingo Institute, named after Shigeo Shingo, was founded in 1989 to promote excellence in the Toyota tradition. The first Shingo Prize for enterprise excellence, later to be dubbed the "Nobel Prize for Manufacturing," was awarded in 1989. In 1993, the institute created a set of assessment criteria to help companies achieve the prize, which were then defined as the Shingo Model. Notable prize winners include Ford Motor Company, Johnson Controls, Steelcase, and Goodyear.

The progression, however, was not perfect, and in 2008 Snyder and his colleagues were getting concerned about the number of companies that won the prize but then were not able to sustain the excellence. "We were saddened by the fact that the majority of recipients during those first 15 years fell off the ladder, so to speak," says Snyder. "We knew something was missing."

To understand the issue better, the institute studied companies that had been successful at sustaining excellence, and companies that hadn't. "We looked at the organizations that kept getting better and better," says Snyder, "and we asked them, 'Why did you do that?' They were able to give us answers to our 'why' questions, and their answers revealed consistent themes, which we were able to articulate in the guiding principles."

The team followed the "five whys" approach where they continually asked them to explain the thinking behind what they were doing. Snyder cites the following example:

Q: Why did you take this action?

A: Because we want to respect our people and give them the dignity of being responsible for their job – both the productivity and the quality. And we want to give them all the resources they need and give them the best checks and balances we can, but we want them to take responsibility. We want them to own the job. We don't want to have somebody coming, looking over their shoulder, inspecting them, and telling them how they should be doing the job all the time. We want to train them to do the work. Why do we train them the way we train them? Why do we give them the ability to make suggestions to how to improve their job? We do that because we respect the fact that they know their job better than anybody else. So let's help them do that.

"We got very different answers from the companies that were not able to sustain it," says Snyder. "Things like 'Well, the engineer left so nobody was watching after what was going on in the process, and it all fell apart.' This showed that the company was following an engineering-driven approach versus a 'people doing the work'–driven approach."

STRENGTHENING THE MODEL

As the study evolved, Snyder and his colleagues began to see that the reason the companies that had fallen off the path was that in spite of having excellent systems in place, they hadn't established a culture to support them.

"Our earlier model just looked at systems, tools, and results," says Snyder. "If they had good Lean systems, good Lean tools, and were getting good results, they would get a Shingo Prize. But we knew we weren't measuring the right things when it came to sustainable excellence." Snyder adds, "That didn't mean that they shouldn't have good systems, and it doesn't mean they shouldn't have good Lean tools. Of course, you have to have results otherwise your business is going to fail. But we knew something was missing. And that's when we got into setting the culture."

The input led the institute to revamp the Shingo Model in 2008. A notable change was a strong emphasis on engaging people throughout the organization. "We went through them one by one," says Snyder, "and we kept hearing these consistent reasons why they did what they did, and we put them into that set of guiding principles. Now, most of those principles had been around for a long time, but we think we've successfully put them into a cohesive unit. They can't be looked at individually because they're so integrated with each other. For example, how can you assure quality of the source unless you're respecting the individual that you're giving the responsibility to assure the quality of the source?"

Prominent in the new model is a set of guiding principles, which are now represented as the bedrock for the model:

- Respect every individual
- Lead with humility
- Seek perfection

- Embrace scientific thinking
- Focus on process
- Assure quality of the source
- Improve flow and pull
- Think systemically
- Create constancy of purpose
- Create value for the customer

Snyder places considerable emphasis on respecting every individual. "When we published the new Shingo model in 2008, we used the term 'respect every individual,'" says Snyder. "We realized that too many people respect some people but not others. And so then the question is, why did they respect someone and not others? There's an element here in saying that some people don't deserve to be respected. So we felt that it was imperative on us to make sure it was clear that you get out of that "deserving respect" because everybody deserves respect. So therefore we need to say respect every individual, every team member, even if it's a part time or temporary person, who has an idea."

HELPING EMPLOYEES SUCCEED

One company that Snyder cites as getting better and better is O.C. Tanner Company, a provider of products and services that support companies' employee recognition programs. The company, based in Salt Lake City, Utah, employs two thousand worldwide, creating a variety of deliverables, including trophies and plaques, software for managing employee recognition programs, and consulting services to help companies implement their programs. The company was an early adopter of Lean, implementing it around the same time as the classic NUMMI and Wiremold experiments were gaining momentum. The company was also an early adopter of the Shingo Principles, and won a Shingo Prize in 1999.

"When we began our Lean journey 31 years ago the word 'Lean' hadn't been coined yet," says Gary Peterson, executive vice president, supply chain and production, and a 35-year veteran at the company.

The company had made its name for offering the best-quality products in the marketplace. "We've always have been the market leader in terms of the best-quality product," says Peterson, "and the best designs and the most creative designs. Going back 30 years, we were primarily a manufacturing company. And that was that was a big differentiator for us."

Maintaining that quality, however, was requiring a lot of rework, and the costs of that were mounting. "That quality came at great cost," says Peterson. "We had real issues; our first-time quality was around 68% or something like that."

As they began their Lean journey, the immediate task was to redesign workflows to make the processes more visible. "We had 28 departments, huge piles of works in progress (WIP) in front of each department, no accountability for quality, and very poor systemic thinking across the entire value stream," says Peterson. "For many people, it wasn't clear what the customer was buying from us."

To bring some order, they reorganized the work to make the entire fabrication process visible to the workers involved in the processes. "By going to one-piece flow and putting everyone into U-shaped cells where every process is there, they're now familiar with every process, and how every team member before and after them added value," says Peterson. "This allowed everybody to think systemically about improvements and about value. So I think being able to see the work differently, to work differently, was a big deal for us."

There were hurdles to overcome, however. The company found that even though the processes were right out in the open, workers were constantly looking to their managers for guidance. "In the beginning, people didn't believe that they had any impact on quality or efficiency, or even safety," says Peterson. "It was, 'That's not my problem, the manager owns all of this. I'm just doing what I'm told, and if it's wrong, it's not my fault.' So we were trying to break that mentality."

What Peterson and his team decided is that the relationship between frontline workers and their managers had to change. In the past, the only contact had been when the manager was responding to a problem and needed to provide guidance. Managers also relied on their knowledge that they had acquired on the job and used that as a precept for showing workers "the right way" to do things. What was needed was more of a coach-mentor relationship that encouraged workers to be more autonomous, and to develop their own problem-solving skills.

"We put in a system that required every manager to sit down every week for five or ten minutes with every person to talk about their week," says Peterson. "Attendance was an issue, safety was an issue, but so was the team output, the team quality, and so forth. So they actually had some metrics that they were tracking. And I think the thing that mattered wasn't a focus on the results. It was the interaction that the manager was having one-on-one with every team member."

The system evolved to become O.C. Tanner's coaching system – one of 30 systems that support the Shingo Principles. Today, the discussions are much broader and more holistic. "I think our coaching system is one of the most important systems that we have," says Peterson. "Every team member sits down and does at least 30 minutes every month with their manager. It's a dual-managed discussion where both are talking about 'What do we need to address here? What can we talk about?' And the whole focus is managers are thinking, 'How can I help you be your best self?' So it may not be necessarily work related. Maybe there are issues at home. We're talking about anything to help you bring your best self to work."

The company also took action to break down the notion that managers have all the answers. Managers and directors are rotated approximately every three years to ensure that they become proficient in the coaching role rather than falling back on their workplace knowledge and desire to apply that directly to situations and problems.

The transition, however, was not without its challenges. While frontline workers frequently adapted, the managers had a tougher time. "I think team members step up to the plate much quicker than your line leaders do," says Peterson. "Line leaders got promoted for doing the things I'm now asking them to stop doing. And they've made a career out of the exact skill set that we don't want anymore. So it's tough. And I hate to say it, but we lost about half of our managers. But I believe the reason we lost them was that there was not a clear message from the top that this is what we're doing."

The journey, nonetheless, has continued, giving workers an unusual degree of autonomy. "Our teams are now self-managed. Each cell of two to seven people have got their own financials that they track every day to understand what their contribution dollars were. Every month the cell, and the value stream, gets a number from accounting that shows them their profit margins. All of their goals are tied around providing more value to the client with less effort. We measure that value primarily, in this sense, in terms of the profitability and the product. When the customer is writing us a check, are they loving it, and can I provide that value with less effort?"

The combination of being respected for their knowledge and having a trusting relationship with their manager has created a high level of employee satisfaction, as the company learned in the surveys it has conducted. "We have certainly found that the combination of psychological safety and giving people the autonomy they need to make decisions has taken us a very long way," says Peterson.

SPREADING THE MESSAGE

Today's O.C. Tanner is a poster child of Lean, and hosts numerous visits from aspiring companies, often through the Toyota Production System Support Center (TSSC) – Toyota's learning group that promotes TPS principles. What visitors notice is the collegial atmosphere that comes from people who enjoy accomplishing tasks together. And as Toyota found, companies that visit hope they become more successful by copying exactly what O.C. Tanner is doing.

The problem with that, of course, is that while the Shingo Principles are generic and can be applied in any business, each company has to develop its own systems to support those principles. "There are no defined systems," says Peterson. "You have to develop those based on what you need. And that's why copying doesn't work. Our coaching system is an exception to that – I think companies could copy that and they'd love it – but probably every other system needs to be tailored to the organization, and what they're trying to accomplish."

There are no shortcuts, however. These systems, and the process of arriving at them, are vital to the journey. "The systems need to make it easier to do the right thing and harder to do the wrong thing," says Peterson. "For example, one of the continuous improvement principles in the Shingo model is focus on process. When something goes wrong, instead of blaming the operator you start asking, 'How did this happen? Why did our process allow this to happen? How do we fix this so that this can't happen? Again, thanks for showing it to us.'"

Each of these systems has an assigned leader. "So our systems, like our coaching system, our idea system, our *gemba* assessment system, our strategy deployment system, our 5S system, our visual management system, our problem-solving system – we have dozens – each one of them is owned by one of our management people or an engineer," says Peterson. "They run the system on the side while they're while they're doing the rest of their work. They are responsible for keeping it fresh or making sure people understand it and are following it or making it better. Usually, people run a system for one to four years or so. And then they turn it over to somebody else."

What makes these systems so effective is that the organization is not siloed along traditional departmental lines, but structured so that employees are accountable to their respective value stream.

"Everybody knows that they're in the press products value stream or the custom products value stream or the distribution value stream," says Peterson. "They know what value stream they're in. And they understand that they're working in combination with what used to be other departments like purchasing, maintenance, engineering, product development, systems…they have people in those groups who are on their teams who are in their value stream cost analysis. They're working together to provide this value. We don't allocate any costs – everything is accounted for in the value stream."

The removal of conventional departmental barriers opens the door for the team culture that now defines the company. "There's no one for a team to point at and say, 'We could have done better if those guys over there…' There is no 'guys over there.' It's all us. We're right here," says Peterson. "And that really is the point of the value stream. Value stream cost analysis is just there to help them understand value, exactly what they're providing, and what's the effort it takes to provide that value. So it gives them a good metric for improvements, and they're not messing around with stuff that doesn't really impact the end result."

AN EVOLVING BUSINESS MODEL

Like many companies, O.C. Tanner has moved more and more of its business into software and services – sectors that are now driving the growth of the company. "As the business changes, and as we've gone to merchandising and technology, manufacturing as a percentage of the total business is shrinking," says Peterson. "And yet our manufacturing remains a competitive advantage for us. I wouldn't say manufacturing drives the business, but it is a point that makes us competitive."

Most companies, facing this transition, would offshore their manufacturing and focus their resources on their growth areas. At O.C. Tanner, they see things differently. "I've had people here from major manufacturing companies – global companies – who can't believe we're manufacturing in Utah," says Peterson, "but manufacturing remains a competitive advantage for us. We do remain competitive on a cost basis. And companies that try to source product like ours from overseas would say, 'The product we just got just isn't like yours.' If you want ours, this is the only place you can get it."

Peterson sees the culture that O.C. Tanner spent years developing as the advantage that ensures sustainable long-term growth for the company. "I think the O.C. Tanner companies are responsive to the market," says Peterson. "I think they're very carefully listening to the customer. They are very nimble on their feet and able to respond to changes in the marketplace and to respond to demands of our clients. And it just feels to me like we're getting stronger and more capable every day. Really, the O.C. Tanner Company is the only continuously functioning company in this space who I think is going to continue to outlast everybody."

WHEN RAPID DECISIONS ARE ESSENTIAL

If a senior leader were described as a military-style manager, most people would assume this person was a top-down autocrat who expected orders to be followed to the letter. This stereotype, however, runs counter to how the US military operates.

"Allowing people to take initiative in the field is very much the American way of doing things," says Sam McPherson, a retired US Army Special Forces commander, a Toyota-trained management coach, and a Shingo Institute faculty member. McPherson often notes the parallels between the US military's field management approach with Lean management methods used by companies such as Toyota.

Because tactical combat plans can be quickly undermined by changing conditions, having to wait for orders from a senior officer can be deadly. Consequently, the responsibility of leaders in the US military is to convey to the field a clear intent of command that allows them to exercise their judgment based on current conditions.

"The beauty of understanding the intent of command is that, as we always like to say, the enemy has a say in your plan," says McPherson. "So if something keeps a specific unit from doing the tactical mission and they understand the intent, they can determine on their own how to achieve that intent. This is why in the American military, we teach mission planning all the way down to lowest level of leadership. And we start doing that in basic training. So we don't have people sitting around waiting for guidance."

Communication, accordingly, is highly structured, and reinforced by culture that begins with basic training. "In terms of intent of command, the operational guidance for the mission is very clear – everybody has to understand the five Ws: **who's** taking the action, **what** they're doing, **when** they're doing it, **where** they're doing it, and **why** they're doing it. The 'why' is very important in the American military. The 5W statement is very specific to your section of the mission, because you're got units on your left and right and behind you, and also, there are parallel missions if you're looking at the terrain."

That "why," McPherson says, is often inadequately conveyed by corporate leaders. "In traditional environments, C-suite leaders don't know the direction the CEO wants to take them," says McPherson. "So the CEO winds up taking tighter control because the staff doesn't understand the mission. That's a communication issue. The countermeasure to that is having people be part of the plan development and then do estimates within their function to support the plan, and then be part of the ongoing communications. This isn't just a matter of submitting estimates – it's the beginning of an ongoing dialogue about what's needed to execute the plan."

LEARNING ON THE FLY

One of the most effective programs for changing the manager's role from boss to coach is the Training Within Industry (TWI) program that was developed by industry and the US government at the onset of World War II.

The situation at the time was dire – automotive factories had to be re-tooled to build tanks, aircraft, and other military hardware to support the war effort. And with all of the experienced factory workers heading overseas to fight, manufacturers had to achieve this without their experienced workforce. Consequently, women and men unable to serve in the military were called upon to fill their ranks.

The effort defied all expectations. The legendary character Rosie the Riveter became a national heroine, and thousands flocked to some six thousand factories to play their part. What TWI provided was an excellent framework for delivering an effective real-time learning environment. As TWI's CEO and president, Scott Curtis, explains, the key to creating such an environment was to transform the role of the manager. Instead of being a "cop" who gives and enforces orders, the manager becomes a coach/trainer who equips workers with the knowledge to do their work according to accepted standards, and to recognize and act on opportunities to improve those standards.

"When it was introduced, TWI was focused on frontline leadership," says Curtis. "The idea was to train unskilled workers to work as a team, and then iterate forward on improving the methods they were working on. There were three core skill areas – leading effectively, which we call job relations, instructing, which we call job instruction, and the skill of improving, which we call job methods – that's what *kaizen* is all about. The idea was that if we could build these core skills in the frontline leader and supervisors, and make sure they were consistent from person to person, then they had a much higher chance of success. And now in retrospect, it was very successful."

The real payoff, however, was the effect of trainers training trainers. "The program was really focused on what they call the multiplier effect," says Curtis. "So you know, let's get a few individuals internally within the manufacturing plants skilled up, so they can deliver this training, and then get those who are trained to then train some more, so that created this multiplier effect. That's how they were able to quickly upskill and spread this within the manufacturing base in a very short period of time."

The TWI program was so effective that it led management guru Peter Drucker to challenge the conventional top-down approach with workers following externally created standards, "The war effort showed that this type of assembly line is neither the only application of the concept, nor in all circumstances the best," he wrote in *Concept of the Corporation*. "It showed further that the concept of the human contribution to production as a minor appurtenance to the machine that was inherent in the orthodox assembly line, is neither the only possible concept nor always the best."[2]

After the war, in what many considered to be a huge lost opportunity, the program was discontinued. Resistance from management could have been predicted. Surprisingly, however, shop floor workers, many weary and shell-shocked, weren't ready for the change.

"They [the veterans] came back to an environment where the supervisor or the workers were working in teams," says Curtis. "They were actively engaged in soliciting the workers' input on how to improve things, and this was a drastic contrast to what they've seen before with command and control, where they just followed what they were told to do. And so they were uncomfortable with it, and that was part of the reason why it was quickly abandoned."

The approach, however, was adopted in Japan and subsequently became an important method in the Lean movement. In fact, TWI provides a great framework for creating an organizational culture where everybody learns together. We'll discuss this further in Chapter 13.

THE OTHER SIDE OF RESPECT

As we've seen, the Top-Down Knowledge Myth is an essential pillar of the established command-and-control management approach. The assumption that managers have all the answers justifies and greatly simplifies the process of controlling all activities through centralized authority.

Command-and-control management, however, is also dependent on another widely held myth – the notion that people in the workplace are externally motivated, and can be expected to be productive when presented with an appropriate mix of rewards and punishment. In the next chapter, we'll look at the Myth of Sticks and Carrots.

TOP-DOWN KNOWLEDGE MYTH TAKEAWAYS

- The assumption that managers have all the answers flies in the face of workplace reality. The resulting management style is disrespectful of workers, and forces managers to hide behind a facade of assumed knowledge.

- When employees are able to share their workplace knowledge and apply it to process improvements, the work becomes more engaging and the quality of information applied to the business improves.
- As managers transition away from the top-down knowledge approach, they must develop their listening and coaching skills, and also, the ability to convey the company's purpose and everybody's role in pursuing it.

6

The Myth of Sticks and Carrots

Myth: Workers are most productive when motivated by rewards and threats

Scientific advances in the early 1900s, as we saw in Chapter 3, introduced new ways of seeing the physical world, which challenged the assumption that the command-and-control approach provides the best way to optimize the productive resources in a company.

That model was further challenged by developments in psychology that gave us radically new insights on what motivates humans. As this school of thought evolved, experimental studies disproved one of the pillars of command-and-control management – the centuries-old paradigm of *Homo economicus*, or the economic man.

Homo economicus depicts humans as rational creatures who act in predictable ways in order to maximize their material benefit. This goal-seeking behavior, the theory holds, will be the primary force that motivates people in their day-to-day work. Accordingly, businesses use external motivators, mainly money, to entice employees to engage in behaviors that management deems to be productive. Sticks and carrots serve as the primary tool for command-and-control management, and if performance is lagging, managers are exhorted to "drive" the system by issuing tougher threats or increasing the rewards for "top performers."

This approach makes a lot of sense – until it doesn't. There is no question that we often respond to external stimuli, whether it's showing up at work early to impress the boss or slowing down in order to avoid a speeding ticket.

But when it comes to bringing our "best self" to work day after day, that external mode of incentive tends to unravel. Research shows that external motivators can produce short-term results, but their influence fades over time. Sustained high performance, on the other hand, requires intrinsic motivation, where employees are driven by the satisfaction of engagement, teamwork, and accomplishment of objectives.

Daniel Pink's excellent book *Drive: The Surprising Truth About What Motivates Us*, surveys the research showing that human beings are not primarily driven by external motivators. Here, he summarizes the disconnect between common management theory and what the research shows:

> "The idea of management (that is, management of people rather than management of, say, supply chain) is built on certain assumptions about the basic natures of those being managed. It presumes that to take action or move forward, we need a prod – that absent a reward or punishment we'd remain happily and inertly in place. It also presumes that once people do get moving, they need direction – that without a firm and reliable guide, they'd wander."[1]

An important component of *Drive* is the work of Edward L. Deci, a professor of psychology at the University of Rochester. In a groundbreaking collaboration with colleague Richard Ryan, Deci demonstrated, in a series of experiments, how external incentives could actually distract people from enjoying a task, destroying their intrinsic motivation, and therefore causing them to be less productive.

In his 1995 book *Why We Do What We Do*, Deci makes the case for a new approach to management that recognizes people's need for autonomy. "One of the most important points that our experiments have illuminated," Deci wrote, "and the basis for hope, is that, although instrumentalities are all too readily used to control, they do not have to be."[2]

Another important contributor who explored the impact of external and internal motivators was Frederick Hertzberg, an American psychologist who founded what's now known as the two-factor theory. What Hertzberg found is that external factors, such as money, don't lead to high levels of motivation, but can demotivate if they are deficient or absent. Hertzberg called these potentially negative influences "hygiene factors" – they include pay, job security, and a clean and safe work environment. In terms of workplace performance, hygiene factors are therefore the starting point, but not the final answer.

Motivators, Hertzberg's research showed, are inherent in the work itself. These include having pride in work well done, having a degree of autonomy, being listened to by management, pursuing inspiring goals, and working in a mutually supportive team environment.

Studies since have shown that people who work in environments where they are intrinsically motivated tend to be more productive and more creative when confronted with workplace problems. They also have better relationships with co-workers and people outside of the workplace, and lead more stable lives.

Creating a work environment that lends itself to intrinsic motivation, of course, is a lot more difficult than simply applying a few formulas. As you will see in the next section, it involves adopting a whole different way of looking at the relationship between workers and management.

BUILDING A COMPANY BASED ON CARING

One of the most passionate advocates for respecting every team member is Bob Chapman, CEO of global manufacturer Barry-Wehmiller. At approximately $3.6B in annual revenue and over 12,000 employees, the company serves a wide variety of industries as a diversified global supplier of highly engineered capital equipment and consulting and professional services.

Chapman is deeply concerned about the way most people feel about their work: "88% of all people feel they work for an organization that does not care for them," he told me. "And 65% of all people would give up their salary increase if they could fire the boss. It's sick. Because it's an economic model that assumes economic gain will create happiness."

Chapman sees the lack of caring, and the resulting workplace stress, as a national catastrophe in the US. He frequently speaks at conventions, think tanks, and government organizations about his leadership philosophy, which goes by the name Truly Human Leadership (THL).

"Hospitals are full of people with all kinds of health issues," says Chapman. "I tell CEOs when I talk to them, 'You're all worried about the cost of healthcare, you are the problem.' Seventy-four percent of all illnesses are chronic; the biggest cause of chronic illness, stress, and biggest cause of stress is the workplace. We are self-destructing a society, and then we write checks to the hospitals to heal all the people we've broken."

Chapman, on his website, cites a CDC finding that "your immediate supervisor is more important to your health than your primary care doctor." Chapman hosts a podcast and one of his guests was Dr. Jeffrey Pfeffer, author of the book *Dying for a Paycheck,* which discusses the negative impacts of workplace stress on worker health.

Multiple studies have confirmed the alarming connections between workplace stress and illness. In a meta-study published in *Behavioral Science & Policy* by Joel Goh of Harvard Business School, and Jeffrey Pfeffer and Stefanos A. Zenios at Stanford University, the results show an alarming correlation. "We find that more than 120,000 deaths per year and approximately 5%–8% of annual healthcare costs are associated with and may be attributable to how U.S. companies manage their work forces," the authors concluded.[3]

EARLY DAYS AS A BUSINESS SUPERSTAR

Chapman's career began as a typical American success story. He had a background in conventional business management, with an undergraduate degree in accounting, and an MBA. Having taking the reins of his father's company after his father died unexpectedly, he put that background to work, growing the company revenues tenfold by making a series of strategic acquisitions. In 1987, Chapman spun off a group of companies through a London Stock Exchange IPO. The offering was oversubscribed 35 times and was written up as a success story by Harvard Business School.

While he was phenomenally successful from a conventional business standpoint – the business has grown from the machine shop that his father started to a multinational conglomerate – he felt that something was missing. A keen observer of people, he noticed how the body language of employees changed in the cafeteria when it was time to go back to work. Clearly, they were not enjoying the work part of their lives, and Chapman had to admit that this was not an environment he would want for his six children.

Global stats, he also noted, weren't favorable – research from Gallup showed an astounding level of dissatisfaction at work. Eighty-eight percent, he noted, felt that their employer didn't care about them, and less than a third felt engaged in their work.

Chapman vowed to change how people were led at Barry-Wehmiller. His business background, however, didn't provide any help for this. "When I was in business school, I was never taught to care," he said. "It was about creating economic value. It was all business models, market cap, market share. I don't remember in my undergraduate in accounting, or my graduate school, ever learning to care or inspire the people I have the privilege to lead. And I never read, never was told, never heard that the way I would run Barry-Wehmiller would impact the way people go home and treat their families, and their health. But the biggest thing we've learned is that the way we lead impacts the way people live."

Working with a group of team members from across the organization, he developed a set of principles, called the Guiding Principles of Leadership (GPL), which established caring for people as fundamental to the job of all leaders in the company. But the question remained, "How do we organize the work in a way that gives workers the experience of working in a caring environment?"

It happened that Barry-Wehmiller had recently acquired a Baltimore-based manufacturer of corrugated paper machines called Marquip Ward United. The company had implemented a number of Lean tools and practices under the leadership of Jerry Solomon, who was also the author of several books on Lean accounting.

In Chapman's first meeting with Solomon, he introduced him to the Guiding Principles of Leadership, and Solomon immediately saw a connection with the challenges companies face when trying to create a Lean culture. Most companies practicing Lean, he noted, never get the culture piece – the same concern that caused the Shingo Institute to revise its model in 2008.

Solomon felt that the company needed was what he called a "delivery mechanism" to integrate GPL with the company's day-to-day operations. How, for example, does a supervisor on the shop floor interact with the people doing the work? Solomon felt Lean and GPL were an ideal fit.

Chapman was skeptical. He had heard that Lean is purely about reducing waste and increasing profits, but not about leading people in a positive way. But he agreed to give it a try, and a number of Lean projects were initiated with the help of outside consultants.

Several months later, a team at a plant in Green Bay had some success with Lean to report, and Chapman flew in to attend the presentation by the consultants. While the numbers looked great from a business standpoint, he saw no reference to GPL, which he had seen as crucial to the Lean initiative. Chapman was furious, and so upset that he had to leave the room. But the leader of the project, Brian Wellinghoff, told him that GPL was indeed central, and begged for another chance.

It happened that the company had an executive meeting scheduled the following morning, and Chapman asked that the people involved in the project, mostly assembly workers, report the projects to the entire executive team. At 7:00 the next morning, one of the workers, Steve Barlament, who was not accustomed to speaking to groups, gave a spontaneous presentation. It was, as Chapman had seen the day before, all about reducing waste and use of space, cutting lead time, and the like. After about ten minutes, Chapman stood up and asked Barlament, "How has this changed your life?"

A long silence followed, and then Barlament said, barely audibly, "My wife is talking with me."

Chapman begged him to explain, and Barlament told what Chapman describes as "one of the most profound stories I've ever heard."

The project, Barlament related, changed everything in terms of his relationship with his work. Previously, it had not been positive – the typical disrespect that most workers complain about had been all too prominent in his life. He felt he was constantly blamed when things went wrong, but when he had suggestions to improve things, nobody listened. He essentially felt like a cog in an uncaring machine, and the resulting lack of self-esteem was spilling over into his family life. As he told the meeting, "I wasn't feeling good about myself, and I wasn't that nice a person to be around."

The Lean/GPL project had given him a new lease on life. "The way we set up the new assembly flow really works," he said at the meeting, "and I can go home feeling that I've done a good day's work, not wasted the day chasing parts or feeling resentful. When I feel respected and know I've done a good day's work, I feel pretty good about myself. I'm nicer to my wife, and you know what's amazing? When I'm nicer to my wife, she talks to me."

Another silence ensued, and then Chapman turned to Solomon and said, "Jerry, we have a new metric for Lean success. It's the reduction of the divorce rate in America."

LOOKING AHEAD

Chapman has stepped back from the day-to-day leadership at Barry-Wehmiller but stays on as chairman. Much of his time is spent evangelizing his message about treating workers like family.

Chapman is clear that he is not opposed to capitalism. What he maintains is that capitalism and treating people well are not incompatible. "I began this journey 20 years ago," says Chapman, "and nobody has ever debated what I am saying as far as the reality of where we are. Nobody debates that leadership is about caring for people. They just have no idea how to go from using people to caring for people. And remember – we've outperformed Warren Buffett for the last five years, and our share price increase has been around 14% per year compounded for the past 25 years. And he's at 9.6%."

Chapman is deeply worried about the condition of American society, which he attributes to the lack of caring that workers experience from their employers. "Look at this society," he says. "Broken. I don't ever remember in my years being more concerned about the future of this country. In terms of suicide, drug addiction, alcoholism, crime, incivility... I mean, I need to go through metal detectors to watch a high school basketball game. There are guards at our schools to keep us from random shooters, barricades in malls, so cars don't drive down. So, the core problem is we do not have a society where we learn to care for others."

The response of many corporations to this has been to support charitable initiatives. "We have a society where we feel writing checks to charity is an act of goodness," says Chapman. "In fact, the greatest act of charity is not the checks we write. It's how we treat the people we lead. That is the greatest act of charity."

Chapman is critical of grand environmental, social, and governance (ESG) declarations that organizations like to publicize. One is the 2019 CEO Roundtable statement mentioned in Chapter 1. "The CEO roundtable came out with a statement that we need to care about more than just the shareholder," says Chapman. "It's a really nice statement, but it's pitiful that they had to say that at all, and they weren't already doing that. And the second thing is, they don't have a clue how to do it. Not a clue."

Since that statement was signed, there has been little or no progress, and the behavior that's so harmful to people has continued unabated. Chapman is outraged that companies actually get good press when they put thousands of people out of work. "If you're on the board of Microsoft, why would you announce to the world that you're going to lay off 10,000 employees?" Chapman asks. "That you're going to hurt 10,000 people you invited into your organization, and have put their hopes in it? And now you're going to hurt them? Because the share price will go up. And guess what happened? The market applauded and the share price went up the next day."

Chapman is very clear on his legacy, but this still surprises people who expect a different answer from somebody who has built a $3.6 billion company. "I was interviewed by people at Washington University (in St. Louis) two years ago, because they'd heard about our culture. And after an hour and a half interview, they said, 'You're the first CEO that never talked about your product.' And I said, 'I've been talking about our product for the last hour,' and I said, 'I won't go to my grave proud of the machinery I built, I'll go to my grave proud of the people who built it.' And that completely caught them off guard."

PUTTING CULTURE FIRST

Lippert is a leading global manufacturer of components for mobile homes and related industries, with 2022 revenues of $5.2 billion and 15,000-plus team members across the US, Canada, Mexico, the UK, the Netherlands, Tunisia, and Italy.

Like Barry-Wehmiller, the company is following a path of instilling a human-centric culture throughout the organization. Its CEO, Jason Lippert, is one of the most prominent proteges of Barry-Wehmiller CEO Bob Chapman. The two have much in common. Like Chapman, Lippert took over the family business at a young age and was phenomenally successful in his youth building the company. He also, like Chapman, felt in mid-career that something wasn't quite right.

"I'd been running for about 15 years," Lippert told me, "but that's probably the equivalent of 30 for most people because I was traveling all over the country and sleeping at the facilities – I don't think I slept for a decade. But it got to the point where I was teetering on burnout. It was just year after year of growth. So I turned to my faith and began to question what my real purpose was. And it wasn't long after that I heard the Truly Human Leadership TED talk, and that's how I got introduced to Bob."

"By coincidence, a friend of mine was looking for a sponsor for his annual leadership seminar here. I sponsor a lot of children and family charitable organizations, but not the leadership stuff, because I feel that money can go better towards families and things like that. But he was begging me to do it, and said, 'Look, if you're the lead sponsor, I'll let you pick the headline speaker.' So I said, okay, if you get Bob Chapman, I'm all in. And two days later, he called me and said, 'Bob's coming.'"

"When Bob came, he sat in a room for two and a half hours with about one hundred of my guys. A lot of them had read his book. He had a microphone and for much of the time we just asked him questions, one by one. 'How did you do this?' ' How did you do that?' It was great, because a lot of things that they had wrestled with and figured out were things we were in the midst of."

Lippert, like Chapman, has found that Lean methods are a powerful delivery mechanism for creating an energized culture of engagement throughout the organization. "One of the things we've found is that Lean has been a great way to engage our team members throughout this whole culture journey. So we've had Lean coordinators, Lean project managers, and all that kind of stuff. We found out that if we could get every human being in the business innovating and thinking about how they can improve whatever they are doing, whether it's quality, safety, efficiency, or anything to make the business better, then the team members tend to light up and be more engaged with the business. And they stay with the company longer if we include them in a lot of those things."

Like many Lean companies, the Lippert organization has a structured program for collecting, evaluating, and implementing employee suggestions. "Five years ago, we started a program called just fix it (JFI)," says Lippert. "We brought JFI into our business, and it's basically, if you see anything wrong in your area, doesn't matter whether you're the janitor, an assembly worker, a team leader, or an executive. There's a process to fix it. It's a simple sheet of paper. And we track that stuff. More than 50% of our workforce have been engaged in JFI, and you know, a lot of these guys and gals on the frontlines get really proud of what they fix to increase efficiency, or safety, or quality in their area. Then they take a video and do a before and after – they really feel a big sense of pride about it. It's about aligning culture, Lean and continuous improvement. They go together."

To make this program work, Lippert trusts his leaders at the plant level to convey the cultural message. "We have 120 locations, and a typical plant will have one hundred people with ten leaders. So, whether it's culture or Lean and continuous improvement, it's really about hammering it in to those 1200 leaders, so they understand what it is and why we're doing it. Then we tell them, 'We're not going to talk to your team – you've learned this, and we want them to learn the same way from their leaders – you!'"

A CHANGING ROLE

Part of the transition of building a culture is getting managers to relinquish their customary role of telling workers what to do based on their allegedly superior knowledge. This wasn't an easy transition, and some weren't able to cope with the change.

"We lost a significant number of managers because of this," says Lippert, "but I put that on us. We promoted people for the wrong reasons. We promoted them because they were here every day, and they knew the business and product and process really well. We didn't promote them because they were great leaders. And they didn't take the job because it promised great leadership opportunities. They took it because it was more money. So we had promoted people for the wrong reasons in the wrong ways, and we had to undo all that once we said, 'Hey, look, these are our core values. We're going to follow them day in and day out. These are the leadership qualities that we're expecting of all our leaders."

Core Value	Leadership Quality
Passionate About Winning	Motivator
Positive Attitude	Servant Leader
Team Play with Trust	Humble - Coachable
Honesty - Integrity - Candor	Effective Communicator

Figure 6.1   Defining leadership qualities at Lippert.
Source: Lippert Cultural Playbook, Page 9.

The new role for managers was to be coaches, not bosses, to listen to and respect their workers, and encourage them to bring their best selves to work. One of the key skill areas is being able to conduct listening sessions, where the manager respectfully asks the worker about their work and their concerns inside and outside of the workplace. This includes coaching employees about their future development – at Lippert, every employee, regardless of rank, has a personal development plan.

In the third year of the culture journey, the company developed a set of five leadership qualities, listed in Figure 6.1, that define what leadership should look like at Lippert.

"We told our managers that if you're a leader here, you need live up to these values," says Lippert.

SPREADING THE MESSAGE

Like Chapman, Lippert is frequently visited by organizations seeking to emulate the company's cultural success. In response to this, the company created its Leadership Academy, which offers a formal coaching program for companies seeking to follow in Lippert's footsteps.

"The culture journey for companies is similar to people's leadership journeys," says Lippert. "What we do depends on where they are in the journey. I had a business in here yesterday that didn't have any core values, and hadn't even thought of that, so they'll have to start by developing a set of values for their people to live by. Some have core values but feel they are stuck, so we work with them based on our experience."

Lippert has published the Cultural Playbook, which provides a framework for the cultural journey. When companies want active coaching, the Leadership Academy provides that as a service. "Companies pay us for that," says Lippert, "but we don't charge a lot of money because our mission is to help other companies figure it out. We'll send coaches to their facilities, or they can bring people into our facilities and participate in some of our activities."

THE ROI OF CULTURE

The point is that culture is essential not only to productivity, but to reducing turnover. "All this starts with having a really solid culture and consistent values," says Lippert. "Because if you don't have that, and people are coming and going all the time, including the leaders, then you can't get any momentum. So that's why we've worked so hard to create a cultural foundation."

Lower turnover is one metric that Lippert uses to convince shareholders that investing in culture produces a strong return on investment (ROI). "Reducing turnover is the easiest, most common metric that people use to measure the ROI on culture," says Lippert. "Everybody agrees that turnover should be reduced, and that culture is a really good way to do that."

On the other hand, most companies aren't doing well. "Bob would say, 80% of people in the country that work for companies feel that they work for one that doesn't care about them," says Lippert. "So what does that say about culture? Not too good. That's why there's so much turnover in business today, especially in manufacturing companies. But at the other end of the data, we have a really good culture and people tend to stay because they say, 'Gosh, I've never worked at a company that's cared about me this much and that gives me freedom. There's genuine intentional behavior towards making sure values are followed, and good leadership is in place, and that's just consistent over time and I can rely on that.'"

"People want to be paid fairly, but money is not the most important thing," adds Lippert. "People want to feel good about where they work, and when they go home, not feel stressed out or anxious or beat down. In my 29 years of doing this and meeting people in businesses everywhere, I've never met anyone that wants to come to work and be frustrated or stressed for 40 hours a week. People just don't want that. But with their horrible cultures, businesses are making that a reality for people every day, all over the country."

Rapid growth can be a culture-killer, Lippert says. "Our turnover was around 125% in 2013," he says, "and it seemed like the more we grew – and we were a growth-oriented company – the worse our turnover got. We were just trying to do more, and it got tougher and tougher on our team members in a not-so-good culture where there was inconsistent values and inconsistent leadership of people."

When the company began to make culture a priority, they began tracking retention – the percentage of employees that remain in the company for the year being measured – and using feedback from employees to find ways to encourage more people to stay. As of 2019, the process of tracking attrition and executing retention and action plans was fully developed, and retention had risen to 72%.

A CHANGING WORLD

Lippert also agrees with Chapman that there's nothing in traditional business education that prepares leaders for the kind of initiatives that are making a difference at Lippert. "It's really sad, but we're doing it all wrong," says Lippert. "I can't think of a thing that I learned in business school that prepared me for what actually needs to happen."

Lippert believes, however, that a lot more business people are starting to talk about this. "There's a whole retooling and reprogramming of the way we think about doing business, and what really makes business effective," says Lippert, "It's about the foundational stuff. You can do Lean and all sorts of other stuff, but if you don't get the foundational culture, leadership, and value principles right, you're going to be spinning your wheels. But if you constantly improve leadership and culture and live out the values consistently, you will retain your people and the business will just keep getting better and better."

BUILDING A CARING CULTURE IN THE CONSTRUCTION INDUSTRY

When it comes to building a collaborative work culture, the construction industry has some special challenges. The physical work environment, for one, is in constant flux – construction sites change every day, and each site is unique. To compound this, changes made by owners while a project is underway often force contractors to re-sequence the work on the fly.

Another difficulty is that a typical construction project involves multiple subcontractors, and relationships between them are often adversarial. Subcontractors who won the business based on low price, for example, are often under pressure to minimize their time on the job site, making them less likely to help out their peers when problems arise.

The construction industry has been working on these problems for decades. The initiative has been led by the Lean Construction Institute (LCI), a not-for-profit organization that promotes Lean principles in the sector. The approach revolves around a collaborative scheduling process called Last Planner©, which uses the value stream paradigm to map out projects. This serves as an alternative to the traditional approach where the general contractor estimates the timelines, and then serves as the enforcer.

The process brings together the general contractor and all the subcontractors – plumbers, electricians, painters – in a collaborative planning process. Participants gather in a room with a project timeline displayed on a long whiteboard. The process progresses from the completion date to the start date. The required finishing date for each phase is determined by the required start date of the phase that immediately follows it.

In Lean Construction, the owner of a particular phase is expected to treat the owner of the next phase like a customer. A drywaller, for example, is accountable to the painter, because delays or quality problems with drywalling can disrupt the painter's work.

As the construction process unfolds, all parties meet weekly, typically for half an hour, to share progress and updates. While the requirement to attend weekly meetings may not be well received initially, participants are quickly won over when they see how group ownership of the schedule reduces callbacks, rework, and conflicts. This makes the jobs more profitable for all parties and reduces stress significantly in the workplace.

GETTING TO THE ROOT CAUSE OF PROBLEMS

Turner Construction is one of the best-known adopters of Lean Construction in the US. Charlie Murphy, who oversees that effort, is a senior vice president of the company, and a frequent speaker at construction and Lean conferences alike. Murphy believes that in order to improve productivity, contractors need to get better at solving underlying problems that occur on job sites. "We [the construction industry] are what could be described as the king of workarounds," says Murphy.

What's needed is a fundamental shift in how problems are viewed and handled. "When you do a workaround instead of solving a problem, you really haven't improved anything," says Murphy. "It's been relatively easy to have people understand problem solving. The harder thing we're trying to achieve is a cultural shift where you're not satisfied with the current state but want to keep improving. So that's what my doctoral thesis will be about."

Many of the problems on jobsites are not readily visible, and Murphy is therefore critical of the notion that jobsites can be managed from an office with the help of an occasional site tour. "One of the problems we have is people not understanding how work comes together," says Murphy. "You don't learn that by just walking the job. You learn it by observing that work activity. We're trying to give our superintendents and engineers observation time to really understand what determines productivity on the job site."

Often what matters are the small details. "You can see the big things, like the steel framing," says Murphy, "but smaller things, like the low-voltage wiring, the ductwork, or the fire alarm system, are harder to see, yet those things can stop the project as easily as the big and more visible things."

Consequently, construction needs the eyes and ears of every worker to help leadership understand the problems and how to solve them. "Leadership engagement, and understanding of what is being done on the front line is an important aspect of this continued learning and improvement," says Murphy. "We let workers know that it's very important to us that they can perform their work properly."

PUTTING PEOPLE FIRST

Getting construction workers involved in problem solving and continuous improvement is job one for Murphy. There is a long history, Murphy recalls from his earlier days working in New York City, of adversarial relationships between workers and management. "Labor unions were very aggressive in promoting things for their members, whether it was pay or benefits or type of work," says Murphy. "Plumbers do certain things, carpenters do different things, and the unions guard those jurisdictions. In the big picture, this wasn't good for the owners who had to pay for this – it cost time and money."

Management was similarly rigid in its approach. "It was also a command-and-control way of operating," says Murphy. "Not that there was no regard for the worker, but the worker certainly wasn't the priority. That was reflected in the safety culture, or just long-term strain on a body when you're doing hard repetitive work. And those workers are the ones that come to the jobsite every day whether it's raining, cold, or one-hundred-plus-degree weather like we had in New York last summer. And I'll say that back then, it didn't look like we cared too much for the workers. But things have changed."

The best place to begin engaging workers, Murphy says, is safety. Construction is one of the most dangerous of all industries, with hundreds of thousands of construction workers injured every year in the US alone. Construction also has the highest fatality rate of all industries. On a given job site, every worker knows somebody who has been seriously injured.

The engagement process, Murphy says, begins with a commitment to provide healthy and safe work environments. It's now common on Turner job sites to see shade tents, air-conditioned break rooms, and Gatorade during hot weather.

"If you really want to improve safety and avoid long-term injuries, you have to show workers that you care about them," says Murphy. "So we've started to take a very different approach. For example, on a high-rise project, we dedicated a whole floor with microwaves, refrigerators, nice bathrooms, and a massage area. So when workers took a break, they knew they were being treated with respect and dignity. The owner even gave every worker on the project a new pair of work boots. That's a very different approach to just saying we care about you."

It's not just about physical health, however. Murphy is working with construction associations in an effort to stamp out graffiti that denigrates and intimidates members of the workforce. "Respect for the worker means creating a workplace where workers don't feel threatened, whatever their background might be," says Murphy. "That's part of keeping a good healthy work environment, and some other contractors in our association are doing this as well. This is something that's been tolerated in the industry for years, but you wouldn't want your son or daughter to be subjected to this, so why should our workers?"

The caring attitude gets integrated into the daily conversation between management and workers. "We do worker briefings at the beginning of the shift, which helps workers understand what's expected of them," says Murphy. "We also bring up safety issues. So it's a different management style – less command-and-control, and more about respecting the workers."

Much of the worker engagement is around investigating recordable incidents. The A3 problem solving process, the variant on PDSA described in Chapter 2, helps determine the root cause of the incident and provides guidelines for making sure it never happens again. The process has been remarkably effective for Turner – its recordable incident rate in New York dropped from five per 200,000 worker hours down to about one.

"We started doing A3s for recordable incidents in 2020," says Murphy. "To me, that was a pretty remarkable turnaround. It shows how adopting an interactive process that emphasizes respect for the worker allowed us to dramatically improve our safety record."

The use of A3s also is helping build skill sets around problem solving in general. "You get people involved in doing the safety related A3s, and then they start applying that to a cadre of problems involving non-safety issues. So, safety became our way of having people become problem solvers. And now we get to the next level of management – let's take that knowledge we've acquired about problem solving and start using if for other things."

The key, however, is prevention, so the real work around safety is building a culture of constant vigilance. This means spotting occurrences that could have led to incidents. "If I were to walk around a construction site and see something unsafe going on, even if nothing happens, that to me is a near miss," says Murphy.

"For example, I saw an insulation worker standing on the top rail of an aerial lift to install a fire safing system that was above the ductwork. Nobody got hurt, and no tool was dropped, but why did the worker put himself in a dangerous situation so he could perform the work? Why didn't the fire safing system get installed before the ducts went in? To me, 'near misses' is our next fertile ground where we can use fact-based problem solving to improve the work and make it safer. It's the next level of improvement."

The key is to stop the work and correct the defective work process on the spot. "I stopped the work, we got the foreman, and created a better way to do the work," says Murphy. "But what I'm really proud of is that the project manager called me the next day and said, 'Don't think I didn't notice what you did. You did what I should have done but didn't.' It's very important to me that person was able to admit that he should have stopped the work. Leading by example is very important to me."

Even more difficult is to use recordable incidents as opportunities to learn. This means avoiding blame and recrimination, and creating an environment where people can speak up openly without fear, but maintaining accountability. "We had an incident where an electrician got an electric shock, and he was hurt," says Murphy. "We did our investigation, and there were multiple causes. Why didn't this person follow the subcontractors' practice when working with this kind of equipment? But one thing I was really proud of was that our superintendent, whose job it was to review the work plan before the electrician started, said, 'I should have stopped the work. We really didn't go through the pretest plan the way we should have.' I appreciate that he was honest, saw how he fit into the process, and how he could have made a difference for the worker. I am also very proud of the environment where we can have these co-learning calls. He felt safe to say that he made an error, and that's a very important part of learning that the environment is right for us to learn. All too often, that kind of meeting is a hostile environment."

THE IMPORTANCE OF PURPOSE

One of the tragedies of modern life is that many people feel a lack of purpose in their work. One leader concerned about this is Mark Borsari, CEO of Sanderson-MacLeod, a Palmer, Massachusetts–based manufacturer in the twisted wire brush industry.

"I think there's a massive crisis of purpose happening not only in the workforce, but in our society," says Borsari. "I think that the reason that unemployment is so difficult is that companies aren't providing a real driven purpose to have somebody engage in for a career."

The result is people jumping aimlessly from job to job. "For a lot of people, changing jobs is like changing an app," says Borsari. "As soon as they find something about their job or a situation they don't like, it's pretty easy to just change and go to something different. The only thing that can make a job stick is seeing the purpose behind the challenges that they have."

It's management's job, Borsari says, to create the conditions in which people can make that vital connection with purpose. "I think it's all about causation," says Borsari, "looking at the things that we've taken for granted lately and realizing that I can't run a successful company if I don't have people show up to do the work. I can't produce on time if my processes aren't as efficient as possible, and I can't get people caring about the product if they don't feel some sense of purpose of doing the right thing. Remove any of those and the numbers the accountants will get don't mean much."

Borsari believes the increase in people working remotely has made it difficult to instill a purpose-driven culture in companies. "I think working at home has had an offset with that," says Borsari, "and I think the lack of company culture has had an offset in that. So not only do people have to be given the opportunity to really do things creatively and be part of a team, but leaders also have to be more pronounced in what the purpose is, and connect their individual purpose with the organization's. I think there's more need for this now than ever."

Often companies, particularly large corporations, try to instill purpose by aligning themselves with environmental, social, and governance (ESG) objectives. Borsari believes that such efforts shouldn't be superimposed, but should flow naturally from well-managed continuous improvement efforts that make companies less wasteful and give employees pride in achieving that.

"If you're doing the right thing and have the right processes, and are aware of optimizing value and all those sorts of things, you don't need to be doing ESG to check that box off – it's naturally there," says Borsari.

The message is getting through – Borsari finds he is able to recruit people from large corporations because they're looking for the sense of purpose that Sanderson-Macleod can provide.

"I believe we're in a transformative time, from a corporate standpoint," says Borsari. "It's very difficult for a large corporation to generate a true and genuine culture. I hire a lot of people from Fortune

500 companies. They come and work for me simply because they need to be part of a culture that they feel they can trust and really work with. They need to feel a sense of connection instead of being just one of a bunch of people."

A CULTURE OF OWNERSHIP

Another CEO who's concerned about lack of purpose in many workplaces is Kerry Siggins, CEO of StoneAge, a Durango, Colorado–based manufacturer of industrial cleaning equipment.

"I think a huge gap that leaders miss is tying the job of every single person who works in the company to the execution of the company's strategy and making sure they understand it," says Siggins. "How do you drive productivity within the company if people don't understand their work and how it's tied to the future of the company?"

Siggins is author of the book *The Ownership Mindset*, and a passionate advocate for allowing workers to have a financial stake in the company in which they work. Today, StoneAge is 100% employee owned.

"Our big thing is that we want to have a healthy work environment," says Siggins. "Most stick-and-carrot comp plans drive people to a low level of health where they're competing against other people, and they're thinking in instinctual terms about how to survive. I think it's a real disservice to people to think that this is the only way to get them to make improvements. But if you're doing things because it's going to improve your life and your teammates' lives, you get to be part of something that's bigger than yourself. It's like we're creating a movement where people are doing things for intrinsic reasons rather than looking for a bigger bonus."

A trend that concerns Siggins is the acquisition of companies like hers by private equity firms that don't understand the challenges that these companies face and fail to see the value that an engaged workforce can provide.

"The problem with private equity is that most of them have never been operators before," says Siggins. "You have super-smart analysts who are taught how to look at financials and extract the last bit of value, but they're not operators. They actually have no idea of the intricacies of running the company, and they look at everything as just resource allocation. But we're talking about human beings! Human beings are not resources, they're human beings. And so that's where I get really disenfranchised with private equity."

Siggins hope that more leaders will begin to see that when it comes to long-term value, people really are the most important asset a company can have.

"Imagine what we could do if we had employees who wanted to show up motivated to work every day," says Siggins. "It's up to employees to contribute to our workplaces and to our culture, but it's also up to leaders to create an environment where there's psychological safety, there's opportunity for advancement, and there's autonomy and responsibility and trust in the workplace too."

WILL THEY TAKE MY JOB?

One of the most prevalent fears of workers is that in the not-too-distant future, they'll be replaced by computer-driven machines. This conversation has heated up as AI-powered tools from ChatBots to robots are seeing growing adoption in virtually every sector of our economy. We'll look at these fears, and what the tech experts are saying, in the next chapter.

MYTH OF STICKS AND CARROTS TAKEAWAYS

- While extrinsic rewards and threats can bring short-term results, long-term productivity gains require an engaged, intrinsically motivated workforce.
- In many companies, employees have a stressful relationship with their bosses, and this impacts both their mental and physical health and their family life.
- Companies can build trust and promote intrinsic motivation by providing purpose to the work and displaying a caring attitude that extends beyond the workplace.

7

The Myth of Tech Omnipotence

Myth: Technology is the answer to all productivity problems

In December 2023, Cruise, General Motors' self-driving car subsidiary, announced that it would lay off nearly one quarter of its work force. The company had invested heavily in a driverless taxi service in San Francisco, hoping to expand to other cities to help defray its high operating costs.

The project didn't go as planned. After a series of incidents, including one where a pedestrian was dragged 20 feet by a Cruise vehicle, regulators ordered Cruise to shut down the service. A statewide ban followed, and the company then voluntarily took all its vehicles off the streets in the US pending the results of investigations.

As more details became known, people were surprised to learn that those San Francisco robo-cabs were not fully autonomous but assisted by humans. According to a *New York Times* report,[1] Cruise had set up a call center facility where a large staff – approximately 1.5 workers per vehicle – were monitoring these vehicles remotely and assisting when there were potential problems. Interventions were occurring every 2.5 to 5 miles.

The setback shows just how difficult full autonomy is despite impressive advances in Advanced Driver Assistance Systems (ADAS) technology, and tens of billions of investment. The auto industry has been telling the public for over a decade that self-driving cars would soon be widely adopted, but as of this writing, the goal posts keep moving.

ADAS, on the other hand, has advanced significantly. Today, a system can take over the wheel to change lanes or park, or apply brakes when approaching a hazard, making the driving experience safer and less stressful.

The Society of Automotive Engineers (SAE) has adopted a standard for ADAS technology. Figure 7.1 shows the progression of autonomy levels. The graduation to Level 5, full autonomy, seems subtle, but it makes all the difference in terms of economics. A completely autonomous vehicle, for example, would allow a company like Uber or Lyft to completely dispense with drivers, or the owner of an autonomous vehicle to hire it out at night as a taxi.

Current predictions indicate that the dream of full autonomy is still a long way away. A McKinsey report released in January 2023 projected that by 2030, only 12% of vehicles sold will have beyond Level 2 functionality.[2]

If a car can park or change lanes by itself, it's fair to ask why full autonomy is so difficult. The short answer is that despite appearances, AI doesn't think the way we do. While humans respond to situations based on a broad understanding of the world, an AI can only act according to the training data that it has been given. Accordingly, much of

Level	Driving Environment Monitored?	Description
0	No	No automation
1	No	Driver assistance, e.g., cruise control
2	No	Occasional self-driving
3	Yes	Limited self-driving
4	Yes	Full self-driving under certain conditions
5	Yes	Complete autonomy, driver not needed

Figure 7.1 SAE designations for autonomous driving features.

the investment in autonomous vehicle technology has gone towards the creation of massive data sets in an attempt to prepare it for every possible scenario.

This brute force approach works in some situations. In the early 2000s, we saw AI-powered computers defeat humans at chess, Go, and of course, video games. But these are finite data environments. While the possible number of chess combinations is astronomically high, it is still finite, and an AI can, through its enormous computing power, access any of them in an instant.

Street environments are different. While there are many recognizable patterns, there is no theoretical limit to the number of possible scenarios. This gives rise to what are called edge cases – rare or unique appearances that are highly unlikely to be captured by even the exhaustive data-collecting exercises.

An autonomous vehicle, for example, will be well trained on conventionally posted stop signs. But if it "sees" a stop sign covered with graffiti, or a stop sign carried by a person, it has no data to tell it how to respond. These edge cases cause autonomous vehicles to act erratically. Some cases are humorous. Others have resulted in tragedy.

Humans, for all their foibles, can apply their broad understanding of the world to assess and respond intelligently to situations they've never seen before. The graffiti-covered stop sign isn't a problem because a person has a general understanding of what a stop sign is, and what graffiti is.

Humans can also learn with extraordinarily little data. A toddler, for example, can learn to recognize the difference between a cat and a dog after seeing only a few examples. AI can only make this distinction after training on millions of images, and even then, it might get confused if the pet is decked out for winter. Humans develop a general understanding of what dogs and cats are, while AI only sees pixels and numbers, and the probability that a particular pattern exists.

This explains why we're such a long way from, say, a robot that serves as a home caregiver. The robot wouldn't "understand" what it was doing if it mishandled a patient because it has no general understanding of what a patient is.

All these problems will be solved, AI proponents say, upon the eventual emergence of AGI, or artificial general intelligence. This will equip machines with human-like intelligence, solving Level 5 vehicle autonomy and a host of other automation challenges.

The definitions of AGI, however, are inconsistent and hotly debated, and forecasts about its emergence range from within this decade to not within this century. Most businesspeople aren't betting on it just yet.

IT LOOKS SO EASY!

It's easy to be awestruck by AI. Its ability to sort through mind-numbing amounts of data and then make predictions, spot trends and anomalies, present complex information in a readable form, or initiate automatic actions has increased both the speed and the accuracy of processes in virtually every sector of the economy. What's more, that capability is increasing at a dizzying pace.

Humans, however, also have phenomenal capabilities that, due to their everyday nature, are easy to overlook.

"There's a very well-known phenomenon that we make assumptions that if something is easy for us, it's easy for AI," says Dr. Alexander Wong, University of Waterloo engineering professor, Canada research chair in the area of artificial intelligence, and a founding member of the Waterloo Artificial Intelligence Institute, "and if something is hard for us and AI does it well, we assume that means that AI does everything very well. For example, since AI can now beat the top players at chess and at Go, people assume that AI must be able to do everything well."

This is evident, Wong says, with simple tasks that we take for granted. "We assume that our neuro motor skills – the ability to pick things up, lift them, and manipulate them – are something that AI should be able to do as well," says Wong. "But when you look deeper, that's actually a super difficult problem. We actually evolved for millions of years to be able to do those things. And so, when we deal with automation, our expectations don't meet reality."

Similarly, we tend to underestimate the sophistication of human tasks that make up a more complex process. One of the best-known cases of this was the widely believed prediction that AI's image-recognizing capabilities would put radiologists out of business. What people missed is that while AIs can train on millions of images – far more than a radiologist will ever see – radiologists pick up additional information from talking with and examining the patient, reviewing health records, or detecting imperfections in the quality of the image.

"You have prominent AI scientists saying that AI is going to solve the radiology problem so that we don't need radiologists anymore," says Wong. "We're just going to take our X-ray images and just pump it into AI, and it will give us the right diagnosis. Guess what? More than five years have passed, and AI systems that fully replace radiologists are still not in place. We're not even close in terms of replacing radiologists and we don't need to."

Wong emphasizes that we don't need to replace people to make significant productivity gains. "The point is that we're making huge headway even when technology is solving part of a problem," says Wong.

Wong suggests that we apply that mindset with reference to self-driving cars. "Do you need a completely full-sized private self-driving car right now for every driver on the road to have widespread positive impact? The answer is no," he says. "AI can help you with your lanes, and cruise control is really nice on long drives, and that's already going to help a lot of people drive safer and more comfortably, which is real positive impact."

THE FACTORY OF THE FUTURE

GM's investment in Cruise was not its first big bet on leading-edge technology. In 1982, amid high anxiety about America's productivity crisis, the company embarked on a bold robotics initiative. The plan was to solve the company's perennial productivity problem once and for all by building what GM CEO Roger Smith believed was the factory of the future – a highly automated "lights-out" facility that operated 24/7 with a dramatically reduced workforce.

The dream of the lights-out factory was a popular one that began to be widely discussed in the 1970s. Technology was so advanced, people believed, that it was only a matter of time before manual factory labor would become a thing of the past.

During the 1980s, GM deployed thousands of robots, conveyors, and other automated machines in functional areas such as painting, assembly, machining, and welding. However, as the automation began to take over increased functionality, the effort hit a wall.

The problem GM faced is that automated lines that operate at high speed and volume are exceedingly difficult and time-consuming to set up, and consequently can only be cost effective in environments that remain relatively static for extended periods of time.

Consequently, GM's new lines couldn't keep up with the rapid changes in the increasingly global market, and the quest for a lights-out factory turned into a financial disaster.

What may have misled Smith and his cohorts who approved these massive expenditures – purportedly as much as it would have cost GM to buy Toyota – is that the financial lens through which they viewed their factories makes automation look much easier than it actually is. As we saw in previous chapters, variation and systemic interdependencies don't show up in the financials. This makes senior managers blind to the inefficiencies in their processes, and the importance of workplace culture in maintaining a highly productive work environment.

Toyota and other Japanese automakers that were decimating GM's market share, on the other hand, were achieving their high productivity not with machinery alone, but by continuously improving their processes. This, as Toyota and other companies have demonstrated, can only come from engaging the hearts and minds of their people.

MANUFACTURING IN TRANSFORMATION

Since the millennium, manufacturers have been adjusting to a marketplace that demands a higher mix of products at lower volumes. This scenario doesn't lend itself well to traditional large-scale automation, let alone a lights-out operation. Consequently, manufacturers are increasingly looking at automation that solves part of a problem.

"With robotics, most processes are not fully at the stage where we can fully automate them," says Wong. "So this notion of collaboration with AI-equipped machinery is now a much more prevalent idea amongst the industries, because they went through the whole phase of 'technology will solve everything.' Then after billions of dollars spent, they realize technology doesn't solve everything. And the key realization they have right now that has earned a lot more success is that technology does not need to solve everything."

The trend has created a growing need for automation that is not only flexible and reconfigurable but can also work in the proximity to humans. This need has spurred the rapid development of the cobot – a collaborative robot that operates at a slower speed so as not to harm humans and has an interface that allows it to be easily programmed by shop floor personnel.

"As long as there's large volume, and as long as things are fixed, stable, and predictable over decades, then the tools for automation have been around for a long time," says Anders Billeso Beck, vice president for strategy and innovation at Denmark-based Universal Robots. "We know how to automate big complex processes. But in a world where manufacturing is dynamic, where you have product life cycles that are short, and where you have variations in your processes, you still wind up having people doing the work."

Traditional robots, however, don't work well in proximity of people. They are fast and powerful – a swinging robotic arm can cause a fatal accident – and generally operate in areas fenced off from humans. And because of the way they are set up and programmed, the processes have to be built around them. This makes it hard to evolve from the traditional mass production model to a process better suited to the high-mix, low-volume markets that are becoming increasingly prevalent.

Part of the trap, Beck explains, is that the popular progression to Industry 4.0 – a loose term for the digitization of virtually every device on the shop floor – is still based on the classic idea of efficiency that was used to justify massive automation projects.

"The big problem was that when you are having a classical Fordian setup for doing mass manufacturing, you also end up putting people in the same position," says Beck. "So you actually have people working as a part of this very structured manufacturing. So you end up with people pretty enslaved to that kind of process."

Today, a perennial labor shortage is one of the most pressing problems in manufacturing. "Human labor has become the scarce resource in manufacturing," says Beck, "so the question of automation becomes 'What does this actually mean to people in manufacturing?'"

The justification for technology, therefore, has changed. "Ten years ago, it was all about 'if I put in a machine there, I can get rid of two people.' That would then be your business case, and you wouldn't be thinking much about anything else. Today, there's a much bigger thought. You might say, 'I've got two people, and I need to figure out, 'How do I get all the production I need to run out of the machines I have on the shop floor?' And those two people need to be able to operate the technology we bring in, to be able to set up the equipment and change batches. They need to be able to own that technology as part of their toolbox.'"

This new way of evaluating automation from a business perspective has been articulated in a concept called Positive Sum Automation. Instead of automation being about employee reduction, it's now more about using automation to make workers, the scarcest resource, more productive.

"Part of our work is just critiquing that management approach, which I think is the classic publicly traded company approach to labor costs, which is that I want to minimize labor costs with automation," says Ben Armstrong, executive director at the Industrial Performance Center at MIT. "The goal should be hours saved in indirect costs as a result of investing in automation."

Whether or not management is committed to saving jobs is beside the point. The headcount-justified business case is simply not working. What academic research has discovered is that the numbers used to justify technology with headcount reductions are no longer adding up. "What we find in study after study is that when companies automate, they're having a really hard time cutting those direct costs," says Armstrong. "When companies adopt robots, for example, they become more productive, but they don't ever really cut costs. They end up hiring more people. What they could do is improve productivity and essentially transform how they grow."

This failure to reduce the numbers through technology has had a devasting impact on global productivity of manufacturing. "The only gains in productivity that we had between 1990 and 2010 were from decreasing worker hours, not from increasing value added," says Armstrong. "But since 2010, we've seen productivity go down because we haven't been able to increase value-add. So that's a shocking chapter in our history."

In describing this phenomenon, Armstrong refers to Robert Solow's "productivity paradox." The term dates from a productivity slowdown during the 1970s and 1980s that occurred in spite of significant investments in technology. The attribution to Solow is based on his comment in 1987, "You can see the computer age everywhere but in the productivity statistics."[3]

MEANWHILE, BACK AT THE OFFICE

While GM's Roger Smith was scheming about building a lights-out factory, companies with large office workforces were applying similar thinking to massive office automation projects. Automated workflows, tech companies promised, would streamline antiquated paper processes, yielding enormous savings in headcount.

Many of the processes targeted were repetitive administrative tasks – order processing, procurement, payroll and benefits, sales forecasting and reporting, project management – the list goes on. As we saw in manufacturing, the question was always "How many employees can we eliminate?"

The thinking behind these projects was similar to the black box approach used in industrial automation – take a functional component in a work environment and automate it. Warned by tech companies and analysts about the risks of falling behind, companies jumped on the bandwagon, implementing massive IT projects in fields such as financial services, retail, government, and healthcare.

These large-scale projects, however, fell victim to Solow's productivity paradox. Despite phenomenal improvements in technology, including personal computers, integrated office software suites, internet connectivity, and cloud computing, numerous surveys have shown, and continue to show, that IT projects that deliver the expected productivity gains are the exception rather than the rule.

"On average, large IT products run 45 percent over budget and 7 percent over time while delivering 56 percent less value than predicted," reported a McKinsey Digital article in 2012. "In fact, 17 percent of IT projects go so bad that they can threaten the very existence of a company."[4]

What these projects were up against, as we saw with attempts at large-scale factory automation, was that the C-suite-level view of the organization doesn't reflect the complexity and the problems that people experience in the workplace. Consequently, the biggest obstacle with these projects was not the technology, but what tech people referred to as worker resistance to technology. People in the workplace, on the other hand, might have referred to this as the consequence of tech people living in a bubble.

This phenomenon has been painfully visible in healthcare, where hospitals have aggressively deployed IT technology in attempts to cut costs. "In healthcare, we're trying to solve problems with technology, and that's not a holistic approach, it's a siloed approach," says Joseph E. Swartz, former administrative director of business transformation for the Franciscan Alliance of Mishawaka, Indiana. "There's so much technology in place now when we go in and try to improve a process, it's like we're working with concrete."

The resulting calcification of workflow processes makes it difficult to make them better. "Before, when it was all manual, it was more flexible," says Swartz, "and we could have a lot of influence on the whole process design. Now we've got all these monuments that are hardwired in place – these software systems that don't move. And with more and more technologies coming in, that's really adding concrete in the process, making it more challenging to make improvements and make change."

Frustration with the disconnect between the tech and the workplace inspired a reform movement in software development called Agile. The approach establishes an incremental approach to software deployment that allows, in PDSA fashion, for developers to get frequent feedback from users as they progress through the various steps of development.

Agile is an alternative to the classic "waterfall" method where each silo – software architects, coders, implementers – completes its work and then passes it "over the wall" to the next team. By the time the product gets to the customer, there are likely to be all sorts of gaps between what the developers have come up with and what customers want.

Agile as a toolkit is widely used in companies, but like Lean and Deming principles, the methodology is usually used only superficially. As several management consultants have pointed out to me, if Agile is only used as an IT tool, it doesn't have the scope to transform the relationship between IT and the rest of the organization.

TALKING WITH COMPUTERS

One of the hottest topics in technology is generative AI, commonly familiar through large language model (LLM) systems such as Open AI's ChatGPT and Google's Gemini. These tools communicate with humans in plain language, enabling extraordinary computing power to be unleashed by means of simple prompts. Pundits predict that LLMs will transform the workplace as we know it, eliminating millions of jobs and streamlining many others.

These tools, however, come with a caveat. "ChatGPT can make mistakes. Consider checking important information," reads the banner below the ChatGPT dialogue box.

The problem is the tendency of LLMs to confabulate, that is, simply make up answers when they can't find the right data. Because these "hallucinations" are so confidently worded, people are easily fooled. I caught ChatGPT hallucinating when I was looking for reviews about a trade show that had occurred a month previously. ChatGPT replied that it couldn't give me an answer because the event hadn't occurred yet. Even when I changed my prompt to emphasize the date of the show, ChatGPT insisted that it hadn't occurred yet.

The fact that LLMs invent answers out of the blue is what makes them dangerous. As a construction executive told me recently, you could use an LLM to check on local building codes for constructing a staircase, but you'd have to check the results – if the LLM can't find a code that it's "looking for" it is likely to make one up.

This is not to say that LLMs can't be useful. In the construction scenario, the executive told me, the LLM could complete 70% of a two-hour project in five minutes, giving the human operator the remainder of the time to refine, improve, and augment it. The project would still take two hours, but the result would be of far better quality.

The problem is that advanced LLM systems require significant resources to operate, and it's expected that companies will need a sizeable payback to justify the expense. Many hope that LLMs will be able to accomplish this by delivering mission critical services such as giving medical or legal advice, or handling customer service calls with no human intervention. But until these systems can be trusted to initiate an action that a company could be held liable for, it's unlikely that we'll see these use cases.

Tech companies have promised for years that the hallucination is a solvable problem, but like self-driving cars, that goal seems to be remarkably elusive despite massive investments in the technology.

"'Scaling' systems by making them larger has helped in some ways, but not others," writes author and AI researcher Gary Marcus in a blog post. "We still really cannot guarantee that any given system will be honest, harmless, or helpful, rather than sycophantic, dishonest, toxic, or biased. And AI researchers have been working on these problems for years. It's foolish to imagine that such challenging problems will all suddenly be solved. I've been griping about hallucination errors for 22 years; people keep promising the solution is nigh, and it never happens."[5]

On the other hand, as Wong notes, we're just beginning to explore the productivity advantages of humans and AI-powered systems working together.

A DISCIPLINED APPROACH TO TECHNOLOGY

The assumption that there must be a technology solution for every problem gets people shopping for technology without considering the alternatives. "When evaluating a possible technology solution, I think it's important to consider a solution that doesn't use technology," says Jamie Flinchbaugh, founder at consulting firm JFlinch. "Add that to the list and compare it with the others. If you end up choosing a technology solution, that's fine, but don't assume. There might be a perfect technology solution, but maybe the non-tech alternative that has no maintenance costs, no training costs, and won't become obsolete is better."

The continuous improvement discipline provides a suitable framework for making that assessment. "A lot of companies that I see that are doing concentrated learning on how to use AI are driving that out of continuous improvement teamwork," says Flinchbaugh. "This is because they recognize that adopting a transformative technology is all about experimentation and learning, and thinking about how work is done. That's the way we should think about how AI comes into our workplace."

Parker Hannifin follows a similar approach. Essentially, the value of the robot has to be proven on the shop floor as a necessary tool to achieve a clearly defined (and quantified) improvement in the process. "When automation is being discussed, we want to go in and take a look at the process and simplify that process as much as we can using our Lean tools," says Parker-Hannifin VP Stephen Moore. "That's one of the first things we do when there's a request to authorize the purchase of some capital equipment like a robot."

Parker uses a hierarchical approach: first, simplify the process as much as possible; second, consider an unpowered mechanical solution, and only if that doesn't work consider the programmed robotic option.

"We're doing a great deal of work to accelerate our use of automation," says Moore, "but when we talk about automation, we look at various tiers. First, we try to simplify the process as much as possible. Then we try to use what we call *karakuri* [deployment of simple machinery such as hoists and conveyors driven by springs, pulleys, counterweights, and other mechanical features]. The next level is simple automation through small, powered devices – maybe a cylinder that actuates and removes a part from a machine, something short of an expensive robot. Once we've looked at that and determined that it's really going to require that robot, now we start to work on implementing that piece of automation."

The results of these investigations are sometimes surprising. "One of our teams was chartered to implement a robot in a cell," says Moore. "This was going to allow for the redeployment of one of the three team members in the cell, and also address a safety concern related to loading and unloading."

Moore split the team up into two groups – one team to work on planning the robot implementation, and one team to find ways to improve the process in the cell. "By the end of the week, we had the production in that area down to only needing two people," says Moore, "and we were able to alleviate all the safety concerns with respect to the loading and unloading of that equipment. So essentially, we eliminated the original justification for purchasing the robot."

The approach, however, isn't opposition to technology. "There are some jobs that are dirty and dangerous, and we do have to automate those," says Moore, "but we always do *kaizen* first." The beauty of this approach is that in understanding the process better, it's much easier to implement the robot once it has been acquired.

"We don't want to automate waste," says Moore. "If we do decide we need a robot, just like we would want to simplify an operator's motions, we want to simplify the robot's motions. Parts presentation and motion reduction are just as important to a robot as they are to a person."

LEAN AND THE NEW ROBOTICS

The new generation of collaborative robots has made the technology far more compatible with continuous improvement environments. "The Lean philosophy is about eliminating waste in many different areas," says Beck, "and that's a very hot area within innovation. In automation, eliminating waste really means 'How do you make things less complicated? How do you have these clean workflows where instead of brute force optimizing you are actually eliminating wasteful processes, and using automation in the places where it really creates value?'"

The advantage of cobots is that because of their flexibility, they can be easily redeployed when a process is redesigned to remove unnecessary steps. "Many robots are used to move things from point A to point B," says Beck. "But in a Lean mindset, that process has low value, and maybe shouldn't be there at all. But what's interesting about cobots is that you can actually put them in value creating processes that occur at those two points, for example, doing the arc welding, rather than doing that low-value process like transportation. So the idea is, let's make sure you don't create this waste that you somehow later have to optimize your way out of."

Because cobots are designed to be programmed by users on the shop floor, they become workplace tools rather than systems imposed on workers. "I think, as soon as when the robot becomes the tool of the operators rather than something that you buy that's huge, complex, and highly customized, it also becomes a tool you can use for continuous improvement in your factory," says Beck. "For us, the question is, 'how do you empower manufacturers to actually take control of what they're automating rather than automation being something you order that has a green-red start and stop button and runs like that for 20 years.'"

FINDING THE MIDDLE PATH

While the technology is evolving to support a more collaborative approach, many people still see automation as a magic labor-saving solution that can be dropped, in black box fashion, into a segment of an operating environment.

"Automation is definitely part of the solution, but it's not the only solution," says Nick Bauer, CEO of Illinois-based manufacturer Empire Group, "and I think the smart money chases automation more than it should. The problem is that robots have to be perfect every time in order to work. A human can adjust for a minute late or a minute early, or if something happens with the power or something like that. To pitch a perfect game every time on a line is statistically unlikely."

People's over-optimism is perpetuated, in part, to the fact that people only hear about success stories. "People are reluctant to share their failure stories," says Wong, "and all we learn about is the positive use cases. Even science reporting is that way – you only hear about the successful experiments."

The question companies need to pursue isn't just whether or not automation will work – it's also how it will ultimately increase the value that the company can provide for its customers. "If you're not automating the right process, all you're doing is doing bad things faster," says Mark Borsari, CEO of Sanderson-McLeod. "Ultimately, the biggest risk I see with technology is making sure everybody understands that there is a tipping point where you're no longer a unique value-add culture that people are willing to pay for. Eventually, you're just cranking out what somebody down the street with a plant full of robots can do."

Companies also need to adopt an experimental attitude about technology where the risks of failure are accepted as part of a learning process. "As an educator, I want students to really understand that when something fails, it's not the end of the road," says Wong. "It's about understanding why it failed, where the potential gaps are, and filling those gaps.

Companies that apply a learning culture to automation will be most likely to succeed, and will create huge growth opportunities for their employees. "There's going to be a huge need for talent – people who can work alongside of AI, or alongside cobots, and are willing to work and learn new skills," says Kerry Siggins, CEO of StoneAge. "If you aren't able to attract those kinds of employees, and if you're not able to help employees whose jobs might be replaced with AI learn new skills, I think you're going to be left behind. So you must create a culture where people want to work and learn. It has to be a workplace where people feel like they're being reinvested in. That's going to be really important."

As Siggins notes, it would be a mistake for a company to ignore the potential influence of AI and other technologies. But the far more common mistake, as we've seen throughout this book, is to undervalue human talent – a mistake that is embedded in the prevailing management system that sees people as cogs in a machine.

Technology is not a magic bullet that will solve productivity problems by itself, nor can it be effective at automating defective processes. But in the hands of an engaged workforce that understands workplace processes and takes pride in optimizing them, technology will be a powerful enabler for the future.

THE MYTH OF TECH OMNIPOTENCE TAKEAWAYS

- Technology can enable enormous productivity gains, but it should not be assumed that there is a technological solution to every problem.
- Companies should think less about using technology to replace people and more about combining the strengths of people and technology.
- Processes should be optimized before being automated in order to reduce the risk of embedding waste within an automated process.
- Technology can improve workplaces by eliminating dull and dangerous work, and making people's jobs more engaging.

PART
THREE

Business Strategies for a Better World

PART
THREE

Business Strategies
for a Better World

8

Productive Strategies for Preserving Our Planet

As we've discussed throughout this book, removing waste from processes is a powerful weapon for improving productivity. It is also the key to ensuring a sustainable future on our planet. Accordingly, saving our planet and improving the performance of a business can go hand in hand.

Many of the practices aimed at mitigating climate change, however, are misguided and inefficient because they fail to get to the root causes of waste. The myths of segmented success and tech omnipotence are largely to blame for this. In this chapter, we'll see how innovative leaders are shattering these myths to make tangible progress against climate change.

HEATING THE OUTDOORS

One of the defining features of a typical Canadian town is its local arena – a facility with artificial ice used for two of Canada's favorite sports: curling and hockey. These arenas are easy to recognize because each has a smokestack-like structure rising out of the roof with steam coming out of it.

The stack is a device called a cooling tower. Its function is to dispel the heat generated by the chillers that cool the ice surface. The irony is that the facility is expending energy to transfer heat from indoors to outdoors during the cold Canadian winter.

"They're actually paying to get rid of that heat after they've moved it by running a cooling tower," says Bruce Taylor, president of Elmira, Ontario–based consultancy Enviro-Stewards. "Then they use natural gas to heat the rest of the arena."

The scenario is typical of the way organizations manage energy. The practice of disposing of heat in one area of an operation while expending energy to generate heat in another is so prevalent that it's embedded in the discipline of energy management. The go-to methods for energy-saving projects are typically technology-based interventions, such as the installation of more efficient heating or cooling systems, installation of solar panels on the roof, or other conversions to sustainable energy sources.

Taylor, in fact, was consulted by the city of London, Ontario, to come up with a plan to make the arena more energy efficient. The expectation was that Taylor would recommend replacing the antiquated systems used to heat the arena with more efficient air source heat pumps.

Taylor had a very different idea in mind. He could have designed a new heating system, and nobody would have questioned it. But as a true believer in doing the right thing, he convinced the city to commission an Enviro-Stewards energy audit on one of the facilities.

The results showed that even during the coldest months of the winter, the heat that was being pumped outdoors through the cooling tower was more than enough to heat the entire building. Capturing that heat, therefore, was a much more effective way to save energy in the facility, from both an environmental and a financial standpoint.

DOING MORE WITH LESS

The conventional approach to making arenas more energy efficient is typical of the way our businesses and governments are addressing our environmental crisis. When facing a high energy bill or a wastewater problem, simply deploy a technology to counteract that.

This makes sense for those who have fallen into the tech omnipotence trap. But a "let's just apply some technology" approach ignores opportunities to get significant gains at a low cost by simply reducing the quantity of resources that are being wasted. If we attack the process to make it more efficient rather than simply counteracting it with another process, we actually increase the productivity of the process while doing our part to save the planet.

When waste goes down, productivity goes up. This is why companies that have succeeded with Lean and Deming's systems approach have not only high productivity, but admirable records on the environment. If you optimize your processes by reducing waste, you simultaneously reduce energy and materials use, and reduce harmful discharges into the air and waterways.

Of course, to make significant reductions in waste, broad initiatives will also be required in addition to companies reducing waste in their processes. These include better insulation on homes and buildings, public transit to reduce vehicle usage, or mandates to reduce disposable packaging.

In his book *How the World Really Works*, scientist and emeritus professor Vaclav Smil chronicles the failures of repeated environmental conferences to make a dent on global warming. Rather than pursue desperate (and unrealistic) measures to end the consumption of fossil fuels, he writes, people need to pay more attention to the solutions that are right in front of us.

"There are enormous opportunities for reducing energy use in buildings, transportation, industry, and agriculture, and we should have initiated some of these energy-saving and emissions-reducing measures decades ago, regardless of any concerns about global warming. Quests to avoid unnecessary energy use, reduce air pollution and water, and to provide more comfortable living conditions should be perennial imperatives, not sudden desperate actions aimed at preventing a catastrophe."[1]

A DIFFERENT VISION

Taylor, a chemical engineer by training, founded Enviro-Stewards in 2000 with a mission of providing environmental and sustainability solutions based on attacking the root cause of problems rather than symptoms. As in the above example, this typically involves assessing where the waste is occurring before prescribing a solution. The work has won his firm numerous awards from environmental organizations in Canada and the US.

While the arena project might sound novel to people who are used to the traditional approach of applying technology to improve energy efficiency, it is typical of the work of Enviro-Stewards. In a project using the same principles, he designed a heat-reusing system at Molson Breweries − a large brewery in Toronto. The system would take heat from the chillers used to cool beer vats and transport it across the plant to be used to evaporate CO_2 for carbonating the beer. Again, the impact will be much greater than the conventional solution of installing a more efficient technology to evaporate the CO_2. The heat and cooling capacity are already in the facility and have already been paid for.

Engineers often take a siloed approach towards efficiency, even when interacting with colleagues in their own profession. Taylor confronted this when he was hired to help a chemical plant save energy by reducing the size of an exhaust fan that was expelling toxic fumes created by a distilling process.

Taylor observed that the problem might be solved differently depending on which engineering discipline was applied. The electrical engineering approach would have been to install a more efficient fan motor to reduce energy costs. This would have provided only marginal energy savings.

Mechanical engineering might have taken a heat loss approach by installing an air-to-air heat exchanger at the exhaust point to recapture the lost heat. That solution would have fared much better, netting energy savings of 60%. The best approach, however, came from looking at the toxicity angle, which revealed that the offending toxic fumes were coming from a single tank. Consequently, the tank was sealed, the fan was eliminated altogether, and the fumes were condensed into solvent that could then be sold to generate revenue.

Taylor's real passion is reducing food waste. The scale of this problem is enormous − a stat Taylor frequently mentions is that if you took the carbon footprint of all the food waste in the world and assigned that to a hypothetical nation, it would have the third-largest carbon footprint in the world (after the US and China). And with nearly a billion people going to bed hungry every night, the problem can aptly be described as a waste that is morally wrong.

Larger corporations are taking notice. Enviro-Stewards is working with Maple Leaf Foods, a large food processing company with 35 plants across North America, to help that company reach its ambitious target of reducing its carbon footprint by 50% by 2025. Based on this work, in 2019 Maple Leaf Foods became the world's first carbon-neutral major food company (while saving $17 million dollars thus far).

Recently, Enviro-Stewards became a provider for food and cleansing product giant Unilever North America, which is pursuing the ambitious goal of achieving zero emissions from their production by 2030. The company knows it's getting something from Enviro-Stewards that diverges from the normal.

"What we're offering is so completely different from what they're getting from other people," says Taylor. "In the reports that they got from others, they're starting at the end of the line – they're telling them to buy fields and fields of solar panels, but otherwise keep doing what they're doing."

Enviro-Stewards took a radically different direction. "We did our first work for them at their plant in Toronto," says Taylor, "and we can cut half to almost two-thirds of their energy in the first place through conservation. This helps build credibility as well as the finances necessary for the remainder of the journey." And as each conservation measure implemented affects the next one, each facility has a customized decarbonization pathway outlining specific measures to be implemented each year with their associated business cases.

Many observers might look at the facility and say, "Where are the solar panels?" "That doesn't make sense," says Taylor. "We have winter here. So put those solar panels in developing countries such as South Sudan or northern Uganda where you get twice as much energy from every panel. Plus, their grid is 100% fossil fuel and ours in Ontario is only 10%. So panels there get 20 times more environmental benefit from every panel. And if you donate the surplus power to these communities, they don't have to use fuel to run generators. So you can use that energy to feed people and get social value out of that investment."

Furthermore, they might totally miss the point about the economic benefits of conservation work. "People may know the (relatively low) cost involved in disposing materials, but they fail to factor in the original cost of purchasing the materials. The problem we have is that this is a low priority for people because they're putting the wrong dollar value on it," says Taylor. "So we have to raise the priority level before anybody will even bother thinking about it. One of the blind spots in business is that they're taught to see things as costs, not lost opportunities."

The connection between efficiency and doing the right thing for the planet is a natural fit using this approach. As we'll see in Chapter 10, Taylor subscribes to a new way of helping communities in the developing world. Spoiler alert – this is about using science and training to help people help themselves.

FALSE ECONOMICS

Given the results of the work of Enviro-Stewards, one would expect that customers would be lining up at their door. While Taylor's firm has a steady stream of business that keeps a staff of 18 engaged in challenging work, his work is often misunderstood and underappreciated. The problem is that when seen through the myopic lens of the myth of segmented success, the true impact of the work is invisible to the people approving the expenditures.

This is clearly illustrated by an Enviro-Stewards success story. Taylor was approached by Jackson-Triggs Winery in Kelowna, British Columbia, about a waste problem. The winery had grown rapidly, and the volume of waste going into the town's sewerage system was straining the town's capacity. In response, the town had ordered the winery to put in a waste treatment plant. The expected cost was $3M, and the winery wanted Taylor to design it.

Taylor did what he always did – conducted a waste audit of the facility. The study revealed that there was a significant opportunity to reduce waste in the plant's processes, and the prospect of reducing that waste presented an attractive alternative to simply treating it. By responding to process defects identified in the audit, the winery was able to cut wine losses by two-thirds and reduced the quantity of wastewater generated in half. This resulted in hundreds of cases of wine being sold instead of being lost down the drain. In addition, the required waste treatment plant had to be only half the size, reducing its cost from $3M to $1.5 M.

Enviro-Stewards, however, didn't share in the financial benefits. Consultants get paid based on a percentage of the project, and accordingly, reducing the size of the treatment plant meant that Enviro-Stewards' fee was similarly cut in half. Had he followed the status quo and designed the $3M plant, nobody would have blinked.

"There's a real reward for overdesign," says Taylor. "We designed a treatment plant that cost $1.5 million instead of $3 million, and we made half what we would have made. That's why consultants don't do this – you give the client the benefit of your expertise, and you make less money."

Taylor finds that similar thinking prevents companies from confronting their waste problem head on. One of the key difficulties is that waste is valued at the cost of disposing of it. A more realistic approach, Taylor says, is to evaluate that waste at the original cost of procuring it.

A manufacturer of ballpoint pens, for example, might not be motivated to reduce its waste of plastic. "Business schools teach you to value that wasted plastic at the cost to dispose of that plastic, not the cost to buy the plastic," says Taylor. Not only are the dollars to procure the plastic lost, but so are all the costs of processing it up to the point where it is rejected. But much of that cost is invisible based on how these losses are reported.

"If you'd actually value it at what it costs to buy it and process it to the point where you've lost it, then you can justify upgrades to productivity," says Taylor. "So the first problem we normally run into is everybody's undervaluing whatever resource it was, whether it's food loss, scrap metal, or whatever."

The metrics governments use in recycling regulations perpetuate this flawed logic by mandating reporting on diversion percentage – the percentage of waste that is diverted from landfill.

$$Diversion\ Percentage = \frac{Weight\ of\ Recycling}{(Weight\ of\ Recycling + Weight\ of\ Garbage)} \times 100$$

"Counterintuitively, if you have a lot of scrap in your process, that actually helps your waste diversion percentage look better, because you're probably sending that to somebody else to do something lower value with that plastic," says Taylor. "But if you put that plastic in a pen instead, then your diversion percentage looks worse, mathematically. Because the amount to landfill's the same but the amount that's diverting is less. So your percentage goes down."

Taylor adds, "A better approach is to track and report diverted plus prevented rather than diverted only."

The same principle of undervaluing waste came to the fore when Enviro-Stewards was engaged to reduce waste at Campbell Soup Company of Canada. The waste problem initially seemed insignificant – the company had conducted waste audits in compliance with Province of Ontario regulations, and those showed that only 1% of waste was not being diverted. These audits, however, assess how much waste goes into landfill, while the vast majority of food loss occurs within the production facility.

Enviro-Stewards did an end-to-end waste audit of the entire value stream, from the receiving of raw food into the plant to final canning and packing of the finished product. The method used was an international standard called the Food Loss and Waste Standard (FLW), which was created by a consortium of organizations, including Enviro-Stewards, dedicated to tackling the food waste problem.

The audit revealed nearly 1,000 tons per year in wasted food that could potentially be avoided, and pinpointed the losses to specific areas in the plant. Improvements in the processes for sorting, peeling, cutting, and canning the products resulted in hundreds of tons of food going into the final products instead of going to waste. The opportunities would reduce the company's greenhouse gas emissions by 4,000 tons per year while saving $706,000 per year in opportunity costs. This project was selected by Clean50 as the top project in Canada that year. The company not only improved its carbon footprint but generated a rapid return on investment for the project.

Another instance of the false economics that companies practice around waste, Taylor says, is the tendency to focus on initial costs and disregard maintenance and other costs that make up the lifecycle cost of a piece of equipment or a facility. Often this delusion occurs when facilities are built with design-build projects.

"What's done with design-build projects is people will hire the same firm to design and build it to get the minimum initial cost," says Taylor. "But with that approach, you automatically get the maximum total cost, because more than 75% of the cost of a facility is to run it. So if you're doing design and build, should you be designing anything different than you've always designed? No, because that comes out of your pocket. Should you buy anything more than the cheapest piece of equipment? No, because that comes out of your pocket. So that maximizes the operating costs and minimizes the durability of whatever you build. And this isn't by accident, it's by design. You automatically get the worst solution."

While many don't appreciate Taylor's vision, his employees do. His work has struck a chord with young engineers who want to make a difference and he has his pick of the best and brightest engineering graduates. "We don't do work that doesn't make a difference," says Taylor, "and because of that, we spend all our time on important stuff – ten of our projects have won national awards. So we get really good people, and we keep them – our turnover rate is about one-tenth of the rate for a typical consulting business. So I can provide a higher-caliber service to my customers because I can keep my people."

TAKING A SYSTEM APPROACH

Bruce Taylor is not the only engineer who is frustrated with the thoroughly unscientific way that companies assess their carbon footprint. Stephen Dixon, an energy consultant based in St. Jacobs, Ontario, whose beliefs align with Taylor's, finds that the metrics evaluating energy managers are often counterproductive.

Dixon illustrates this disconnect with an event around the time of the great recession in 2008. "I was the energy consultant for a large factory in the mid-2000s," recalls Dixon, "and in early or mid-2008, I got a panic phone call from the energy manager. He said that the efficiency numbers that they had worked so hard to improve were now getting worse."

Like many factories, the efficiency was assessed in relation to the amount of product being shipped – the ratio was mega-joules of energy per kilogram of product. In hindsight, the cause was obvious. The economic meltdown of 2008 had precipitated a huge drop in sales, and production had been reduced significantly. However, with the fixed energy costs of heating and operating the plant remaining the same, the cost per kilogram of product was now a higher number.

"When we actually went in and properly analyzed his data, he was as efficient as he ever was," says Dixon. "He was doing all the right things – the decline in efficiency was completely caused by the drop in production volume."

The lesson from this is that the ratio – energy consumed in relation to the amount the plant produced – is a false indicator of energy efficiency of the plant because it can change independently of any energy reduction efforts that the energy manager undertakes.

As we've seen with so many other businesses, people tend to view the aggregate numbers myopically without a view to where they came from. The factory energy consultant was focused on a principle that, he believed, told him everything he needed to know about the efficiency of the plant. Invisible to him, and to his superiors, was the potential influence of a black swan – an event like the 2008 crash that essentially put an offset into the equation, causing all the number to be different from previous expectations.

Helping companies recognize the truth behind energy-related data is central to the work of Dixon's consultancy, Knowenergy. An early student of Deming's philosophy, Dixon applies a systems approach to energy projects. He is also a strong proponent of the Deming Chain Reaction – the observation that costs go down as quality improves.

"When you do a good energy project," says Dixon, "you get direct and indirect energy savings, you get improvement in the reliability of your equipment, you get better safety, better air quality, and higher productivity. But many companies would run all of these as separate projects." The problem is that with siloed budgeting, there is little incentive to expand the scope of these projects to produce wider benefits. "Maybe a much better solution would cost a little bit more, but the benefits would go to somebody else's silo."

Like Taylor, Dixon is constantly battling silos, even within his own profession. Energy projects, for example, fall under a different silo than waste projects. Dixon learned just how deep this siloed thinking is when he was a student.

The tendency to take a siloed view has deep roots, Dixon explains. "I have degrees in both physics and systems engineering," says Dixon. "I found that physics tends to be reductionist, where you expect that you can understand a system by analyzing all the subsystems. But systems engineering is a lot closer to the collectivist approach that we see in biology, where it's always the interaction between the elements that really dictates the overall behavior of a system. In system design, you

learn very early on that you can't describe a system as the mathematical sum of the parts — it's always the interaction, whether it's a technical
system or a human system."

In energy projects, the ratings of the components don't guarantee
a successful outcome. "I can pick the best motor with a very high efficiency rating, a very high efficiency pump, and a piping system that has
incorporated all the best practices of reducing friction and encouraging flow with the minimum amount of power," says Dixon. "But if I
mismatched the three of those things together, I don't get an efficient
system, especially if the system is oversized."

The problem is that nobody's looking at the performance of the
entire system. "Different people have responsibility for different parts,"
says Dixon. "So, the efficiency often suffers in the lack of communication between them."

Helping people communicate, therefore, has become a major focus
of Dixons firm. "In my earlier career, my job was to run around plants
doing energy audits and finding ways to improve the efficiency of technology. But I realized as I went through that process that I was walking
by a lot of operational improvements, and I really wasn't afforded the
time to get down and really understand the operations."

Then came an epiphany that would transform his business. "I ran
into a social anthropologist I was working for, and she said to me,
'Steve, you're never going to crack this energy nut, not unless you
deal with the people.' So here was a social scientist," he says with
a laugh, "calling me out on my engineering practice. So that was a
huge epiphany for me. And from that point forward, I adopted an
approach to my work based on the fact that with energy projects, we
are dealing with three elements — the technical, the behavioral, and
the organizational."

Dixon uses a Venn diagram to illustrate the importance of this (see
Figure 8.1). The idea is that to create a successful project, you need
to make sure that you're in the zone where these three areas interact.
"There are lots of things you can do in each of those circles," says Dixon,
"but it's at the intersection of these circles where you have success in
energy management."

The typical culprit here is that technically oriented approaches —
often driven by a technical vendor promising miraculous results — see
the involvement of people as a distraction rather than an enabler.

Figure 8.1   Diagram used by Stephen Dixon.
Source: Created by author based on description by Stephen Dixon.

"I'm a believer in building automation systems," says Dixon, "but if you disengage the people that are working in the building on a daily basis, the consequences of that can be quite significant."

Often, people responsible for maintaining facilities will fight automation systems, rendering them ineffective. Putting tape over photo sensors or electric heaters under thermostats are classic examples. "People are quite ingenious," says Dixon, "and if they're not engaged with a technology, they'll find a way to defeat it."

Dixon saw an extreme example of this when a company installed an AI-driven control system on a crop-drying operation – a very energy-intensive process. The following spring, the engineers went back to look at the system and how it had performed, and found, to their dismay, that most of the functions had been overridden by the operators.

"They hadn't engaged their people, so nobody understood the system or how to use it," says Dixon. "The system might have performed well if it had been left alone, but there was no way of knowing that. So the cost of not engaging those people was enormous."

Engaging people, however, isn't just a matter of getting buy-in – operators often know more than the engineers designing the systems and have knowledge that can vastly improve the potential effectiveness of those systems. Dixon believes that leaving such people out is simply a bad design practice. "You can either engage people and leverage their energy, knowledge, ingenuity, and commitment, or you can disengage them," says Dixon. "When they're not engaged, it costs you, and it puts the automation at risk."

Dixon applied this principle on a steel plant project. "In a smelting operation, you have people with many years of experience who are sitting behind a control panel every day," says Dixon. "In that situation, we've found that it's best to respect the knowledge they have – there's no way that I, as an energy person, can have anywhere near enough knowledge of that process, and the intricacies and nuances of that furnace."

Successful improvements come from overlapping the tacit knowledge from people's years of experience and the technical engineering expertise that specialists like Dixon bring to projects. "I know about the physics of that furnace," says Dixon, "and if I can provide the right information to those operators, that's when the magic is going to happen in terms of efficiency."

To illustrate, Dixon uses the table shown in Figure 8.2, which is based on a comparative study of energy projects in four buildings. Note that Building 1 actually recorded negative savings!

When Dixon shows this at conferences, he gets a lot of nods. "People with experience know that these technological solutions aren't going to work if you don't engage with people," he says.

THE INCREMENTAL ASPECTS OF ENERGY SAVINGS

Energy saving isn't just about projects. As per Taylor's observation that 75% of the cost of a facility is in its operation, operational improvements are where many of the savings will be found. However, those savings aren't often found in convenient and easy targets – energy losses are typically the sum total of hundreds or even thousands of small anomalies. Consequently, involving people who know the facility, not just operators, has to be an ongoing commitment.

BUILDING	APPROACH	SAVINGS
1	Technology Only	–3%
2	Technology Only	4%
3	People Only	16%
4	People & Technology	23%

Figure 8.2 Energy savings from different approaches.

Dixon spends much of his time encouraging and training people to think differently about energy. As we saw earlier, when energy projects are guided by a sincere effort to reduce energy loss, they will generate efficiency gains in other areas. Dixon often makes the connection between energy improvements and other improvements that have nothing to do with energy.

"I was working for an auto parts manufacturer, and as part of the assessment, I looked at their historical energy data," says Dixon. "When I analyzed that data, I noticed that there was huge improvement in energy efficiency in January 2002. So the question was, what had changed that made this possible?"

It turned out that the company had engaged its employees in a 5S project. Bringing cleanliness and orderliness to the plant had, in fact, uncovered significant energy savings as a byproduct. "The 5S project wasn't focused on energy per se," says Dixon, "but it actually improved the energy situation quite markedly. I think they got a 16% reduction in electricity consumption."

What's interesting is that 5S is based on the idea of incremental improvement. You don't "5S" a plant by imposing a high-level plan – instead, you engage the hearts and minds of all employees who introduce improvements which may be very small but contribute to making the facility a better place to work.

This is in stark contrast to the "big bang" energy projects that gain lots of visibility and are therefore favored in large organizations. "There are lots of people who want to go after those big projects," says Dixon. "I actually don't like the word 'project' because that tends to be time-delineated – people set up a task-specific team, complete the project and then everybody moves on."

If, on the other hand, everybody is engaged in improving the work environment, you've got something sustainable. "I would rather go after little things that become part of this continuous improvement mindset that you have to adopt with energy," says Dixon. "So we'll look at a small incremental improvement, measure it, and lock in the gains."

Dixon uses this approach in group events aimed at uncovering energy saving opportunities. "One of our most successful events these days is somewhat like a Lean *kaizen* event where you get a group of people together to explore creative ways of making improvements," says Dixon. "It's essentially an energy treasure hunt involving a whole range of people that are widely familiar with the facility from working in it day by day and are neither supervising nor operating energy-saving systems."

The events begin with some basic instruction about energy and how various losses occur, and then some explanations of the energy picture in the subject facility. "We show how these principles are playing out in the particular facility by looking at graphs, charts, and historical information," says Dixon. "Then we invite people in the room to identify opportunities to improve."

Once opportunities are identified, Dixon works with participants and various tools to quantify the potential gains from implementing an improvement. "Many people have a good idea, but they don't know how important it is because they don't know how much energy is attached to the idea," says Dixon. "So we try to attach numbers to the idea to increase the importance of it in everybody's minds. This really increases engagement, and it also gives employees ownership of the idea, because it shows how the benefits of the idea can be tracked."

Experience from these events shows that energy expertise isn't necessarily the determinant of the best ideas. "We did a treasure hunt exercise in a manufacturing business," says Dixon, "and the person who came up with the best ideas was not the person who operates all the systems, but a member of the cleaning staff."

This shouldn't be surprising. Waste can show up anywhere, and cleaning staff are typically most familiar with the entire facility, and as well, with the work habits and attitudes of the people that occupy it. An energy manager who spends most of the day in the office and tours the plant occasionally will not have this familiarity.

The key here is breaking down the idea that energy saving is a silo that should be managed exclusively by a specialist with a specified role pertaining to energy. "The reasons these projects work so well in energy is because energy is nobody's job and everybody's job at the same time. As soon as you establish a title like energy manager, that can have a negative impact."

IT'S ALL ABOUT PRODUCTIVITY

If we reimagine productivity as not just a financial indicator, but a metric for doing more with the resources we have, the work of Dixon and Taylor is really about increasing productivity. "If you've defined productivity simply as the number of dollars that you get out of a process for what you put in, that's very limiting," says Dixon, "but if I redefine the term productivity in a way that allows people to see other dimensions for growth in the numerator, then these kinds of improvements really represent how the organization is being more productive."

Many people entering the workforce are actively seeking companies that are committed to the environment. If companies do this right, environmental projects could become a catalyst for engaging employees in continuous improvement journeys, leading to higher productivity and sustainable growth.

9

A Prescription for Better Healthcare

ealthcare, our most important industry, is widely regarded to be in a state of crisis. Much of the problem can only be solved on a national level. However, there is also trouble within the walls of caregiving institutions. Here, productivity is determined by number of positive patient outcomes in relation to the resources applied, and by this measure, many hospitals are struggling.

In this industry, the myths run rampant. Care delivery is badly segmented. Problems are too frequently seen through a myopic financial lens. Many employees feel unsafe, disrespected, and intimidated. And finally, software systems are often superimposed upon wasteful processes, making these processes very difficult to change.

In this chapter, we look at how leaders are confronting the myths in an effort to change all this.

A ROADMAP FOR A BETTER SYSTEM

In June 2023, *Health Affairs Scholar* published a paper titled "The Better Care Plan: A Blueprint for Improving America's Healthcare System," which was co-authored by a group of highly respected US healthcare executives. The paper cited rising concerns about high costs, difficulties navigating the system, and the alarming frequency of injury or death due to preventable medical errors.

"Care is expensive, fragmented, highly variable in quality, and too often unsafe," wrote the authors in the introduction.[1] The paper calls for sweeping changes to how health services are delivered, paid for, and evaluated. "Healthcare is in serious shape," says Dr. John Toussaint, one of the co-authors of the paper, former hospital CEO, and founder of the healthcare improvement organization Catalysis. "We've been saying this for years. But the number of adverse events and safety events in healthcare is just astronomical. 1.2 million people will be injured at hospitals this year. 1.2 million! That means that if you get admitted to a hospital, there's a 25% chance of some sort of adverse event. Now, some of these injuries are going to be minor, but a third of the cases are going to be serious."

Quality, however, is much more difficult to quantify in healthcare because aggregated numbers don't typically capture the severity of the problem. "When you go buy a refrigerator, you're typically thinking of quality in relation to cost," says Toussaint, "but in healthcare, that doesn't compute because it gets so convoluted, frankly, from the standpoint of value. So what I look at personally, from the standpoint of a patient, is 'What is the desired outcome that I'm after? And how does the team perform at that level?' So the big thing in healthcare now, which I'm totally for, is patient-reported outcomes, and seeing more and more data around that. Because in the end, that's the value equation. Did you get better or not?"

Bringing transparency about patient outcomes to create a more accountable system, however, faces formidable resistance. Breaking the deadlock needs to begin, the authors say, by reforming a fee-for-service model that provides no accountability for patient outcomes. "We cannot improve our nation's healthcare system by continuing to pay for the volume of care produced under our deeply rooted fee-for-service system," say the authors. "We also cannot improve our nation's health without developing credible, transparent, standardized, validated, timely and understandable patient safety and quality outcomes reporting."[2]

The fee-for-service model, essentially, lets providers off the hook for quality issues. To remedy this, the authors propose transparency regarding outcomes. "If there's bad surgery, that should be reported," says Toussaint.

"Along with that, there needs to be oversight around patient outcomes, and a realignment of incentives to compel providers to compete on patient safety and quality, access, and price."

Much of the attention in the paper, however, is about how to change how healthcare services are organized and delivered in order to improve outcomes. Central to this is moving from a siloed, hierarchical approach, which is essentially resource-centric, to a patient-centric approach, which emphasizes the end-to-end journey of the patient through the system.

As we've seen in other fields, the quality of the outcome depends on the effectiveness of the teamwork as much as it depends on the skill of the practitioners. Consequently, the paper identifies team-based care as the essential foundation for creating better outcomes.

"Team-based care is central to providing better care," say the authors. "Provider organizations that invest more in team-based primary care have better performance on measures of clinical quality, patient experience, utilization, and cost."[3]

An important deterrent to teamwork, Toussaint says, is the established hierarchy that assumes that the doctor knows best and is fully qualified to tell other team members what to do:

> "In healthcare, we clearly need highly trained experts. Let's take the example of the neurosurgeon. That doctor is highly trained to do a specific task that takes years and years of learning. There's no question that he is the only person that can do this task. But it's also assumed that he should have control over everyone else in that process because he's the highest trained, generally the most intelligent, etc. This means he gets input on every single part of the process that he doesn't have a clue about. So the problem is that people like that start to meddle in every part of the process they don't understand. And so you wind up with a terrible process. Then the neurosurgeon blames the nurse or the anesthesiologist or another team member, but it was him who caused the problem."

The neurosurgeon, for example, may not be up to date on all the latest sterilization techniques, the nuances around lab tests, the operation of equipment, or the preparation of tools and medications. "If he would just stay in his role and do his one thing and allow members of the team to figure out what to do before and after he makes the incision, the process would work way better," says Toussaint.

What's needed is the same systemic approach that Deming promoted. "The challenge is trying to understand systemically something as complicated as brain surgery, and how each one of the members of that team are just as important as the other members," says Toussaint. "And that's despite the physician having 15 years of training versus three for a nurse, as each role is critical to the outcome of the procedure."

A key cause is the traditional way in which doctors are trained. "I think the situation is getting better," says Toussaint, "but when I went to med school, there was no talk about teamwork. Zero. It was all about me as leader."

A contributor to the problem, Toussaint says, is that the existing model is essentially a physician-centric structure. Physicians are typically the most expensive resource in the system, so utilization is optimized on a "physician first" basis, that is, by maximizing the physician's billable hours.

This can also cause a physician's time to be unwisely allocated. With doctors engaging in areas where they have little or no expertise, they are not only creating potential harm, but spending their precious time on tasks that could be better completed by others who have specific expertise, and are more readily available and less expensive.

The resource allocation problem applies to nurses as well. When he was CEO at ThedaCare, a regional medical center in Wisconsin, Toussaint led a major campaign to improve the productivity of nurses. "It was very difficult to define nursing productivity," says Toussaint, "so there's no single right approach."

The challenge is that the determination of what work is actually productive in improving outcomes depends on a multitude of factors. "In nursing, productivity is very specific to the work, and to the people who are doing the work," says Toussaint. "So a lot of it gets down to roles and responsibilities. And what we found is that a lot of the work nurses were doing could be done by staff with much less training. We really needed nurses to do knowledge work, not bathe patients. We could hire other people to do that. So increasing nurses' productivity was about taking away those tasks where their experience and expertise wasn't required."

A leader in the teamwork approach, Toussaint says, is Mayo Clinic. "One of the reasons Mayo Clinic has been so good is because they have from the beginning established teamwork as the core element to delivering care. When you go to Mayo Clinic, no matter what you go there for, you see a team of people, not all doctors, but a team where they're looking at this from a systemic perspective. There are very few places you can do that."

Toussaint and Leonard L. Berry, an academic and healthcare advocate, published a paper through the Mayo Foundation for Medical Education and Research titled "The Promise of Lean in Health Care" in 2013. While the need is daunting – improve quality and efficiency while controlling costs – Lean is up to the task, the authors note, but not a magic bullet.

"Lean is not a program; it is not a set of quality improvement tools; it is not a quick fix; it is not a responsibility that can be delegated," say the authors. "Rather, Lean is a cultural transformation that changes how an organization works; no one stays on the sidelines in the quest to discover how to improve the daily work. It requires new habits, new skills, and often a new attitude throughout the organization from senior management to front-line service providers. Lean is a journey, not a destination."[4]

AN ARMY OF PROBLEM SOLVERS

Teamwork in healthcare isn't only about more efficient delivery of services. It's also about solving the myriad problems that arise in any complex environment. With patient harm occurring in 25% of hospital admissions, the urgency of solving these problems cannot be overstated.

Patient harm incidents are due to defects in the delivery system. These defects, however, are not glaring targets that a senior manager or a consultant could identify; instead, they are due to thousands of small problems that are only visible to people working on the front lines.

Medication error is an important component of the patient harm statistic, causing hundreds of thousands of adverse drug incidents, and thousands of patient deaths in American hospitals every year. However, the root cause for this problem rarely shows up as a glaring defect that can be flagged by a senior manager or consultant – likely there is an array of contributing problems. Maybe the labels on the medication vials are confusing or difficult to read. Maybe people handling the medication don't have sufficient lighting to read the labels properly. Maybe medications are stored next to other bottles that look very similar. Maybe the manner in which a medication is presented on a tray creates confusion.

Sometimes, the cause is even more subtle than a physical defect. According to a Kaiser Permanente staff memo by then-CEO George Halvorson, nurses conferred on the medication error issue, and posited that nurses handling medication are often distracted due to frequent interruptions, and that this can contribute to errors. A team of nurses experimented with a novel solution – a nurse handing a medication would wear a bright yellow sash as a sign that this person should not be interrupted.[5] Results were impressive, and the solution, named the KP-MedRite, was rolled out to all of the Kaiser Permanente facilities.

No manager can solve all these problems. What's needed is an army of problem solvers – frontline people who deal with the medication process every day – to propose and implement solutions. This means training people and making sure they are empowered to speak out when they see problems.

EFFICIENCY AND WAIT TIMES: A PERSONAL STORY

One of the best ways to understand the challenges that healthcare facilities are facing is to analyze how a typical patient flows through the system. The idea is to look at the patient's entire experience, starting with entering the facility seeking help and ending when the condition has been resolved.

I experienced a patient view of the system a few years ago when my late father, then 95 years old, was experiencing a severe nosebleed. The condition had occurred on and off for about a week, but this time, it was much worse and the usual interventions – applying ice and pressure – were no longer working. Because it was evening, I called his family doctor, who was also a friend and neighbor, at home. The walk-in clinics were closed, so he recommended that I take him to the emergency room at the local hospital.

We arrived at hospital at around 8:10 p.m. The ward is a small ER with no trauma center, so my father's situation was fairly typical of their evening caseload. There was a line at admitting, but it wasn't too bad – we got my father signed in at around 8:20 and then took our seat in the waiting area.

We waited until about 9:00, when an assistant came out and directed us to an examination room. After five minutes, a triage nurse arrived. He looked at the nosebleed, gave my father some fresh gauze compresses, and made some notes. Next stop, doctor.

We were directed back to the waiting room, where we waited for another two and a half hours. Fortunately, we both had brought books to read. I was also pleased when my sister Lisa joined us. Finally, at about 11:30, an assistant came out and directed us to an examination room.

After about 15 minutes, members of a care team arrived in succession – first a nurse, then a billing administrator, and then a doctor. Everybody was very friendly. The doctor asked my father questions about his health, examined his nose, and installed a small inflatable balloon-like device in the affected nostril to apply pressure to the area. He also made some suggestions for the general practitioner about blood pressure medication. Then the nurse returned to sign off on the discharge paperwork. All this took about 11 minutes. We left the facility shortly before midnight, tired but happy to get the situation resolved.

Our situation was fairly typical for that facility, and the service we received was in line with what we had expected. And given our expectations, we would have given the hospital a good rating.

But when we look at the incident through a value stream perspective, we get a very different picture. Let's look at how my 95-year-old father spent his time at the ER (see Figure 9.1).

To get the patient-centric view, we calculate the flow efficiency, that is, the time spent getting help compared with the time spent in the facility. In my father's case, the flow efficiency is 17 minutes divided by 230 minutes equals 7.4%. Now, if an organization were to advertise that it is 7.4% efficient, nobody would be impressed.

THE PIPE DREAM OF FULL UTILIZATION

Most hospital administrators don't look at efficiency from the standpoint of my father's experience. Their definition would be based on how fully utilized their resources are. If the admissions coordinator, the triage nurse, and the physician's care team are fully occupied with no idle time,

	Minutes Spent in ER		
	Receiving Care	Waiting for Care	Total
Sign-in by admitting coordinator	2	8	10
Pre-exam by triage nurse	4	40	44
Device installed by doctor, medication advice given	11	165	176
Total	17	213	230

Flow efficiency = Care Time/Total Time = 7.4%

Figure 9.1   Example of how a patient's time was spent in an ER facility.

and expensive equipment like MRI machines are solidly booked, the operation is judged to be highly efficient.

The resource efficiency idea comes straight out of the Myth of Segmented Success. If we assume that the efficiency of the hospital is the sum of the efficiency of its components, it all seems to make perfect sense. But as Deming would say, a hospital is a complex adaptive system, and if management doesn't understand the system, events will quickly get out of control.

Swedish consultants Niklas Modig and Par Ahlstrom studied this problem in their book *This Is Lean: Resolving the Efficiency Paradox.*[6] As the authors explain, a focus on high resource efficiency is not only bad for patients, but is also, in the long run, self-defeating for hospitals from both a care and a financial perspective.

The problem is that long throughput times tend to generate a number of secondary problems that create more work for the hospital staff. In our case, for example:

- The long throughput time means there are far more patients in the facility than there would otherwise be. If my father's total throughput time was 60 minutes instead of 230 (flow efficiency of 26% instead of 7%), there would be, on average, approximately 75% fewer patients in the facility at any given time. Waiting capacity is not free – waiting rooms, bathrooms, and other amenities have to be sized and maintained for, in this case, four times what the patient load would be if patient flow were better managed.

- The high number of patients in the ER mean that lots of people need to be monitored. What if my father's situation had gotten worse, and the bleeding had become unmanageable? Then admitting, or triage, would have to interrupt their work to expedite his care. Juggling multiple patients reduces efficiency.
- The long-elapsed time means it's hard to maintain continuity. What if the doctor had a question for the triage nurse? There's a good chance that the triage nurse's shift ended during the time my father was waiting. This means that the doctor might have to repeat work that the triage nurse already did, wasting valuable time.
- Long wait times and large numbers of patients in the facility cause stress for patients and for staff. Patients get angry and complain. And in a stressful environment, mistakes are more frequent.

To sum up, poor flow efficiency increases the volume of patients in the facility and causes hospital staff to be saddled with superfluous work. This includes fixing mistakes, redoing tasks because of the long time elapsed, rejuggling queues because of emergencies, or dealing with irate patients. What's needed is a holistic approach to removing waste from processes in order to achieve flow efficiency and resource efficiency. Later in this chapter, we will look at how a leading hospital is accomplishing this.

You might wonder, however, why wait times are so sensitive to high resource utilization. It turns out that there's a mathematical principle that throws some light on this.

The principle involved is called Kingman's Law, developed in 1961 by British mathematician Sir John Kingman. The law states that as the utilization of a resource approaches full capacity, the length of the queue time – in this case, the wait time in the ER – increases exponentially (see Figure 9.2).

Once a resource gets to around 80% utilization, wait times for that resource spiral out of control. The steepness of the curve depends on how variable the queue items are. In an ER, today's caseload is likely to be quite different from yesterday's. Consequently, the high utilization that looks so good to the finance department is almost a guarantee that

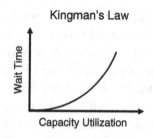

Figure 9.2 Kingman's Law.

there will be long wait times in an ER. And with those long wait times, the superfluous work of everybody involved in the care value stream will increase dramatically.

All this underlines the urgent need to eradicate waste in healthcare processes.

A COMMON VICIOUS CIRCLE

The queuing problem is by no means limited to healthcare. Any institution that keeps people waiting in line is subject to this. People confront this when they wait at:

- Airport security
- Restaurants
- Government offices
- Retail bank branches
- Call centers

Again, this will be invisible to managers who see the workplace only as a collection of assets that need to be utilized.

COPING WITH FINANCIAL PRESSURES

While continuous improvement is a proven method for improving quality while lowering costs, and is established as the only sustainable way to control costs in the long term, hospitals are perpetually caught in a Catch 22 situation where they are pressured to lay off the very staff that they need to make the improvements that will ensure their long-term survival.

Joseph E. Swartz, who we met in Chapter 7, is all too familiar with this conundrum. As a leading advocate for process improvement in healthcare, he has led over two hundred Lean and Six Sigma improvement projects and is co-author, with Mark Graban, of two Shingo Award–winning books: *The Executive Guide to Healthcare Kaizen*, and *Healthcare Kaizen: Engaging Front-Line Staff in Sustainable Continuous Improvements.*

"Our healthcare system is pretty much like everybody else," says Swartz. "Every five years we discover we are not making enough money, or our margins are dropping. Labor is about 60% of our costs, so that tends to be the target. So what invariably happens is they bring in a McKinsey, and they come up with ways to chop out labor."

Margins improve for the short term, but then problems start to emerge. "After a year or two, people get tired and burn out from over-work. So they stop working the extra hours, and the system deteriorates. Then we get called in to fix problems, and what we usually find is that the problems exist because they laid off 5 or 10% of their staff."

Those consultants who recommend the cuts often don't understand the effects on the system that cutting will have – they are meeting a dollar savings target. On one of Swartz's first healthcare projects, he traced a problem back to the laying off of 20% of the phlebotomists in a particular area. "What happened was that the phlebotomists were not able to keep up with the workload," says Swartz, "so nurses had to come in and assist or take over for them in order to safely serve our patients. But nurses make twice as much as phlebotomists, so that was not sustainable."

What needed to be done was to simplify the process by applying Lean methods to identify unnecessary steps and other causes of waste. "I had to go in and work really hard to help the team think through ways of making their work simpler, easier, and faster," says Swartz. Having work areas well organized and the right tools within easy reach helped to improve the productivity of the existing staff. We got good results, but it was a lot of work – maybe a year."

Now a veteran with a track record, Swartz has strong credibility with senior management, but the battle against arbitrary headcount reduction is ongoing. "When I see a situation like that, I try to get leadership to give me more staff for a few months so we can improve the processes first," says Swartz. "The idea is to get everything working the way it should be in terms of serving our patients, and then apply Lean methods to simplify the processes. Once the process is more efficient, you can bring down headcount. It doesn't always work that way, but that's how I think it should be."

Ultimately, however, organizations need to move from cutting to survive to having a long-term plan for sustainable growth. In terms of his own leadership team, Swartz is optimistic.

"I noticed a shift in our leadership maybe ten years ago where they became more conscious of growth," says Swartz. "We started to hear things like 'You can't cut your way to prosperity.' Our leaders are starting to think about where we're growing, and how we can help that growth. We've been working on a big initiative lately, and growth is the first thing they looked at."

BUILDING RESILIENT TEAMS

One of the outcomes of the COVID-19 pandemic is that its impact on many workplace environments has put staff well-being on the corporate agenda. Nowhere is this more critical than in healthcare.

The pandemic has caused, and at this writing continues to cause, untold emotional stress and physical harm to frontline healthcare workers. Burnout is a constant risk as staff deal with the threat of illness to themselves and their families, a myriad of extra work around pandemic safety, and extended shifts due to staffing shortages.

One organization singled out for its expert handling of this challenge is Salem Health in Salem, Oregon. The 644-bed facility, the largest hospital in Oregon, has had more than its share of challenges. Its staff of 5,000 serve 500,000 people who represent the neediest population groups in the state, with patients plagued by poverty, obesity, diabetes, food insecurity, and mental health issues. The ER, the busiest in the Northwest, has 100,000 visits a year.

That so many in need depend on this facility provides the organization with a defined purpose. "Our True North is 'How do we make sure we remain essential for the future to take care of the health and well-being of our community?'" says CEO Cheryl Nester Wolfe.

In response to the enormous stress on staff, the organization launched, in early 2022, a program called Staff Engagement & Resiliency

Advocates (SERA), where each division has an embedded well-being advocate charged with implementing staff surveys, monitoring situations that cause stress, counseling workers, and spearheading process improvements to increase staff well-being. The program was adopted based on the success of an earlier initiative in the hospital's ER department.

"The project aim was to replicate the following outcomes: decrease emotional exhaustion, improve emotional thriving, and emotional recovery," reads a description on the hospital website. The high engagement in the project – evidenced by over 16,000 staff interactions – shows a promising trend, but as Nester Wolfe stresses, there is much work to be done.

STEPS IN A LONG JOURNEY

While a project like SERA looks like a convenient standalone initiative that would be replicated by other hospitals, Nester Wolfe is clear that this is not something that was accomplished in isolation, but part of a long-term cultural transition that the hospital has been engaged in for years.

Nester Wolfe has been involved with the cultural transformation since 2007, when she joined Salem Health as chief nursing officer. The hospital executives had investigated adopting Lean healthcare in the early 2000s, and had made visits to ThedaCare in Appleton, Wisconsin, where John Toussaint was then CEO. "I think that sparked the thinking of the executive team at the time," says Nester Wolfe, "but they didn't think the organization was ready for it. So Lean was sort of sitting in the background when I joined the organization."

As a nurse who rose through the ranks, Nester Wolfe understood the power of worker recognition and teamwork, and in her leadership role, initiated preparations for Salem Health to become a Magnet-certified hospital.

The Magnet certification program was established in the 1980s to promote excellence in nursing. There was a nursing shortage at the time, and the program's elements were created based on the practices of hospitals with low nursing turnover. What the program provides is a framework for establishing a continuous improvement culture throughout the organization. It emphasizes many of the cultural aspects of Lean – focus on patient outcomes, adoption of scientific problem-solving tools, wide staff participation, and respect for the knowledge and skills of frontline workers.

"Magnet certification is a designation that very few hospitals in the US have," says Nester Wolfe. "It's about excellence in care, not just about nursing, but about the entire organization, and how you continuously improve to provide better care."

The work provided the prerequisite environment for a Lean transformation. "Just before we got our Magnet certification," says Nester Wolfe, "I talked to the CEO and I said, 'I think we're ready for Lean.' We didn't have the right tools for improvement work, but we had the structure with our staff to help us make them work. So once we started with Lean, the improvements started happening."

While the path now seemed abundantly clear, Nester Wolfe, who had become COO of the hospital, and the CEO saw the enormous implications of the transformation that lay ahead. Accordingly, they consulted extensively with the board of directors to make sure they were in it for the long haul. "We spent the next year with the board," says Nester Wolfe, "making sure they understood what the journey looked like. I didn't want this to be a typical 'flavor of the day' initiative that happens so often. So there was lots of education, for example, people coming in from Boeing, and at the end of the process, we held a formal board vote to establish this as our management system. So the CEO, I think, had wonderful foresight in establishing this firmly as the way we operate."

The result of this ironclad commitment is that Nester Wolfe, now CEO, expects the program to endure after she retires. It also means that Lean is fully entrenched in the organization. "Lean is our management system," says Nester Wolfe, "so we have embedded it throughout our organization. There's no department, no physician group that's employed by us that isn't part of this."

One of the hallmarks of the Salem continuous improvement journey is that physicians are not just in support of the program, but actively involved in studying and learning Lean methodology and leading improvement through the hospital's Physician Leadership Institute. "We've been doing that for multiple years," says Nester Wolfe. "It's really about a whole organizational approach to leadership that is centered on continuous improvement."

The work within the Institute morphed into the hospital's first staff resiliency project, which was initiated by the hospital's chief medical officer, Ralph Yeates. "Ralph had a heartfelt passion around physician burnout. So I asked him to bring in a consultant so we could analyze the problem and figure out what we needed to do to support them better."

The project really took off when the hospital brought in Brian Sexton, a psychologist from Duke University who specializes in safety and team resiliency. His work involves organizational assessments, teaching and mentoring, and problem-solving – an ideal fit for the improvement culture at Salem.

The presentations he gave to the staff were game changing. "He did sessions for the entire staff, and I've never heard so much buzz in the organization," says Nester Wolfe. "The way he talked about the topic and the data gave us a very different thinking approach."

The scope of the work quickly expanded from preventing physician burnout to fostering resiliency for the entire staff. "The question became, how do we progress this work on resiliency in the organization?" says Nester Wolfe.

The initiative led to a pilot in one of the most stressful environments in the hospital – the emergency room. "We did a pilot in the emergency room to see if having a staff advocate embedded in departments would make any kind of discernable difference with our staff and their feelings about resiliency. And the results blew us out of the water."

The program was extended, and there are five staff advocates now on staff. "They're embedded in each division, so they're part of the team," says Nester Wolfe. "They have counseling skills and are available in the moment to talk to staff and help them get what they need to keep going in these trying times."

One of the problems related to resiliency is that healthcare workers are often subject to verbal abuse and even violence. "A year and a half ago, we started an initiative we call harmful words and actions," says Nester Wolfe. "I'm a registered nurse, and in the past we just considered this part of the job. But we needed to break away from that thinking and make sure staff knew that they also had rights. So we went after that wholeheartedly, and have made it clear that this is something we would no longer tolerate."

The initiative, however, didn't end with an executive proclamation – the organization has applied the same data-driven approach to improving the situation as it does to other organizational problems. The improvement work continues, with new methods being tested and systems being adjusted and refined.

The point is, healthcare is a very personal profession, and it makes workers very vulnerable. "We work in an environment where staff are incredibly dedicated to taking care of people," says Nester Wolfe, "and you should be treated completely with respect by everybody. And you should expect to feel safe in your workplace."

When the pandemic arrived, Salem Health was facing one of the toughest caseloads in the country. However, with years of experience dealing with resiliency issues, the hospital was able to circumvent much of the suffering that staffs in other hospitals were experiencing.

IMPROVEMENT IS PART OF THE CULTURE

The high level of trust, earned over years of work, has not only helped relieve stress and suffering for staff members, but helped galvanize high engagement in continuous improvement activities. Consequently, all staff members are expected to take an active role in improving the standards that govern their work. This includes contributions to large strategic initiatives, improvements based on tracked metrics, or ideas based on observations of the daily work.

At Salem, all staff are made aware of the high-level projects that the hospital has undertaken. "There's a list of hospital-wide strategic initiatives," says Nester Wolfe. "Depending on their role, workers can contribute improvements towards that. Everybody is expected to, and we track that. An EVS worker, for example, might participate in an effort to reduce infection rates. They're expected to look at their environment and look for areas that need improving. Improvements that would impact that strategic initiative."

Excessively long hospital stays are a major challenge that Salem Health has been working on. "We're doing massive length-of-stay work right now," says Nester Wolfe. "Long stays are what's pulling hospitals' financials down, and it's also a quality problem – the longer you keep people, the more likely they are to get infections or have complications in the hospital."

The problem increased during the COVID-19 pandemic. "Through the pandemic, our length of stay started rising, and it's stayed higher," says Nester Wolfe. "So we've put a team together for that – it's a team of clinicians, primarily physicians and clinical leadership staff. My CFO is leading the team."

The actual improvements take place on the front lines and are reviewed daily in the established daily huddle process. "We have daily patient care huddles to review quality issues," says Nester Wolfe. "This includes staff at all levels – physicians, nurses, physical therapists, care managers – anybody who's involved with the care of patients in a particular unit. In relation to the length-of-stay initiative, they discuss how they can move a patient through the system in a more organized, expedited way that doesn't compromise quality."

To ensure quality isn't compromised when length of stay is shortened, for example, the team is also monitoring readmission rates to ensure that changes in procedure aren't causing patients to be discharged prematurely.

One of the challenges that had to be overcome was insufficient data. "We have systems in place to monitor length of stay," says Nester Wolfe, "but we didn't have that when we started. But now we can look at length of stay every week and say, 'Are we within that zone of improvement that we've set for ourselves at this phase of the work, or not? If there's an outlier starting to happen, what is the reason for that? And what is our next innovative work in terms of where we need to go?'"

While the implications of problems are significant, it's up to the team to determine the direction. "I'm not making those decisions," says Nester Wolfe. "The team will look at the data that they've been collecting, and they'll make the decisions about the next phase of the work to improve what they believe is the problem."

The work is showing tangible results. "We've been able to reduce our length of stay pretty significantly," says Nester Wolfe. "We're not where we want to be yet, but this is an example of whole teams doing this work. And we've really started to improve our bottom line." While the big projects might make headlines in healthcare magazines, the small steps – opportunities for improvement that can only be noticed by people close to the work – are also essential.

Many length-of-stay projects are specific to the clinical nature of the work. One project, for example, targeted a reduction in length of stay for gastric bypass surgery, which is used for patients suffering from obesity. A team of surgeons and a program coordinator used a four-step problem-solving methodology, a standard approach used at Salem, to design and test a pathway for a shorter stay while monitoring quality metrics to ensure that the shorter stay didn't adversely affect ER visits or the readmission rate. The project exceeded its target, with 51% of patients discharged on day one instead of day two.

Improvement initiatives, however, aren't necessarily linked to strategic initiatives. Projects are everywhere in the organization. The nutrition services team recently took on a problem with delays in meal delivery with a 94.4% success rate. The vascular access department dramatically reduced infection rates connected with central line catheter insertion. A financial team reduced notification time for updated contact information from nearly 10 minutes down to 15 seconds. Hundreds, and ultimately thousands, of improvements like this all add up.

"The work that staff do on the small improvements is just as important as the work we do on the strategic initiatives," says Nester Wolfe. "These are the proverbial pennies in the jar, because they save time and save money in the work environment. But we don't limit it, and it doesn't have to be financially driven at all. It can just be about something that makes the job easier."

Ideas are solicited through good idea cards, where staff submit ideas for improvements in their work area. "We have a tracking system for these," says Nester Wolfe. "Our staff are expected to contribute one per year, but they do many more than that. We have 100% participation."

Many of the suggestions come in response to quality data, which is readily available to all staff. Catheter-associated infections is one example – any worker who touches this process is expected to be looking for possible improvements to bring the number down.

Good idea cards aren't just something that goes into a suggestion box, however – all staff members, regardless of the department they work in, are trained in methods that allow them to use data to assess potential areas that need improving, and to evaluate the results of improvement initiatives in a scientific way. Each department has a quality tool for assessing, implementing, and tracking improvement initiatives based on that department's specific metrics, and using this tool is part of the Lean work of every employee.

Most initiatives start locally, but sometimes expand. "These initiatives are typically unit based but are shared across divisions when there are common issues," says Nester Wolfe. "We're striving to get better all the time. There are so many places we can get better. We live in a very complex environment. And when you have 5,000 problem solvers helping us every day, that's very powerful."

LARGER CONCERNS

The work of healthcare reformers is inspiring, but unfortunately, their efforts are doomed to be severely limited without a national strategy to support them. As Cheryl Nester Wolfe says:

> "I think we do our part, which is to reduce as much cost as we can and to continue to be more and more efficient by eliminating waste in the organization. But we can't solve the national conversation on our own. Oregon can't solve it in isolation either. To me, and I've been doing this a long time, we really have not made a break from the pay-for-services model where we're getting paid based on contractual rates and volume. We have made, I think, zero progress in changing this. There have been attempts, but they haven't worked very well. There has to be a national complete revamp of the healthcare payment system in order for true reduction in costs."

The accomplishments of leaders like Nester Wolfe demonstrate what an effective healthcare system could look like. One can only hope that our national leaders are listening.

10

An Entrepreneurial Approach to Breaking the Poverty Cycle

Poverty is a complex and persistent problem calling for a range of solutions, including food relief, education, healthcare, technology support, and measures to improve local economies. What's not widely discussed, however, is that, contrary to the top-down knowledge myth, people in poor communities often have the best understanding of the barriers that they face. Therefore, if given the chance, they can become effective change leaders in bringing themselves and their peers out of poverty. We'll look at that approach in this chapter.

A PHONE CALL THAT CHANGED EVERYTHING

On a Sunday evening in 2001, Mauricio Miller was interrupted during dinner by a phone call. At the other end of the line was Jerry Brown, mayor of Oakland, California, who was also a former governor of the state and was to return to that office in 2011.

Brown was clearly irritated. In front of him was a federal grant proposal from the Oakland Private Industry Council (OPIC) to create youth programs in the city. Now, most mayors would have been thrilled with the prospect of millions in federal funding coming into a city's poorest communities, but Brown didn't see it that way.

As an OPIC board member, Miller was aware of the proposal, but didn't know the details. Brown sent an assistant to Miller's house with a copy of the proposal and told him to call him back when he'd received it.

Reviewing the proposal, Miller could see that the program would be funded by the US Department of Labor. The $10.2 million in grant money would be used to hire 120 social workers, employment experts, and administrators, and to open three community youth centers.

When Miller called back, Brown got right to the point. "Doesn't this sound like poverty pimping to you?" he asked Miller.

The term stung. Miller had first heard it 1966 at a Black Panther rally on the University of California at Berkeley campus, where he was a student. The highly derogatory term describes how people – primarily social services professionals, who are by no means poor – benefit personally from funding for poor communities, likening them to exploitative agents who deal between prostitutes and their customers.

The Black Panthers, who originated the term, were strong advocates for self-determination in Black communities, and early proponents of the Black Power movement. They were also vocal critics of then-president Lyndon B. Johnson's war on poverty, which, they claimed, employed a lot of social workers but didn't actually help poor communities.

Brown's comments struck home. While Miller was a respected leader in the social services sector with a national profile, he was frustrated by the slow progress of the war on poverty. His intuitions were reinforced by census data showing that 75% of families living below the poverty line move above it at some point, yet 50% of those relapse within five years. His life work, he felt, was only about creating stopgap measures, and he felt like he had failed.

"Like other nonprofit leaders, I blamed the lack of fundamental change on having too little money and too many restrictions," recalls Miller in his book *The Alternative: Most of What You Believe about Poverty Is Wrong.* "He [Brown] countered that after thirty years of a war on poverty the social service sector's primary accomplishment was to make living in poverty more tolerable for the few that fit our ever-changing eligibility criteria to get into our programs. I quietly agreed."[1]

Brown then issued a challenge that was to change Miller's life. If money or restrictions were not a problem, what would he do to actually make a difference? Brown instructed his assistant to set up an appointment to discuss what he came up with.

For the next three weeks, Miller pondered the situation, but made little progress. None of his experiences running social service programs provided even a clue about what an ideal solution might look like. When the meeting finally arrived, he was virtually at a loss.

As Miller recalls in *The Alternative*, Brown didn't waste any time. With no greeting, he asked, "So, what would you do?"

"Well, I don't know what I would do," Miller told him hesitatingly. "But my mother figured out what to do to get me out of poverty, and I think every mother, father, or guardian will know the best way to get their own families' lives together."[2]

Miller half expected he would be thrown out of the mayor's office. Here he was, a 20-year veteran in social services who had overseen millions of dollars in government programs, admitting that he didn't know how to get people out of poverty.

Brown, however, was listening intently. Encouraged, Miller then related how his mother, Berta Miller, had struggled her entire life with poverty but had somehow found a way to save money so Miller could attend the University of California, Berkeley. Hardworking and entrepreneurial, she was a talented seamstress who made ends meet as a self-taught bookkeeper.

Miller recalled his childhood memories of visits by social workers and other "experts" who provided advice on how Berta could manage her life better to get out of poverty. What she had really needed, however, was not the advice that social agencies customarily provide, but help acquiring a sewing machine so that she could achieve her life dream, which was to start a sewing business. Unfortunately, nobody ever asked her.

Miller then shared some of his observations about people who had emerged from poverty. People from Irish, Chinese, and Cambodian immigrant groups, he noted, had thrived by establishing mutually helping communities. What was needed to get people out of poverty, he explained, was not help programs for individuals, but programs that helped people in communities get each other out of poverty.

Miller also had data showing that it's not lack of motivation but lack of resources that traps people in poverty. In addition, those who do escape help others in their communities succeed, and they're far better at this than outside agencies.

Then, in a rambling proposal, Miller related how he would set up an agency that would work with communities to collect data on where the best opportunities were to support community-based initiatives. He had already experimented with a computer-based journaling system, he told Brown, so he would build a platform where people could share their data and their concerns. The organization was to be a learning organization that would discover ways to get out of poverty.

Instead of looking for the neediest people, the organization would focus its efforts on identifying and assisting those most likely to lead positive economic change within their communities. There would be no social workers or other advisors – the assumption was that people in poor communities, like his mother, knew how to get out of poverty. They just need some roadblocks, financial or other, removed so they could achieve that.

Miller knew from personal experience that poor people have pride, just like everybody else, and find that being told how to "stop being poor" by an outsider who has never experienced poverty is outrageous and demeaning.

Furthermore, his training as an engineer, and his first job at Union Carbide, had taught him to think outside the box. "As an engineer, one of my roles was to be creative," says Miller. "Union Carbide had a whole program of innovation that was open to everybody. They were always looking for ideas."

All this was a radical departure from the conventional approach that Miller had championed for so long. Brown, however, was not looking for status quo. After further questioning from his assistant, he pledged full support for the program.

A NEW KIND OF AGENCY

The meeting with Brown led to the founding of the Family Independence Initiative (FII). Under Miller's leadership, FII helped thousands of families in the US start businesses, acquire homes, and send their kids to college. There were no social workers and no set programs. Instead, it works with people in the communities to collect data, and then finds resources to help low-income families fund their own initiatives.

Accordingly, FII was set up as a learning organization. Families that signed on with FII used an online journaling system to provide detailed monthly updates on their income, savings, education, health, family, and housing circumstances. FII compensated the families for their time spent recording this information.

The data guided FII as it channeled direct investments in people and communities, and the ongoing exchange of information encouraged families to take initiative. Specialized FII-affiliated funds awarded scholarships, funded small business start-ups, matched family savings, created networking resources, paid for family activities, and supported alternative financing arrangements, such as informal lending circles.

Giving advice, however, was strictly off limits – that, community members were told, should come from their peers. Peer advice, Miller explains, is more relevant to the problems that people in poverty encounter, and when people turn to their own community for advice, it builds ties that help people rise out of poverty together. It also removes the stigma of paternalism that so many associate with the help sector.

TRANSFORMING THE SECTOR

One of the barriers to promoting peer-driven change, Miller says, is the academic establishment that cranks out legions of social services professionals. "All of us in this privileged position are told that we're going to be the leaders," Miller told a group of help sector peers on a podcast. "We're told it is us that are going to offer solutions. And just that very fact that we're made to believe that we can solve anybody else's problems is crazy. You know, my mother would never have accepted any of you or even me to make decisions for her. She was very determined person. And so it was the same thing with all our friends and our families."

When Miller presents to academic audiences, he is often asked to cite university-backed studies that validate his conclusions. He explains that his work can't be validated in this way.

"When I was teaching at Princeton," Miller says, "people kept asking me, 'Aren't there any Harvard studies that you could put on your reading list?' The problem is that to teach, you're supposed to have academic research to back it up. But I didn't learn what I learned from reading books – I learned it from watching people, and what I saw when I was growing up. So this wasn't acceptable to be able to teach at Berkeley or Princeton."

Another institutional problem is that large donors seek to fund large projects that make headlines. While mass initiatives can clearly help millions of people and save lives, the mistake people make is to see them as cures for world hunger and poverty. What these mass-scale initiatives are doing, essentially, is deploring desperate poverty while at the same time accepting what Miller calls tolerable poverty.

"There are instances where large-scale initiatives can be great," says Miller. "There are instances where we just hand out food, especially if people are in a crisis. The problem is that it takes up all the air in the room. What I'm concerned about is not just getting people out of extreme poverty, which is what Bill Gates wants. It's not just about giving out fishing nets and mosquito repellant. Even if you get them up to a level where they're living in tolerable poverty, the gap between rich and poor is continuing to grow because we don't have the upward mobility that it'll take to bring those six or eight billion people closer to at least the middle. And we're losing ground all the time."

A SYSTEMS APPROACH TO COMBATTING POVERTY

Jason Schulist, like Miller, is an anti-poverty activist with an engineering background. Schulist has master's degrees in electrical engineering and management from MIT, and spent much of his career shepherding three successful corporate Lean transformations.

In 2016, Schulist founded the Generative Local Community Institute (GLCI), a Wisconsin-based not-for-profit organization dedicated to using scientific methods to help communities address thorny problems such as breaking the cycle of poverty.

"I've always been interested in different ways of addressing problems," says Schulist. "In the auto industry it's efficiency and Lean manufacturing, in the utility industry it's a network optimization problem, and in the paper industry it's a continuous process manufacturing problem. So the problems are different, and in communities, it's also different."

Community problems are highly complex, Schulist notes, and defy high-level packaged solutions that academics in the helping sector are often perpetrating. What's needed, he says, is a scientific approach. "Community problems are complex," he says, "meaning they're part of the complex adaptive system science. What that also means is that you can't 'solve' these problems because there are no answers. There's only the ability to modify patterns."

One of the problems GLCI was asked early on to support was a perennial one in the US – matching individuals with jobs; manufacturers were desperate to find employees, and many unemployed people weren't finding work. The question was, how can we break the disconnect here and find stable employment for more people in the community?

"Pre-pandemic, we were trying to match people with jobs," says Schulist. "We had many jobs available, and we had many people who didn't have jobs, but somehow they weren't getting together."

The first step was to research the pay levels necessary to support sustainable employment that would take a person out of poverty. "We needed a 'stabilometer' – what metrics would enable people to break out of that cycle of poverty? The local community performed a multi-variant analysis of all the data and found only one statistically significant variable – if you can get $18 an hour in our area, you probably wouldn't slide backwards in your wage," says Schulist. "And if your wage was $23, you'd have a stable living wage."

The institute was sponsored by a community group, the Basic Needs Giving Partnership, to facilitate the process of finding local companies that had $18-per-hour job openings, and people who didn't have $18-per-hour jobs. Then several community stakeholders followed a series of PDSA experiments to connect the people with the jobs.

Schulist and community members quickly learned that the existing methods such as job fairs weren't working. "For a typical job fair, a prospective employee would have to bring a resume and dress a certain way," says Schulist. "But many people who don't have jobs have been told their whole life that they're no good and can't achieve anything. So now a company is asking them to come in a suit that they don't have and to bring a resume that they've never written for a manufacturing job that doesn't need either of those."

The Basic Needs Giving Partnership and GLCI worked with a local packaging equipment manufacturer to try a different approach.

Candidates were invited to an event where they could go on a tour of the plant, meet people, and then apply and be interviewed on the spot. "So they invited many people with no job or a low-paying job, and what happened is that no one showed up," says Schulist.

The next step was to find out why the experiment hadn't produced the expected result. "To see why this didn't work, the team went one by one to all the people who said they were coming and didn't show up," says Schulist. "They gave a variety of reasons. Some said they were scared. Some didn't have transportation. So we reflected on this and proposed a countermeasure. The next time, we would support with a handler or a sherpa – somebody they trust – to bring them to the job fair."

The tactic was used in subsequent job fairs organized by the community. "All of a sudden now we are matching jobs with people," says Schulist.

The institute has also been studying the role of entrepreneurship in getting people out of poverty. Schulist was recently challenged by a business leader who believed in giving back to communities but was tired of being repeatedly asked to help solve the same problems over and over again.

In response, the institute is seeking to fund a cluster of local businesses that can serve as a self-supporting ecosystem within a community. "Our hypothesis is that if we can launch multiple businesses concurrently in our community, we can use the surplus cash generated by those businesses to help the employees and the community flourish," says Schulist. "As a community member, you're investing in people, by donating money to launch these businesses that then creates the cash to enable people to flourish."

Possible businesses in the cluster include a grocery store, a coffee shop/restaurant, a laundromat, a yoga studio, an incubator kitchen, hydroponic food growing, and venue space. The generative business network is being structured as a single workers cooperative with multiple divisions – one for each business. The cluster will employ approximately 90 people, and all are paid a living wage ($24 as of 2024 in Appleton, Wisconsin). The businesses are located within a one- to two-mile radius and each division supports the others. If the restaurant is empty, one of the servers can go and work in the grocery store.

The initiative is also employing industrial principles to maximize the asset use to increase profitability. Laundromat equipment, for example, can be used at night to clean the uniforms for a nearby service business or hospital. The kitchen incubator can be used at night by a local bakery.

Plans are underway to test the concept in Appleton, and then promote the learning on a broader scale so that it can be replicated. A current "pre-prototype" that Schulist is monitoring includes support by the Embassy Center MKE, a Black Assembly Church of God in Milwaukee, that is very active in its local Sherman Park neighborhood. The cluster consists of an incubator kitchen, a grocery store, a laundromat, and a community center. GLCI is also in conversations along the same lines with interested community groups in other cities – a small town in Colorado; Santa Barbara and Grass Valley, California; Tel Aviv; and a refugee camp in Greece.

When looking at the benefits of an investment, however, it's important to put a human perspective on productivity. "When it comes to productivity, people tend to think about return on investment (ROI) in dollars," says Schulist. "But we like to refer to it as ROF – return on flourishing. At GLCI, I am the CFO – chief flourishing officer. If you're investing community-wise, you really want to get flourishing as your output. So instead of just thinking about economic value, we want our return to include broader benefits such as spiritual, mental, intellectual, social, or emotional well-being. When we invest money in communities, what we're looking for is more productivity in the ability to help people be more spiritual, more intellectual, and feel better physically."

THE ROLE OF GOVERNMENT

Most people would agree that governments have a key role to play in solving poverty and other social issues. Governments, however, have a reputation for being slow, bureaucratic, and unaccountable to the public.

To address this problem, a growing number of federal, state, and local governments around the world have established agencies to promote Lean practices within government. In the US, one of the most prominent of these is Results Washington, a state agency that promotes public-sector performance management and continuous improvement. The agency tracks statewide performance metrics in five goal areas:

- World class education
- Prosperous economy
- Sustainable energy and clean environment

- Healthy and safe communities
- Efficient, effective, and accountable government

The results, posted on the Results Washington website, include everything from high school graduation rates to road safety to the number of electric vehicles in the state.

One of the most challenging tasks for governments is bringing different agencies together to solve complex problems. "Based on the metrics analysis, we do a lot of cross-agency projects," says Results Washington Director Mandeep Kaundal. "Right now, we often look at things from an agency lens. What Results Washington wants to do is paint the whole picture of the landscape for the leader."

To achieve this, the state established a public performance review process through which cross-functional issues are discussed in the presence of the governor. "In this forum we bring cabinet agencies together to present the overview, problems, and next steps," says Kaundal. "We also have customers sharing their perspectives (lived experience, what's working and not) with the governor. These public performance reviews are part of our strategy to reduce the silos between mission-aligned agencies and enhance collaboration to maximize benefits for the Washingtonians."

The proceedings of the forum are livestreamed on TVW, an online news channel that shares ongoing state government activity with the public. In 2023, 11 cross-functional issues were discussed, including social and infrastructure issues, and the pursuit of climate-related targets.

"One of the successful ones we did a few years back was to improve our recidivism rate, which was fairly high," says Kaundal. "So we brought a number of agencies together to find the root cause of the problem."

The agencies included Washington State Patrol, Corrections, Health, Social and Health Services, Employment Security, and Licensing. "Each agency provides its service to this customer base, depending on their area" says Kaundal. So, after six or seven months of facilitated dialogue, we narrowed the problem down to a single root cause – people coming out of prison weren't getting their driver's license in time."

The problem, the team discovered, had a snowball effect – without a driver's license, the returning citizens couldn't find work, then couldn't acquire housing. At the urging of the governor, the agencies involved then created a game plan to start the licensing process before the person's release from prison, thereby breaking the vicious circle.

Results Washington also tracks employee engagement for government workers. In 2022, an impressive 90% reported that their supervisors treat them with dignity and respect, and 79% reported that they find meaning in their work.

GOING GLOBAL

With six billion people in the world who are either poor or at the edge of poverty, Miller realized the work at FII could only ever be a drop in the bucket – what was needed was an organization that could instill a new way of thinking about poverty.

In 2018, Miller founded the Center for Peer-Driven Change (CPDC) with the purpose of reforming the helping sector based on the lessons he had learned from growing up in poverty, and during the early days of FII.

In describing the work of Center for Peer-Driven Change, Miller cites decades of lackluster results from well-intended large-scale programs.

"Every president of the US has come up with their own initiative," says Miller, "but they were never able to scale these programs. The Western idea is that because Amazon is able to grow, that must be the only way to do it. But that is not how social change scales."

Peer-driven change is about working at a micro level to seed initiatives that scale all on their own. As examples, Miller cites the success of immigrant communities in the US. One example of that began with a Cambodian refugee starting a donut shop in Los Angeles. Once successful, he helped family and community members replicate his success. The movement spread like wildfire – within 10 years, more than 80% of the donut shops in California were run by Cambodians.

"These are all about people helping each other peer-to-peer within communities," says Miller. "Those efforts scale and they scale naturally without some kind of outsider doing it. I've been doing this work for over 40 years, and I do not have a program that can scale like that."

One of the keys to these success stories is the presence of natural leaders, who Miller calls positive deviants, in communities who help others once they have succeeded. "Positive deviants set a tangible example that peers in similar circumstances can follow," writes Miller in *The Alternative*. "Often, they help others to follow the path they have established.

As peer role models, they are more effective than leaders, teachers, or trainers."[3]

In parallel with his work at CPDC, Miller also founded the Community Independence Initiative (CII), which works with communities according to the original principles he established for FII in the US. The organization is supporting projects in Africa, the Americas, and the Philippines.

CII seeks out these leaders using a process Miller calls affirmative inquiry. It's not expertise they are looking for, but that special attitude of wanting to succeed and help others. One of the conditions for assistance is the understanding that once you succeed, you are obligated to help others follow in your footsteps.

The idea behind this is what Miller calls mutuality – an innate desire of people to help each other. Citing *Drive* by Daniel Pink, Miller describes the motivation that provides the energy behind these growth success stories. "Pink breaks this down into several categories," he told me. "Number one is you want to do well for yourself and your family. The second is that you want to learn and create. The third piece is that you want to impact others, maybe your extended family, or the community. I feel that what's motivating those families to help each other is the last two."

What makes these initiatives spread is intrinsic motivation – people get satisfaction out of doing something significant. Miller cites a success story in Liberia where a group of positive deviants who had signed up with CII were the catalyst for a series of well water purifying projects.

"This was a group of families we worked with in the city of Buchanan," Miller explains. "They've been really successful with their businesses – their incomes on average have increased over 400%, and they want to give back, which is part of our philosophy – if you're successful, you owe."

The group had heard on the radio that there was a nearby village where two hundred people had contaminated water, and they saw this as their chance to give back. After consulting with the villagers and confirming that they wanted help, the group took the initiative to find a well expert, who assisted on a voluntary basis, and put a budget together. With the help of a small investment from the village and the provision by CII of a water pump, the well was producing good water in a shorter timeframe than expected. Two hundred people who had suffered intolerable problems due to polluted water now had clean water. Their lives were transformed.

Then came the magic. "The word spread around the city of Buchanan where there's lots of contaminated water," says Miller. "So now, all of a sudden, other groups are forming. Now that they know it can be done, we're seeing well projects all over the city. And this whole idea that we as everyday people can actually solve problems is spreading to other areas. Now we've got a group dealing with ocean pollution due to a lack of toilets in a fishing village, and another dealing with a garbage problem. So we're seeing all this self-organizing, but the big catalyst was that one group – five of our original families – that was able to get that village of two hundred clean water."

Once the word gets out, others are inspired. "What we see happening is a combination of inspiration and fear of missing out," says Miller. "People see the success of these projects, and that people in their communities are being recognized all over the world. So they say, 'We could do that.'"

As positive initiatives spread, Miller says, they reach a tipping point where growth starts to really take off. CII is using technology to accelerate this. "Technology can play a big role," says Miller. "At the Center for Peer-Driven Change, we're using technology to help people share information. For example, people in Tanzania and Kenya are going to be connecting with people in Liberia."

The center, however, is not interested in accumulating data. "We're not extracting information," says Miller. "We're in a supportive role to help people communicate with each other. It can actually be a movement, and technology can allow it to expand across the globe. We already have Liberian families talking with Filipino families. We've already done it in the US with Hispanic families in Boston talking with African American families in New Orleans."

Miller hopes that over time, the Peer-Driven Change model will be recognized for what it is – the truly sustainable and scalable alternative to bringing people out of poverty.

CLEAN WATER INITIATIVES

Another champion of self-determination for economically deprived communities is Bruce Taylor of Enviro-Stewards, who we met in Chapter 8. As part of his commitment to give back to communities, in 2004

Taylor started a branch of Enviro-Stewards called Safe Water Social Ventures (SWSV). The organization, like CII, isn't just about providing outside help — it's about acting as a catalyst for change that can develop its own momentum.

More than one-quarter of the world's population, according to UN statistics, don't have clean water to drink. Dependence on contaminated water often leads to severe illness and death. Even when the illness is treated, the impact of medical expenses and long hospital stays is devastating to families. Furthermore, some hospitals utilize half of their capacity for illness caused by contaminated water.

SWSV helps local entrepreneurs produce and sell low-cost biotech filters call bio-sand filters. These can be built with local materials, are strictly low tech, and require no electricity or chemicals to operate. And rather than take his staff to annual team-building retreats, Taylor brings his staff, all trained engineers, over on annual trips to provide instruction on testing water, creating business plans, and building the filters.

The bio-sand filter works on a multilayer principle. Beneficial bacteria in the top sand layer consume the harmful bacteria. The filters are simple but effective — they remove 99% of viruses and 98.5% of bacteria from the water. The cost for a filter that will serve a household is $100 — the same as it costs for a single injection to cure typhoid. A single filter can provide safe water for seven people for 25 years or more. Adoption of these filters also prevents deforestation from wood fires previously needed to boil water.

Taylor has seen his efforts scale into multiple biofilter construction facilities, supporting dozens of projects, and saving thousands of people from suffering due to bad water.

Taylor's takeaway from his experience is remarkably similar to Miller's. "When you ask North Americans what poverty is, they'll say that it's a lack of money and stuff," says Taylor, "so therefore the answer to poverty is money and stuff. But if you talk to somebody who's in poverty, they'll say, 'I have no power to change my situation. I'm like garbage, humiliated.' So we're trying to solve the problem the wrong way."

SWSV helps local entrepreneurs acquire both technical and business skills they need to succeed. "We teach them how to do a market assessment and create a business plan," says Taylor. "Then we show them how to test water, how to make the filters, how to sell them, and how to run a business. All that is available for free." One of the training tools, for example, is an interactive board game that helps learners understand how to operate a safe water social venture business.

Taylor solicits the participation of corporations in funding these efforts, and 100% of donations go into price discounts for economically disadvantaged families and launching of new projects, and contributing is an efficient way to offset their water consumption. Taylor's clients save millions of dollars, as noted in Chapter 8, and the Safe Water Ventures Project provides an ideal opportunity to share some of those gains with communities that are less fortunate.

AN END TO TOP-DOWN THINKING

Top-down countermeasures can temporarily alleviate the symptoms of poverty, but as we've seen above, they have a poor track record at lifting people out of poverty permanently. What's needed is an approach that cultivates the resourcefulness of people who are intimately familiar with poverty through their day-to-day experience. They are the experts, and by respecting their knowledge and capacity to take initiative, we can help them remove barriers in order to improve circumstances for themselves, their families, and their communities.

This same approach based on respect is also needed to remove roadblocks so that people with diverse abilities, who are commonly referred to as disabled, can have meaningful and productive careers. In the next chapter, we'll look at how some innovative leaders are working on changing attitudes in order to achieve that.

11

Rethinking the Meaning of Disability

One of the most unfortunate aspects of command-and-control management is that it often judges people based on how they fit into the org chart and not on their capabilities. This is particularly difficult for people with disabilities, and it also deprives companies of the proven advantages that come from a diverse workforce.

There are two myths at play here – the Myth of Segmented Success, which sees people as interchangeable components, and the Top-Down Knowledge Myth, which tends to reinforce stereotypes about people with disabilities. In this chapter, we'll show how leaders are countering these myths and demonstrating the unique contributions that people with diverse abilities can offer.

IT BEGINS WITH THE CHILDREN

Northwest Center, based in the Seattle area, is all about changing attitudes. Founded by a group of Seattle moms in 1965, the center works to remove barriers that people with disabilities encounter at school and at work.

Northwest Center began as a traditional charity that advocated for children who, on account of their disabilities, were denied access to education. As the center grew, it opened a school for children who couldn't find placement elsewhere. The parents led the fight for the first state law to grant access to public education to people with disabilities and paved the way for the federal Individuals with Disabilities Education Act (IDEA). The Center also drew support from the Seattle Parks and Recreation Department.

As the children attending the school grew older, the Center began to develop job training and employment advocacy services for them. That evolved eventually into the establishment of a portfolio of businesses that would be organized so that they could provide employment for people of various disabilities, including an electronics assembly plant, an assembler of gift kits for corporations like Starbucks, and an industrial laundry service.

The people employed at the businesses had various abilities – autism, sight and hearing impairment, mobility impairments, and so on. The business model behind this was that the Center operated two kinds of businesses – companies that employed people with disabilities that ran at a loss, and companies that employed non-disabled people that made profit to subsidize the other companies.

The subsidized companies were typical of make-work scenarios for people with disabilities. The workers were closely supervised by social workers, who made sure that no undue demands were made on their "clients." The experience certainly had a positive impact on those people's lives – showing up for a job was much better than sitting around at home or in a care center all day – but it was based on the false premise that because of their conditions, they weren't capable of useful work.

That changed in 2008 when the center hired Tom Everill, a veteran leader from the aerospace industry, as CEO. Everill was well versed in operational excellence and a follower of Deming's approach and believed that there was no reason companies couldn't hire people with disabilities and make a profit. So rather than asking, 'Is this a program or a business?' the new approach was about evolving from either/or to both/and.

DISSOLVING THE STEREOTYPES

Under the leadership of VP Mike Quinn, a veteran Lean practitioner who was willing to fully commit to the both/and mandate, the businesses began to transform. Applying his well-trained eye to the businesses, Quinn concluded that bad processes, not disabilities, were the reason those businesses weren't profitable. Applying Lean principles, Quinn began to transform the businesses. Within three years, they were all profitable. This proved beyond a doubt that with the right work environment, people with diverse abilities can work productively.

Then came the surprise. As the businesses developed, Quinn discovered that people who had so-called disabilities were actually outperforming non-disabled people. This became particularly evident when the packaging business, which was assembling gift baskets, received a phone call from Starbucks, a major client. The caller said that they were surprised by the quality – there were many thousands of kits, but no mistakes. Starbucks had never had a vendor deliver that level of quality.

The key was that the Center had an individual with severe autism in the quality control department. While a non-disabled person would find their attention waning after a half hour of watching the same kits go through the line, this individual, Chance, could check thousands of kits without making a mistake. What is considered a handicap turned out in this case to be an extraordinary talent. The Center found that people like Chance performed far better than non-disabled people in other areas of the business as well, including electronic assembly.

The success of these companies led to a redefining of the both/and approach. Now it was "because," that is, creating work environments where businesses could thrive because of the unique skills of people with diverse abilities.

"These businesses are all operating on principles of profitability and growth through inclusion," says Gene Boes, a veteran executive from Microsoft who took over as CEO in 2017. "That allows us to prove to companies that there's a really good business case for inclusion. This isn't theory. I tell businesses, 'Let me show you the P&L.'"

The portfolio of companies today includes an industrial laundry, a facilities services company, a printing company, and a company that provides services to Amazon. Northwest Center now employs over one thousand workers.

I had the privilege of touring one of those businesses in 2015 – Northwest Center Laundry Services. Thanks to the special abilities of the workers, the business delivers a quality boutique service to high-end hotels. The secret is that the individuals who make up the workforce notice the little things – a brown spot on a towel – that most workers would miss, and consequently, Northwest Center Laundry can charge a high price for this superior service.

The work environment, I could see, was calm and focused. The workers are not "charity cases" but able workers who are earning their way. Social workers were present, but very much in the background.

However, when Boes took over in 2017, the work environment at Northwest Center Laundry Services had deteriorated. "When I took over, the laundry business was struggling," says Boes. "It was operating in fits and starts, it was inefficient, and it was not profitable. Honestly, there was a lot of talk about the people there – who's leading it? who are the workers? and so on."

The business was successfully transformed, but not in the conventional way. "The only credit I'm going to take in the transformation is that I was smart enough to describe what I wanted and get out of the way – we basically turned it over to the very people that we were told weren't working and needed to be replaced in order for this to be profitable. We turned it over to them, and we asked them to transform it. We set the goals, and then said, 'Tell us what you need, tell us how it should work.' They were able to examine the processes, because they're the ones that live in it every day."

The result, Boes said, is a much more impressive business even compared with what I saw. "The layout is very different, the processes are very different, but it's roughly the same people. So it wasn't a question of kicking out the people. It was about stepping back and asking, 'What really needs to be done?'"

A notable change is that the job coaches and social workers have disappeared. "The laundry represents our workforce population, of which 60% have disabilities," says Boes. "We pulled out the job coaches and social workers – now, there are employees, including managers and supervisors, who support each other. To me, this is a workforce the way it's supposed to work."

Another aspect of the Center's diversity is that it has employees who speak 17 different languages and represent 15 different national origins. "A couple of our employees don't have language," says Boes, "but our employees know how to support each other and know how to work together. And if I asked who there has a disability, you wouldn't be able to tell me because it's not visible. What's visible is ability."

Boes is passionate on the subject of inclusion and feels it's not just about helping a particular demographic, but about mutual respect. "We cannot reach our potential until we allow everyone to engage and contribute," says Boes. "The value of inclusion is not about charity or fixing or doing anything to the disability community. For me, it's really a human thing. It's about allowing everyone to engage and contribute – that's what makes us better."

Boes speaks from personal experience. His daughter Tori is on the autism spectrum but is capable of making a productive contribution to a workplace. "My 30-year-old daughter is on the spectrum – she doesn't have language," says Boes, "but I don't expect anything less from her than what she's capable of. I don't give her a pass because she has a disability."

The challenge is that barriers to inclusion are embedded in conventional business systems. "Unfortunately, society puts people in boxes," says Boes. "The truth is, that's a disservice to us as well as them."

Clear communication, therefore, is essential. "We let employees know that we expect them to be successful," says Boes, "but also, we ask them what they need from us so that they can bring their best self to work and be successful."

The center's business customers are taking note. "We're a vendor with Amazon," says Boes, "and we rated number 4 out of 56 vendors for quality. We were the only not-for-profit out of the companies surveyed – we were in no way in a separate category from the other companies."

TAKING ON "ABLEISM"

Central to the challenges that people with disabilities face in workplaces is a definition of human productivity that falls far short of incorporating the diversity of human capabilities. The term used to describe this narrow thinking, ableism, represents one of the most significant organizational barriers to productivity.

While one in six people have a disability that could impact their employability, ableism remains stubbornly invisible. "I didn't know what the term 'ableism' was until I was 22 years old, which is pretty shocking," says Nora Genster, senior director of the Employment Transformation Collective at Northwest Center. This is especially surprising since Genster herself has used a wheelchair since she was a child.

A graduate in foreign service from Georgetown University in Washington, DC, Genster is on a mission to fight against the prejudices that had made her life painful at times, and also limited the opportunities of organizations to appreciate what people with diverse capabilities can offer. "I came into Northwest Center with a pretty strong viewpoint," says Genster. "What I think is great about being at Northwest Center is the ability to look at this issue from both an economic but also from a social justice perspective."

The two perspectives, she says, are inseparable. "I really, I don't think there's a way to look at the economic reality of the country without understanding all of the other social systems that go into that," says Genster.

Like racism, ableism is centuries old. The problem accelerated with industrialization, which narrowed the definition of physical work. "As industrialization came to the front, everything became 'Well, how much can you produce?'" says Genster. "And those who couldn't meet that [narrowly defined] physical demand of production went by the wayside. So we have built a workplace landscape that demands a particular neurophysical type of person with little variation."

One of the most shocking hallmarks of this attitude was the existence of so-called "ugly laws" that made it illegal for many people with disabilities to be seen in public. Such an ordinance in Chicago prohibited people judged to be "diseased, maimed, mutilated, or in any way deformed" from appearing in public spaces, and that wasn't repealed until 1974.

The Americans with Disabilities Act (ADA), signed into law by President George H.W. Bush, put an end to such laws, but, like racism, deeply entrenched prejudice against disabled people persists. "We have systemic oppression of disabled people because we've spent centuries enforcing a favoritism to physically typical neurotypical individuals," says Genster.

Today, that systemic oppression is firmly embedded in employment and management practices. "The way that we define disability and the way that we define employability in the United States are historically and legally very closely tied together," says Genster. "When we look at your ability to receive or not receive disability benefits, or when you look at your disability status as a veteran, it's tied to how much you perform."

UNCOVERING HIDDEN BIASES

Genster runs workshops with corporations to help them change their attitudes, as part of a broader business that offers services, solutions, and support that remove workplace barriers to accessibility. "We're focused on inclusion, but what really is at the front of my agenda is to build anti-ableist workplaces," says Genster. "And ableism, of course, is to disability what racism means to people who are not White, and sexism means to people who are not male. But ableism is only recently making its way into the consciousness of the general population. So, if a company comes away from an engagement with us, and everyone on their corporate board now knows what ableism is, I'm happy with that outcome."

What surprises the executives in her sessions, Genster says, is that the problem is much larger than they expected. According to a 2023 Boston Consulting Group study, 25% of people surveyed by a third party acknowledge that they have a disability, but employees with disabilities "significantly underdisclose to their employers."[1]

"Essentially, we've built a workplace that is antagonistic to perhaps 25% of our population," says Genster. And these attitudes aren't just inhumane – they also harm the bottom line. According to a 2018 Accenture study, companies identified as leaders in disability inclusion have 28% higher revenue, 30% higher economic profit margins, and double the net income compared with other companies surveyed.[2]

"This is a result of ableism," says Genster, "where we have systemic oppression of disabled people because we've spent centuries enforcing a favoritism to physically typical neurotypical individuals."

The stigma about being different is so painful that many disabled people cope by trying to hide their disabilities. "I think that in America, we have a real obsession with independence," says Genster. "From my perspective, there's really an obsession with demonstrating that we're not disabled, because disability requires dependence. So we want to say I'm independent, I don't need help, and I'm not disabled. And that plays a real role in how bad we are at talking about disability and how bad we are at recognizing when we ourselves are disabled."

People are accommodated all the time in the workplace, Genster says, and this same flexibility should apply to people with disabilities as well. "Every single person in the workplace needs accommodations," says Genster, "and they have the right to claim that within reason. Jeff needs to go pick up his kids from school one day a week and leaves at 4:30 instead of 5:00. Susie gets distracted easily and needs to wear headphones. We do this all the time. But when we attach a disability to that need, then people get really skittish, which is not surprising given the way people view disabilities."

What's needed, Genster says, is a rethinking about how workplaces manage diversity. "What I would really like to see companies doing is creating what I call a proactive culture of accommodation, wherein we are assuming that every person is going to need something. We are making it really clear how to ask for what you need. And we are making really easy systems to navigate to get what you need."

One of the hurdles to overcome is that employers, when asked for accommodation along lines they are unfamiliar with, are suspicious of the employee's motives. "When there is a request, there's a tendency to ask, 'What is this person trying to pull?'" says Genster.

Creating a culture of accommodation, Genster points out, needs to involve not just disability specialists, but all managers. "Because accommodation plays out amongst your team and with your manager, it makes no sense for disability and inclusion work to be the sole province of HR. It has to be something that everybody is learning about and has the skills to navigate successfully."

However, as we've seen in other situations where managers are confronted with the ways in which they impede productivity, changing the management style to one of proactive accommodation is an uphill battle.

"What has been really fascinating to me is exploring how to break out of silos of HR," says Genster, "because what is unique about disability inclusion in the workplace is that it actually requires that you do things differently. And I think that perhaps that's true for all sorts of historically marginalized folks, but you have to have different processes – you have to literally do your work differently."

The training, therefore, isn't a how-to guide for handling various disabilities, but a kind of awareness training where executives are encouraged to listen to employees and look for red flags. "You need to have a spark in your brain that flickers when these things come up," says Genster. "We're focused on engaging with the CEO and strategic leaders to establish inclusion and anti-ableism as a professional skillset – one that needs to be developed if you're going to be an effective leader and effective manager and effective teammate."

In the workshops, Genster questions leaders on their systems, and how those might be reinforcing ableism. For example, a CFO might have an onerous process in place for approving expenditures regarding accommodations. The hurdles that companies create for disabled people – hurdles that impede their productivity – tend to be invisible to people who don't share the disability "We are demanding that employees work with what I'm going to call archaic systems," says Genster. "You are asking people to, instead of actually producing a widget or managing a project, spend their time navigating artificial barriers."

Genster has personally confronted such barriers. "I worked in an office that did not have automatic buttons on the bathroom door," says Genster, "which meant that when I needed to use the bathroom at work, I had to ask my co-workers to let me in and let me out of the bathroom. How productive do you think I was on days when my co-workers who I was comfortable with were not in the office?"

For many managers, the problem is "out of sight, out of mind," as the popular expression goes – while managers often dictate how employees spend their time, those same managers disregard time wasted through processes that they have created. "There is an attitude that as a manager, I don't care if an employee unnecessarily spent 10–15 hours a week navigating these unnecessary barriers, just so long as I don't have to think about doing things differently," says Genster. "I think they see that as a sunk cost."

During the training sessions, people are often shocked when they learn how pervasive ableism is, and learning how they might need to change their ways often makes them uncomfortable, Genster says. "When I was speaking at Microsoft, I got a question along the lines of 'What if a manager can't learn these skills?' My answer was, 'Then they're probably not a very good manager.'"

The point is that respect for individuals, in all their diversity, is not just something that should be practiced in an HR department – it should be a universal principle of management. "This maybe sounds trite, but we see a style of managing that demonstrates a real lack of creativity," says Genster. "I don't know if it's anybody's fault, but we've built all kinds of management systems that really demand that workers fit themselves into those systems rather than creating a system that fits the workers. So I really see that played out over and over again with disabled people in the workplace."

BUILDING ANTI-ABLEIST ORGANIZATIONS

In parallel with Genster's work to bring anti-ableist thinking into organizations, Northwest Center is taking the ableist prejudice head on as they encourage companies to hire people with disabilities. In many cases, the Center is encouraging companies to "steal" employees from their successful and profitable operations.

"We have a team called the Employment Transformation Collective," says Boes, "and they're really focused on helping the employers think about inclusion." Boes finds that while companies are unsure about how to move forward with inclusion, they are listening, and for good reason – finding adequate staff is at the top of the agenda for many executives, and the inclusion of an untapped demographic that could account for 25% of the population is too good a business opportunity to ignore.

"I think people are starting to think about this differently," says Boes. "With so many unfilled positions out there, employers are looking at the world differently, and understanding that they have a responsibility to support their employee base in a way that's going to make them most productive."

The problem, Boes says, is that people don't know how to go about accommodating workers with disabilities but are willing to ask for help. But it's not just methods that Northwest Center provides – it's a different way of thinking.

"We place candidates in sortation facilities," says Boes, "and Amazon is one of our clients. Recently, we had a candidate that we wanted to place in one of their facilities who was deaf. The manager insisted that wasn't possible because, with forklifts and machinery moving around, it wouldn't be safe for a deaf person."

The job coaches examined the environment and devised a simple solution – install mirrors in the person's work area. The manager agreed to give it a try. The experiment was successful, and the employee worked safely and became highly productive in her new role. But then came the surprise. Amazon discovered that if mirrors were added to the workstations of other employees, the overall safety record in the facility improved.

"This is an example of how all boats rise when you think about the problem differently," says Boes.

In fact, this kind of different thinking can become a catalyst for productivity throughout the organization. Recognizing this, senior leadership at Amazon gave some of its general managers an unconventional directive. "Amazon's leadership went to the GMs of some sortation facilities that were performing below expectation, and told them, 'You're performing below expectations, and we're going to help you get better by requiring you to hire people with disabilities.'"

The managers were incredulous – hiring people with disabilities, they would have thought, would make them perform even worse. "There was resistance, of course," says Boes, "but after one hundred days, there was a complete mindset shift with those managers. What they thought was a punishment was actually helping them see a new direction, to the point where one of the GMs said, 'I don't want to hire anybody but Northwest Center people.'"

Boes thinks companies should look at inclusion as a partial enabler for solving a wide variety of business problems. "When we went into the Amazon challenge for the sortation facilities, our mandate was to help them go after five business problems – attrition, absenteeism, productivity, quality, and safety."

With Northwest Center employees, who have been denied the dignity of work for much of their previous years attrition and absenteeism aren't problems. "Our clients are happy to be working," says Boes. "They show up every day, and they are loyal to their employers."

Consequently, companies that hire Northwest Center people can count on an ROI from lower turnover. "Take your turnover rate," says Boes. "Let's say we're going to reduce your turnover rate by just 10%. What does that translate into dollars? Yes, it's a little more expensive on the front end. But your return is tenfold."

One of the methods that Northwest Center has used is to provide an alternative to the arcane HR recruiting process that leaves out so many candidates. "The conventional approach is that one submits a resume, steps into a conference room, and talks to a bunch of people, and then gets a job offer based on what's articulated in a conversation and what's written on a piece of paper. That for me is a broken process – we really need to look at the world differently."

Overall, Boes thinks that people should think about ability, not disability. "There is not one role at Northwest Center, or in my opinion, anywhere, that's not appropriate for a person with disabilities," says Boes. "Someone with a disability can do my job, and maybe they can do it better."

"The key is not disability, it's about ability," says Boes, "and I think that's all employers need to know – that there is no job opportunity that's out of bounds, and that there's no reason why you shouldn't consider a candidate with a disability as long as they have the ability to do the job."

WE CAN DO BETTER

With a sizable portion of the population living with a disability that affects how they fit into the workplace, the time to bring these people into the fold is long overdue. This is not just about doing the right thing for the benefit of a particular demographic. Disrespect for people with disabilities is a symptom of flawed thinking about how individual people contribute to the workplace.

If an organization has a culture where people with disabilities can contribute to their full potential, this will help create an environment where all employees can contribute to their full potential. A company's ability to benefit from the diverse skills of people with disabilities could therefore be seen as a bellwether of how effectively the company utilizes the productive talents of all of its people.

12

Joy at Work

When Deming criticized the top-down command-and-control approach to management, one of his most passionate arguments was that it destroys people's natural inclination to find pride and joy in their work. In this chapter, we'll learn about how joy at work was established as the founding principle of a thriving software firm.

A NEW KIND OF LEADERSHIP

Menlo Innovations CEO Rich Sheridan, who we met in Chapter 3, is one of the most vocal critics of corporate hierarchies and their tendency to interfere with people's innate desire to do their best work. Menlo, a thriving custom software developer and consultancy based in Ann Arbor, Michigan, was founded with the purpose of building a company where people can gain joy and satisfaction from their work.

Many people know Sheridan through his bestselling books *Joy Inc.* and *Chief Joy Officer*, and for his numerous public speeches, podcasts, and TED talks. He began his career as a coder working for a small entrepreneurial software firm based in Ann Arbor. That firm was soon acquired by a larger software company, Interface Systems, and Sheridan was exposed to the culture and mechanisms of software creation in a hierarchical corporate environment. He also became conscious of his own career and began to have concerns about how the corporate ladder operates.

"I had noticed something early on that really stuck with me," says Sheridan. "When you're going up the career ladder, it's pretty natural to look at the people who are two or three steps ahead of you and use them as a sort of model. 'Who would be a good model or mentor for what's coming next in my career, even just as an example to observe?' There were quite a few along the way where I would look up to him or her and say, 'They look successful. I should try to emulate them. I should figure out what their magic is.' But the weird thing was, these people who I admired most would eventually get fired unceremoniously – just pushed out the door."

In spite of his concerns, Sheridan advanced rapidly at Interface Systems. The company was growing at breakneck pace and became the fastest-growing public company (based on stock price growth) in Michigan. Yet that growth came at a great cost – the pressures of making the numbers were taking their toll on the very people whose productivity was the lifeblood of the company.

Sheridan soon found that he was being taken away from what he loved most – collaborating closely with his customers. "As one of the lead technical people, I knew the products I was in charge of designing and building incredibly well," says Sheridan. "And because we were this tiny firm that was very entrepreneurial, I knew our customers really well. I knew what they wanted. I knew how it worked for them. I knew everything about them."

Sheridan remembers getting assigned to a project he was very excited about. He told his boss that he couldn't wait to meet with the potential customers. The boss had a different view. "I don't want you meeting with customers," he said. "I need you to spend your time programming. Sales has already met with the customer, and the project is all defined for you."

But even worse, managers were gaming the system to make their numbers. Sheridan was outraged, for example, when a VP priced one of the components in a deal below cost because the profit on that wasn't reflected in his compensation plan. "The insanity I saw at every public company I worked for was that we would do all these unnatural things to make this quarter look great," Sheridan told me. "And then we would begin the next quarter in the hole because of all the short-term dumb decisions we made to make the first quarter look good. So then you do the dumb stuff even sooner in the second quarter, and that makes the third quarter even harder. And I would say, 'Who are you kidding, guys? All you're doing is moving deckchairs around on the Titanic.'"

The experience had taken all the joy out of the profession that Sheridan had once loved. Rather than enjoy creating great products for customers with his team, he was perpetually fighting fires. Customer complaints and project delays were an everyday occurrence. Colleagues shouted at each other during meetings. Family time suffered, and vacations were impossible to schedule. Sheridan felt there was no way out.

"On the outside, I was still viewed as a great success, grabbing promotions and raises and greater responsibilities." Sheridan wrote in *Joy, Inc.*, "But although I was still succeeding in the eyes of the world, that didn't matter to me anymore as I stared daily at my life of quiet desperation."[1]

Nevertheless, Sheridan continued to be regarded as a superstar, and in 1997, a new CEO, Bob Nero, offered him a promotion to VP of research and development. Initially, he balked at the idea. "For years before Bob's arrival, I had lived in fear of my organization and I certainly didn't want to sign up for the uncapped personal commitment that came with the executive seat of a public company," wrote Sheridan in *Joy, Inc.*[2]

Nonetheless, he accepted the role with the understanding that his mission would be to build "the best damn software team in Ann Arbor." With the CEO and the board of directors on side, Sheridan began to experiment with new ways to organize the work. His guiding question was, "How can we have a business environment that preserves the joy that I and many of my colleagues experienced from creating high-quality software products?"

THE PSYCHOLOGY OF JOY

A similar question was posed nearly 50 years ago by a young psychologist, Mihaly Csikszentmihalyi. He had been deeply affected by the Nazi atrocities of World War II, and resolved to apply his academic talents to help make a better world. At age 16, after hearing a lecture by Carl Jung, he decided that psychology was the field where he could achieve that.

At age 22, in 1956, Csikszentmihalyi emigrated to the US and subsequently earned his PhD at the University of Chicago. His interest, however, was not along the lines of the conventional thinkers of the time such as Freud and B. F. Skinner, but on the path suggested by Carl Jung's humanistic approach. Csikszentmihalyi became a professor at the University of Chicago and began to work with his students on a series of experiments in what he called autotelic experiences, that is, engagement in an activity where the person is self-motivated to achieve a particular goal.

His work led to defining a concept he called flow (not to be confused with production flow), which describes a state of high engagement and concentration that results in both enjoyment of an activity and high achievement. He was fascinated by the superb concentration and dedication to tasks observed in rock climbers, musicians, chess players – people that got completely absorbed in what they were doing, and by channeling their energy so effectively, got superb results.

"What makes these activities conducive to flow is that is that they were designed to make optimal experience easy to achieve," he wrote. "They have rules that require the learning of skills, they set up goals, they provide feedback, they make control possible. They facilitate concentration and involvement by making the activity as distinct as possible from the so-called 'paramount reality' of existence."[3]

Csikszentmihalyi defined the "flow channel" as a zone in human consciousness where a combination of skills and challenges enable total engagement in an activity that is free from fear and anxiety, yet also free from boredom. As a person gains skills, the channel moves to higher levels, motivating the person to rise to greater challenges.

"In our studies, we found that every flow activity…provided a sense of discovery, a creative feeling of transporting the person into a new reality," Csikszentmihalyi wrote. "It pushed the person to higher levels of performance, and previously led to unheard-of states of consciousness. In short, it transformed the self by making it more complex. In this growth of the self lies the key to flow activities."[4]

Csikszentmihalyi suggests companies and their employees need not subscribe to the age-old notion that work is intrinsically unpleasant. "In theory, any job could be changed so as to make it more enjoyable by following the prescriptions of the flow model," he wrote. "At present, however, whether work is enjoyable or not ranks quite low among those who have the power to influence the nature of a given job."[5]

REMOVING THE BARRIERS

As mentioned in the preface, many people love what they do but not the company they work for. "I love my work," they might say, "I just can't stand all the other stuff that I have to deal with." So how can we avoid the "other stuff"? And what's a leader to do to create an environment where employees can focus on their work unencumbered by bureaucracy?

In his search for answers to these questions, Sheridan was inspired by the work of Kent Beck, one of the founding members of the Agile movement, and one of the architects of a nonconventional approach known as Extreme Programming. The approach is far more collaborative than the conventional model where "geeks" worked independently of each other and kept their code as part of their own cache of tribal knowledge. Continuous feedback loops were established to ensure that an ongoing project was aligned with what the customer wanted. Releases were broken into smaller components that were frequently tested and verified. Code was continuously shared among team members and standards were established to facilitate collaboration. And rather than striving to be lone geniuses, programmers often work in pairs at a single workstation, bouncing ideas off each other as they move forward. And finally, no all-nighters – programmers were expected to work reasonable hours to avoid burnout.

Sheridan was also impressed with the collaborative work environment at Ideo, the influential design firm. He showed the executive team a *Nightline* video depicting an Ideo team responding to a challenge to design an innovative shopping chart and construct a working prototype in one week.[6]

The video shows employees working side by side under considerable pressure to meet a deadline, but rather than fighting each other, they were all working hard while supporting each other. Although they were exhausted at the end of each day, they were clearly having a great deal of fun. The team was highly diverse, consisting of marketers, engineers, production experts, and product designers. The experience looked like directed chaos, such as what one might experience on an athletic field, but the common goal connected people together. Even Sheridan's harshest critics got on board.

Sheridan began to run a series of experiments with his teams. He started with two programmers working together at a shared workstation and tested various aspects of the collaborative Extreme Programming model. After several weeks, he was stopped in the parking lot by one of those programmers, who said he was having so much fun he didn't even see this was work that the company had to pay him for.

Encouraged, Sheridan pushed forward with Extreme Programming. The culture change was significant. Programmers were giving up what had been their sources of pride and satisfaction – individual recognition, a private office, "ownership" of code they had created, uninterrupted focus on their own work. The payoff, however, was enormous – products were shipping on time, no more technical disaster and all-night fixes, increased customer satisfaction, no more internal competition, and a relaxed and supportive team atmosphere where people could feel safe.

Over the following months, Sheridan rolled out the innovative approach to the entire team, and the company's performance continued to defy expectations. The stock price climbed in a short time from $2 a share to $80 a share. In 2000, a Silicon Valley suitor acquired the company at a huge valuation – a success that the CEO Bob Nero attributed to Sheridan's campaign to transform the programming group.

Then, in early 2001, Interface Systems became a casualty of the dot-com meltdown, and Sheridan, for the first time in 31 years, was without a job. It was clear, however, that the crash had been beyond the control of Sheridan and his team, and he vowed to continue the effort that had been so successful.

STARTING AFRESH

Sheridan and colleague James Goebel founded Menlo Innovations in June 2001, only a few months after the demise of Interface Systems. In order to avoid some of the problems he had seen in his early career, Sheridan chose to grow the company organically without outside capital.

"I chose a very special version of entrepreneurship," says Sheridan, "that involved not taking any outside funding and not getting any bank loans. I therefore ended up in a place of enormous freedom."

Outside funding, Sheridan explains, pressures companies to prioritize short-term results. "I think there's a game that's played out in the public markets in particular, and also in private equity and venture capital markets, where there's pressure for you to beat expectations," he says. "What you have to do is set expectations, and then beat them by a little bit every quarter in order for your stock price to rise."

Accordingly, there's a disconnect between financial interests and the work that provides joy for employees and satisfaction for customers. "Somewhere along the way, there's a breakage between the people who actually care about this business – the people who work in it and the people they serve out in the world – and just taking care of shareholder value," says Sheridan. "And somebody comes in – maybe an institutional investor – and says, 'I don't give a hoot about your employees. I don't care a bit about your customers or your product quality or anything. Just hit those numbers.'"

The self-funding approach has allowed the company to focus on its work, its customers, and its people, not on the demands of outside financial stakeholders. "There's burden, of course, because you're carrying your team members, and you have to figure out how you're going to earn the revenue and the profits to keep that going," says Sheridan. "But there are none of those quarterly death marches."

Sheridan and his team have grown the company by relentlessly pursuing the mission to "end human suffering in the world as it relates to technology." The team has expanded from the original 6 to 50, and the company recently moved to a new office. Today, the company offers not only software and design services, but consulting for companies that are seeking to emulate Menlo's unique (and award-winning) work culture.

Sheridan now spends much of his time evangelizing the joy-at-work principle in public speeches, webinars, and his books. The business also hosts frequent tours; thousands of people, intrigued by the success of Menlo's unconventional approach, come to Ann Arbor every year to visit the Menlo offices.

"We've been in business for 22 years, and we've opened our doors to the world," Sheridan told me. "We share everything we've learned in my books, and in physical tours, virtual tours, and training classes."

Visitors will immediately notice the informal atmosphere. Often, two people are working together at a single workstation, and there are no signs of bosses telling people what to do. This is in stark contrast to traditional environments, which, Sheridan believes, isolate people from each other and deprive them of human companionship.

"I am neither an expert nor a student of such things," wrote Sheridan in *Chief Joy Officer*, "but I suspect that our most powerful human fear is the fear of loneliness or abandonment."[7] Accordingly, the physical work environment has none of the attributes normally associated with running an efficient knowledge-based operation. There are no private offices, and no barriers between workstations. People mill around and interact freely. And in contrast with what people expect to see in a busy office, there is lots of laughter in the air.

"We are an in-person company that provides no electronic tether lines to work outside the office," wrote Sheridan in *Chief Joy Officer.* "Thus, we all work together all day long, five days a week. We know this is very controversial in some circles, but we believe you lose something important when you are not together."[8]

In what people would find strange for a high-tech company, employees are banned from being "wired in." "Our system encourages eye contact and proximity," wrote Sheridan in *Chief Joy Officer.* "Because of this, we ban ear buds and headphones, as we want people to be available to one another."[9]

Similarly, the company has abandoned the fundamental idea of the personal computer. At Menlo, computers are shared, typically by programmers working in pairs on a single machine. This surprises visitors.

"One of the fun parts of tours, especially with visitors who don't know us well, is watching their reaction to seeing people sharing computers," says Sheridan. "They start looking around, and then it finally dawns on them, everyone seems to be paired. So they ask, 'You have two programmers sitting on one computer, sharing a keyboard and a mouse back and forth all day long. Wouldn't it be more efficient to put them on two separate computers and let them move forward themselves?' And so this turns into a fascinating discussion. And then they ask the question that's been burning in their brain since they realized what we're doing: 'In this environment, how do you measure personal productivity?' And I smile and say, 'I don't care.'"

"And then they ask, 'What do you mean you don't care?' Personal productivity, I explain, is about optimizing the parts and expecting that somehow this is going to optimize the whole. What we cultivate is team productivity – for us, getting a team of humans to work together is the holy grail of management."

People are even more surprised when they learn that the pairings are not permanent. "And the way we do it is we build relationships by putting people together, and then we switch those pairs every five business days at least," says Sheridan. "And the amount of stuff we get for free – cross training, mentoring, onboarding, learning new technologies, finding problems before customers – all these are natural byproducts of two people using one computer. This approach has probably solved

30 problems that I can't even describe to you, but I know the five that I needed."

BEYOND THE METHODOLOGY

Sheridan's work on culture parallels the engagement work we've seen with Lean companies. Consequently, he has become a sought-after speaker by the Lean movement. Other movements, such as Agile, have also sought to claim him as one of their own.

"I regularly get invited to speak at Lean conferences," he says, "but I'm not quite sure I deserve to be here because we never really pursued Lean. It's similar with Agile, and some other movements that have pursued us. In our world, we had some big problems to solve, and it just happened that in some ways the tools of Lean made sense to us."

Sheridan was also pleasantly surprised when somebody showed him a hand-drawn diagram by Deming that closely reflects the values Sheridan is promoting at Menlo. The diagram shows how constantly being measured and judged through grading in school, merit systems, incentive pay, and numerical quotas systematically drives down enthusiasm and self-esteem. The diagram, shown in Figure 12.1, appears in the printed version published in *The New Economics*.

"This is one of the most amazing things I ever saw," says Sheridan. "He shows how life begins in school, and how the system of constantly being rated beats down and humiliates people throughout their lives. I found this well after I wrote *Joy Inc.* and I was amazed at how much Deming talks about the word "joy" – joy in work, joy in learning, a joy to work with. Chance for cooperation. No loser – everybody wins."

What's important here, as Sheridan pointed out to me, is that regardless of the management philosophy that you ascribe to, there are some universal elements. Companies that continually rate and rank their employees and pit them against each other create a toxic environment that destroys intrinsic motivation and joy at work, and leaves people beaten down and humiliated at the end of the day.

Dispensing with these artificial barriers opens the door to a whole different way of working. You don't have to be a follower of any particular methodology to understand that.

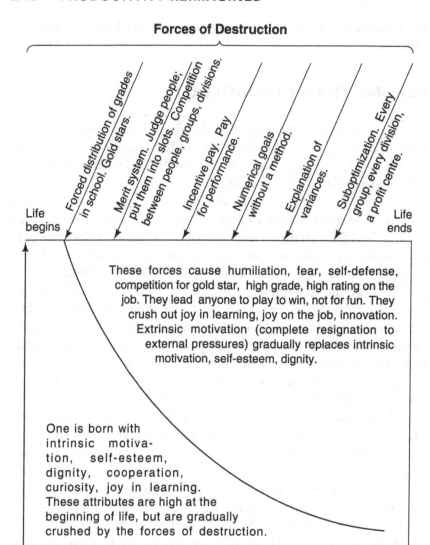

Figure 12.1   Deming's forces of destruction diagram.

Source: W. Edwards Deming,. The New Economics for Industry, Government, Education., Cambridge, MA: Massachusetts Institute of Technology Center for Advanced Engineering Study, 1994, p. 122, Fig. 10.

PART
FOUR

Moving Forward

13

We Can Do This!

In the preceding chapters, we've shown why most companies have a productivity problem. We've also outlined how innovative leaders have countered widely held myths to achieve, through continuous improvement, sustainable growth that benefits all stakeholders.

In this chapter, we'll look at the steps that leading companies have taken to transition from the traditional command-and-control approach to a productivity-driven model based on employee engagement and continuous improvement.

Let's start with a recap of our two hypothetical companies outlined in Chapter 2:

Company A follows traditional top-down management practices. Leaders determine how the work is to be done and give orders to their staff accordingly. Individuals, functional groups, and departments are treated as independent entities under centralized control. Pay and promotion are determined by individual performance according to a set of predetermined criteria. Employees are ranked and encouraged to compete with each other.

Company B is managed as an interactive system where people and functional teams depend on each other. Supervisors aren't expected to have all the answers, and they rely on frontline workers to share their workplace knowledge and take an active role in improving their work processes. All employees know they are participants in a team culture pursuing common goals, and solve problems together to move the company forward.

When organizations follow the Company B approach, as you've seen from the examples in this book, there's no need to sacrifice the viability of the business in order to serve the interests of all stakeholders. People are essential to improving real productivity, and the work is challenging, engaging, and inclusive. Productivity growth achieved this way allows companies to do more with existing resources, benefiting both the bottom line and the planet. And the principle that cost, quality, and speed are not mutually exclusive but improve together leads to higher value for customers and ensures the company's economic viability. Everybody wins, as Deming noted, under this scenario.

THE CASE FOR ACTION

Many conversations about management reform center on changing behavior in order to "do the right thing." So let's be clear – what we're advocating here is not risking the future of a company in order to pay workers more, improve quality, or reduce carbon footprint. This is about removing these trade-offs once and for all by transitioning to a system where the company thrives by nurturing its employees, customers, suppliers, and surrounding communities.

Given the trajectory of today's global problems, I believe that to do otherwise is unsustainable. Furthermore, I believe that companies managed according to the Company B paradigm will have a growing competitive advantage over companies stuck in the Company A mold. Here's why:

- **Adaptability:** Companies today face growing uncertainty. To cite the popular acronym, we live in a VUCA world – one that is Volatile, Unpredictable, Complex, and Ambiguous – a world in which the imminence of "black swan" events of equal or greater impact than the COVID pandemic is now taken as a given. This puts Company A, with its dependence on forecasts and fixed assumptions, at a perilous disadvantage. Company B, on the other hand, has both the trained workforce and the company culture to operate as a complex adaptive system, making it inherently resilient to an increasingly unpredictable business environment.

- **Hiring:** According to many surveys, executives rank attracting employees as their top concern. Most employees, however, report that they are not engaged in their work – quiet quitting is just one symptom of that. Consequently, companies that continue to treat employees like cogs in a machine will suffer increasingly from high turnover and low productivity. Companies following the Company B approach are winning the talent wars, particularly among young people who want to make a difference in the world.

- **De-globalization:** The COVID pandemic has served as a wake-up call for the vulnerabilities of global supply chains, and Western economies are seeing an unprecedented movement towards bringing production closer to home. New supply chain dynamics will force many companies to build new capabilities from scratch, calling on higher levels of creativity and innovation. Companies with engaged workforces will have the edge as they adapt to these new global realities.

- **Climate change:** We're just beginning to see the effects of global warming. Extreme weather, flooding, fires, drought, and unbearable heat will get more prevalent and intense. Shortages will emerge, regulations will get tougher, and businesses will be under increasing pressure to do more with less. Companies that have built strong cultures for adapting to changing conditions and continuously improving productivity with minimal resources will significantly outperform their rivals.

BECOMING COMPANY B

The journey to create an engaged workplace culture for sustainable productivity growth is one that never ends. Bama Foods, Parker Hannifin, O.C. Tanner, Barry-Wehmiller, and Design Group have been at it for decades, and they show no signs of letting up on the quest to learn and get better.

While the companies we've studied have much in common, each of their journeys is unique, and there is no set roadmap. Every company must create its own path according to its circumstances, its people, and its own compelling vision for the future.

That said, there are eight steps that companies typically follow on this journey:

1. Explore and discover.
2. Assess the current state.
3. Create vision with substance.
4. Build trust.
5. Create a safe environment.
6. Train and transform.
7. Raise the bar.
8. Share and learn.

Once again, these steps are intended to be illustrative as opposed to definitive. With a change of this magnitude, there is no alternative to strategic advice from a qualified coach or consultant.

EXPLORE AND DISCOVER

Continuous improvement draws on various schools of thought, including engineering, psychology, accounting, statistics, and management theory. Accordingly, the people I've spoken with have been inspired by a wide variety of books, seminars, and podcasts. The subject is a source of pride and passion for people who live the journey, so the quality of literature on the subject is first rate.

This journey, however, is all about culture, and culture has to be seen to be understood. It's essential, therefore, to visit companies and get a sense of what an engaged work environment feels like. Companies such as O.C. Tanner, Parker-Hannifin, Barry-Wehmiller, Salem Health, Vibco, and Menlo Innovations are very generous about offering tours. There are many others.

These tours, however, aren't of the typical "show and tell" variety. Employees in these companies see themselves as teachers and collaborators and are eager to share their knowledge and get honest feedback from visitors. Some even invite visitors to sit in on improvement sessions.

In addition, the point of these visits is not to find something to copy. Many people have told me that they learn the most from visiting companies in completely different lines of work. Hospital staff often go to visit factories, and vice versa. Remember, this is all about people and processes, not about the specific work that is done.

Accordingly, a visit to a company is not about seeing machinery, workplace processes, or organizational charts. What's far more important is to watch people closely. What does the work environment feel like? How do people solve problems? How do supervisors and their reports interact? How do people in the workplace support each other?

One word of caution – senior management must be actively involved in these tours. The Company B approach involves fundamental changes in how a company operates, and this can't happen without the active support of the CEO. The host companies will be well aware of this and will not likely take you seriously if your senior management team isn't committed.

ASSESS THE CURRENT STATE

As many leaders who have traveled the continuous improvement path will attest, the systemic barriers are formidable. It's advisable, therefore, to ensure that the scope of the proposed transition is fully understood and supported by the entire senior management team and the board of directors. The Five Myths provide a hint of what lies ahead:

1. The Myth of Segmented Success

    Most organizations have disjointed organizational structures that sabotage efforts to create a collaborative work environment. These include organizational reporting structures, incentive plans, and established divisions between different work groups, all reinforced by the physical layout of offices, plants, and supply chains.
2. The Myth of the Bottom Line

    GAAP accounting numbers are the final word in most organizations for evaluating progress and making important decisions about strategic and tactical issues, but as we saw in Chapter 3, those numbers are often false or misleading. While reengineering accounting systems to reflect true productivity takes time, it's important to understand at the outset that the accounting reports that might have been considered to be scientifically accurate are highly suspect.

3. The Top-Down Knowledge Myth

Many people who manage and supervise others have built their careers on applying their knowledge in order to tell people what to do. As we've seen, the applicability of that knowledge is often highly questionable and even harmful. This authoritative role, however, is very hard for many managers to relinquish – recall that companies on these journeys can lose half of their management teams along the way. The shift might also be hard on some frontline workers who have grown comfortable with the status quo.

4. The Myth of Sticks and Carrots

External motivators are simple mechanisms that require very little imagination to implement. Creating a work culture driven by intrinsic motivation, on the other hand, requires extraordinary skill in communicating goals and objectives, listening to employees, and creating a teamwork environment where all employees, regardless of rank, are learning together. Many people in leadership roles will struggle with this.

5. The Myth of Tech Omnipotence

Technology has captured our imagination for over a century, and many are convinced that computer-powered machines will soon be capable of doing any work that a human being can. This exuberance derives in part from the Myth of Segmented Success, which oversimplifies the replacement of a given process, in building-block fashion, with some form of automation. The hard lesson, as we saw, is that the unique ability of humans to operate within complex adaptive systems is not something that technology can easily replace.

It takes phenomenal leadership and dedication to overcome these deeply entrenched ways of thinking, and the journey is a long one. Fortunately, the transition is supported by an inclusive community of true believers who have dedicated their careers to helping others. Traveling this path means joining this vibrant community.

CREATE A VISION WITH SUBSTANCE

Continuous improvement demands more out of employees than merely showing up for work – the expectation is that everybody will take initiative on an ongoing basis to improve the processes in their work environment. Consequently, all members of the workforce must understand the "why" behind the work.

Clarity of this kind makes special demands on leaders. There's no longer a fixed agenda; what's needed instead is an inspiring vision that specifies the purpose of the company, and a set of supporting goals and objectives that allow any individual employee to connect daily job functions with the pursuit of that vision. If the institution is a hospital, providing compassionate healthcare services for people in need is a vision that all employees can be engaged by. Increasing earnings per share is not.

What we're pursuing here is also very different from the aspirational goal and mission statements that companies typically display in their lobbies, websites, and annual reports. In most cases, these are marketing slogans with little substance. I saw this clearly when I attended an environmental conference some years ago. The event included presentations by a number of large corporations and industry associations. There were impressive looking slides about their corporate responsibility programs, and how the CEO was personally behind these efforts. The presentations were also very candid in their assessment of climate change.

Only one company, however, was actually sharing its targets for reducing its environmental impact. This was not a large corporation, but a small furniture manufacturer that had adopted Lean methods to remove waste from its processes. In a series of modest text-only slides, the presenter showed the company's aspirational targets for reducing scrap, chemicals, and energy; its progress in reaching those targets; and its plans to do even better.

When I questioned other presenters about their specific targets and accomplishments, nobody had anything to share – not even an industry association that was touting its commitment to the environment.

So let's be clear – what we're talking about here is creating aspirational goals that we intend to pursue rigorously with the active participation of every employee in the organization.

Conveying the Message

As Deming stressed, a system must have a purpose, and therefore, conveying constancy of purpose is one of the most important roles of leaders.

The leaders you have met in this book know where their companies are headed. When Barry-Wehmiller talks about its vision of "showing what's possible at the intersection of great business strategy and profound care for people," this is supported by a written set of principles that govern the company. At Menlo innovations, the mission "to end human suffering in the world as it relates to technology"© is engrained in the day-to-day work of every employee. O.C. Tanner has built its management structure and its workplace culture around the vision of "helping every employee thrive at work."

These companies have made long-term commitments to a set of values and have successfully built engaged workplace cultures in which every employee is aware of how their daily work connects with that purpose. And yes, they have achieved excellent financial results because of their people.

Creating a vision that's supported by a system of values and objectives is clearly no small undertaking, and furthermore, it's a process that needs to be refreshed and reviewed on a regular basis. The companies that have been at this for many years stress that they are still learning.

A Multi-Level Approach

In the Lean world, the term "True North" is often used to describe an aspirational vision reinforced by a number of supporting objectives, goals, and targets. Here's an example of how such an approach manifests at different levels in the organization:

- Level 1: An overall vision that will inspire every employee.
- Level 2: Principal barriers that stand in the way of achieving that vision, and aspirational targets to eliminate them. These might include defects, wait times, safety incidents, employee turnover, or costs.
- Level 3: Campaigns to aggressively attack those barriers with the active participation of the entire workforce. A company will

typically set an annual target for the entire organization, to be pursued in team-like fashion.

- Level 4: Individual efforts by employees to make incremental improvements against the barriers.

Advanced Lean companies often use a formal strategy deployment method to organize the multi-level pursuit of goals and objectives that ultimately support the purpose of the company.

A Vision for Better Healthcare

To visualize how vision can be connected with work on the front lines, let's look at a fictional case study based on real-life scenarios. A small hospital wanted to make radical improvements in the quality of care that it offered and decided to engage on a continuous improvement path.

First, they chose a True North vision: to become the safest and most compassionate hospital in the region. The leadership team considered how they could objectively measure progress towards that vision. For safety, they chose a metric tracked by a third-party organization. Costs, wait times, harm statistics, and employee and patient survey results were also used.

With the mission, direction, and methods of measurement in place, the team established a set of sub-goals, which represented overcoming the barriers that stood in the way of achieving the vision. Goals for eliminating these barriers were, in the Lean tradition, aspirational in that they were based not on what people thought is possible, but on the ideal outcome. The barriers they chose were:

Patient harm: Hospitals are notoriously unsafe – as we learned in Chapter 9, 25% of hospital admissions result in some kind of harm being caused to the patient. Becoming the safest hospital meant reducing that number significantly. Ideally, however, patient harm should never happen. The True North Goal for patient harm, therefore, was set at zero.

Wait times: Awaiting care in a waiting room or a hospital bed is one of the most painful aspects of the patient experience with the health system. A sick or injured patient who needs care shouldn't have to wait. Accordingly, the True North Goal for wait times was set at zero.

Staff disengagement and burnout: Disengagement and burnout are epidemic in healthcare, affecting as much as half the workforce. This is unacceptable in a profession where patients depend on staff members for compassionate and competent care. There was clearly much to be done to alleviate the challenges staff were facing, but the leaders realized that the true sign of success would be high employee engagement. Consequently, they set the employee engagement target at 100% – measured by one improvement per employee per year.

Unnecessary expenditures: Waste is another malady plaguing our hospitals. A 2019 study revealed that waste accounts for approximately 25% of US healthcare spending.[1] In an era where hospitals are struggling to meet their caseloads with limited resources and balance their budgets, every bit of waste is intolerable. Again, the True North Goal was set at zero.

Once the plan was established, the hospital leadership began to pursue targets in each of these categories with the idea that all of these would move the hospital forward towards the vision. Each of these was broken down into pursuable sub-targets.

Medication error, a persistent problem in many hospitals, was one of the areas identified. The problem can have multiple causes. Sometimes the labels on medication vials are hard to read. Other causes could be how medications are organized in a storage area, how they're presented on trays, poor lighting, or supply chain issues. The staff was able to reduce this by nearly half in the first year.

The results, however, didn't come from senior management innovation or brilliant observations from consultants, but dozens of small process improvements that were proposed, designed, tested, and codified by the people that knew the environment the best – frontline employees, including doctors, nurses, orderlies, receptionists, and cleaning staff.

The staff proceeded to attack other patient harm areas, including patient falls, hospital acquired infection, and length of stay in the facility. In each case, staff identified incremental problems, proposed solutions, and took charge of implementing them.

The hospital captured the top safety rating in the region after only four years, thanks to thousands of staff-initiated incremental improvements, and a near perfect score for employee engagement.

BUILD TRUST

As we saw throughout this book, continuous improvement means asking employees to actively participate in a transformation that will improve what the company does with existing resources.

Building trust, therefore, is essential, and can require significant effort. In some work environments, employees are already angry, or resigned to just soldiering on with as little effort as possible. Furthermore, many companies have attempted to implement various "flavor of the month" reforms, causing any new initiative to be met meet with considerable skepticism.

Without a foundation of trust, continuous improvement initiatives can also be interpreted as veiled attempts to impose quotas and other external constraints in order to get people to work harder. That skepticism can be heightened by the fact that productivity improvements will lead to fewer people being needed for specific tasks. The immediate question then is "If I improve the work so that fewer people are needed, will I get fired as a result?"

In the Lean community, many companies, including Wiremold, have made written commitments that employees would not be laid off because of the efficiencies gained through continuous improvement. While not all companies are able to commit to this in writing, there needs to be assurance that employees who participate in these efforts aren't in danger of putting themselves out of work. Nobody can be expected to engage in projects that are going to get them fired.

Many companies have also made the mistake of starting a broad transformation without buy-in in hopes that employees will eventually come around. The extensive study by the Shingo Institute described in Chapter 5 shows just how misguided that approach is. And if there's a single lesson from this book, it's that the leaders we have met recognize the importance of putting culture first.

Another deterrent is that many people have learned to navigate the old system – even game it – and see the new paradigm as a loss of status. Those who have risen through the ranks are survivors of the traditional management system at the very least, and at worst, people who have successfully gamed the system to their personal advantage. Managers may see their MBO agreements as entitlements that ensure their bonus and shield them from any criticism of their work.

Conversely, some managers might be relieved that they no longer have to pretend to know all the answers. In a continuous improvement environment, seeking answers from frontline workers is a plus – note that at O.C. Tanner, managers are coached explicitly *not* to give answers, and once they've gained considerable knowledge in their area, they will be transferred to an area where their knowledge is very limited.

Trust isn't just about trusting management, though. People have to trust that if they admit to a co-worker that they have a weak area and need help, this won't be used against them. Salespeople shouldn't be afraid to admit they can't answer a customer's question. An engineer shouldn't be afraid to ask an operator about the specifications of a machine. And a junior professional should never be afraid to ask a more senior counterpart to explain something.

Meeting People Where They Are

Sometimes the challenge of building trust can seem insurmountable, particularly when it's been difficult to get employees even to show up for work.

In 2018, Maryland Thermoform, a Baltimore-based manufacturer of thermoform products and components, was struggling with poor financial performance and strained management–worker relations. (The business became Mercury Plastics MD in 2020 when it was acquired by Mercury Plastics Inc.)

"When I joined in 2018, the company was failing miserably," says General Manager Carl Livesay. "There was an abundance of challenges; most of all people were treated poorly. We had a 25% attendance problem – every day, one in four people were either late for work or didn't show up. The company treated people poorly, and the people treated the company poorly. It was an adversarial relationship."

Livesay had an impressive track record turning companies around using Lean methods. However, he knew that there was a lot of work to be done before even uttering the word "Lean."

"If you're going to transform a business, you've got to first meet the people where they live," says Livesay. "You can't change people to fit into your mold, because they won't fit. But what you can do is learn what theirs is, and then you can help them change on their own."

Where the employees lived, Livesay says, was in difficult financial circumstances. They needed more money to feed, clothe, and educate their families, and to have a secure roof over their heads. Stable employment and sustainable prosperity for them and the company was the objective that engaged them.

"I explained to the people that the company wasn't doing well, and that we needed their help," says Livesay. "I said, 'If you help us fix this, we will take a good portion of the money and turn it into better compensation, better benefits, and a better working environment.' Nobody believed me at first – to them I was just another outsider telling them what to do – so it took time to build their trust."

Job one was listening to people, not just about their work but about their lives. Livesay became aware of the challenges people were facing outside the plant first, and only then did he explore what they were facing on the job.

What Livesay needed initially was not people working harder but sharing their perspectives on workplace realities. "You've got to know firsthand the challenges that you're facing," says Livesay. "I don't build parts personally, but I make sure that people who are building parts know that I'm standing beside them, supporting them. I'm asking how they're doing and 'How can we make your job a little bit easier? If you could change one thing, what would it be?' You'd be shocked at how many good ideas come from just a simple conversation like this."

A Transformed Company

Livesay's efforts to build trust paid off significantly – after only five years, Mercury Plastics has transformed from a poorly performing company with terrible morale to a profitable company characterized by an engaged work environment. Sales have nearly doubled, output per worker has increased fourfold, and scrap – an expensive waste in the plastics industry – has decreased by more than 60%.

"Our culture here stands out," says Livesay. "Visitors frequently comment about how happy people are here and how enjoyable it is to visit our plant. There's no backbiting, no drama, and we just don't have those common problems."

This isn't just a matter of getting a few perks – workers know they are trusted to take the initiative, and when there are problems to solve, they are rising to the occasion. "Today, our business will run no matter who's in charge," says Livesay. "We've got the people in place who are very comfortable making decisions and taking action. We call it a first responder attitude. When problems arise, everyone heads in that direction."

Livesay's skill at building trust has made him successful at bringing people into the workforce who are recently out of prison. "I hire a lot of returning citizens," says Livesay. "We get about a 60% success rate out of returning citizens, whereas people off the streets, the success rate is 40%."

Livesay looks for candidates who have served eight to ten years. "These people have lost just about everything," says Livesay. "Their families have left and often forgotten them, their friends aren't there anymore, nobody writes them, and nobody cares about them. Once they are finally out, now they need to rebuild their life from absolute zero, and they're looking for a hand up, not a handout. We treat them with respect. We don't care who they were eight years ago, we care who they are now."

CREATE A SAFE ENVIRONMENT

One of the most powerful ways for a company to earn the trust of its employees is to demonstrate that it is willing to put safety above all other priorities. The importance of safety cannot be overstated. Note that when Wall Street analyst Cliff Ransom evaluates a company's ability to move forward with continuous improvement, safety is the first indicator he looks at.

Toyota has always designated safety as the one KPI that cannot be superseded, and emphasized that when a situation develops that could threaten the safety of a worker, the work must stop immediately and cannot continue until the threat is resolved. This has become one of the pillars of the Lean movement.

To make real progress with safety, companies need to show not only that they comply with all mandated safety standards but are committed to a relentless campaign to reduce safety incidents to zero.

Often, this involves a battle against an existing culture that sees safety as an annoying distraction. Every year, thousands of incidents occur where a worker took a shortcut or defeated a safety feature on a piece of equipment in order to keep up with a demanding work schedule. A safe work culture means that workers know that their own safety takes priority over finishing a job on time.

Safety is a bit like buying insurance – you're spending your time focusing on something that hasn't happened. A strong safety culture, however, can become a source of pride for every person in the organization, enhancing the way people collaborate and solve problems.

When a safety incident occurs in a Lean company, the emphasis isn't on reporting and blaming – it's all about finding the root cause of the incident so that changes can be made that will prevent it from ever happening again. And when a senior manager brings work to a halt because a worker is at risk, this sends a powerful message.

The Lean approach to safety is that an incident or near miss is the result of a defect in a process. Accordingly, the procedure for finding the root cause of a safety incident is identical to investigating a quality problem that caused a major recall. Consequently, safety can serve as a training ground for investigating workplace problems and improving processes, as we learned from Charlie Murphy at Turner Construction in Chapter 6.

The establishment of regular 5S events can be a powerful enabler for a safety culture. Orderly work environments are safer, particularly in an industry like construction, and 5S also helps build teamwork around safety and reinforces management's commitment to a safe and humane work environment.

Safety isn't just about physical environments, however – psychological safety is also vital. "You have to provide a safe working environment," says Livesay. "And I don't just mean safe as in injury. I mean, if somebody does something wrong or makes a mistake, it's got to be okay for them to bring that forward without fear, retribution, or penalty."

Psychological safety was also seen as a prerequisite for a continuous-improvement culture by Toyota when it was working to transplant their culture to North America and other parts of the world. "Even the best-laid plans for endless problem finding, problem solving, and improvement will eventually fail if a workforce believes that their efforts and improvements won't further their job security, their careers, and their lives," wrote Toyota's Nate Furuta in *Welcome Problems, Find Success*.[2]

Companies sometimes have to deal with circumstances where many people feel threatened on account of their ethnic or religious background. The construction industry in New York City, where the problem was particularly acute, collaborated in an anti-graffiti campaign to combat this.

One of the best ways to create psychological safety for people of all backgrounds is to stress the value that diversity brings to a company. At O.C. Tanner, for example, diversity is celebrated because it brings different perspectives to problem-solving, leading to better solutions.

"We have a lot of ethnic diversity in our factory – every team looks like a mini–United Nations," says O.C. Tanner VP Gary Peterson. "So that's really powerful, because when they're talking to a problem, they don't get to groupthink quite so quickly. When we get any 20 people in a room, they have different backgrounds, different experience, different ways of learning, and different ways of seeing the world. So with all those perspectives, if you can get everybody to engage in the conversation, you're going to get phenomenal results."

Both psychological and physical safety are paramount in healthcare, and that has been particularly acute during the pandemic. As we saw at Salem Health, the company-wide staff resiliency initiative has been key to establishing the high level of trust needed to build an improvement culture while facing considerable challenges.

Another key to creating psychological safety is removing the anxiety many people feel when their managers visit their work area.

"How you talk with workers is extremely important," says Empire Group CEO Nick Bauer. "The classic question people often ask is 'What can we do to help you do your job better?' I've found that this puts people on the defensive – it implies that they're not doing something right. Or they might be thinking, 'I don't need any help from you – I can do it all myself.' So we switched the vocabulary to 'What bugs you? What is annoying about your job?' That way, we get thousands of ideas, and they're not defensive."

TRAIN AND TRANSFORM

One of the primary tasks in the continuous improvement journey is turning the workforce into an army of problem solvers. This requires a combination of analytical skills to understand the physical environment in which they work, and equally important, the people skills required to collaborate with others in order to study and implement scientifically tested solutions to problems.

Furthermore, people are learning to work in an environment in which the traditional manager–worker relationship is transformed. Under this arrangement, workers agree to self-manage according to the requirements of standard work, solve problems when they occur, and lead initiatives to improve work processes when opportunities arise. Managers, in return, agree to respect their direct reports as colleagues, and to follow their directives for removing barriers to completing or improving their work.

Because much of this involves unlearning habits acquired in a conventional command-and-control business environment, it takes years for this kind of transformation to fully mature. As Gary Peterson points out, people are still adjusting at O.C. Tanner 25 years into the journey.

What's needed, therefore, is a company philosophy that celebrates continuous learning and recognizes that it never ends. A senior employee needs to value learning just as highly as a new hire who is just out of school.

Workforces that Learn Together

Perhaps the most widely read thinker on continuous learning is scientist and MIT lecturer Peter Senge, whose longtime bestseller *The Fifth Discipline: The Art and Practice of the Learning Organization* established some widely used definitions of the learning organization.

In that book, Senge looks at learning through a much broader lens than most corporate training departments. That scope is illustrated in what he calls five crucial disciplines:

1. Personal mastery: A personal commitment to be always learning
2. Mental models: Ongoing study of the rules and assumptions that govern the organization
3. Shared vision: Articulation of a shared purpose that all employees can follow
4. Team learning: Open communication to foster knowledge sharing and team collaboration

5. Systems thinking: Engagement of all employees in understanding the systemic aspects of their work and solving problems based on the interdependencies that occur

Systems thinking, the fifth discipline, is, according to Senge, the most critical of all in that it encompasses the other four. "I call systems thinking the fifth discipline because it is the conceptual cornerstone that underlies all of the five learning disciplines of this book. All are concerned with a shift of mind from seeing parts to seeing wholes, from seeing people as helpless reactors to seeing them as active participants in shaping their reality, from reacting to the present to reacting the future."[3]

These five points, particularly with Senge's emphasis on systems thinking, are remarkably similar to Deming's System of Profound Knowledge, as Senge acknowledged.

The highly successful training programs developed by Training Within Industry (TWI) to support America's World War II effort provide an excellent methodology for delivering this kind of learning environment, and they are widely used in the Lean community. As Scott Curtis, TWI's CEO explained in Chapter 5, the key is to place managers in a training/enabling role.

This was fundamentally different from the conventional training approach that manufacturers had practiced for decades. The idea was that learning was not an occasional adjunct to the work, but a daily part of it. Workers, accordingly, didn't just acquire specific job skills – they also learned methods for improving the work with existing resources. Leaders focused on building collaborative teamwork where problems could be solved in a non-confrontational way.

A point that can't be overemphasized is that collaborative learning is a powerful culture builder. As we saw in Deming's Forces of Destruction diagram in Chapter 12 (Figure 12.1), the traditional learning format often humiliates people and creates unhealthy competition. Collaborative learning, on the other hand, promotes dialogue through the learning process, and helps build a culture where cammraderie and listening are key priorities.

"A good job is literally the person on your right and the person on your left," says Mary Rudder, Director of Communications at Barry-Wehmiller. "It's so important that people feel that they are valuable, are listened to and heard, and have a way to contribute."

Introducing coaching as a management competency is, of course, something that can't happen overnight. Many managers have thrived in a top-down work environment and regard their knowledge as their key to their power over others, and to their own job security. Therefore, learning is not limited to acquiring new skills or knowledge, but also includes an important component of unlearning. And unlearning, as any adult will attest, is considerably more difficult than learning.

Practical Skills

The disciplines of maintaining standards, solving problems, and improving workplace processes call for the acquisition of a large variety of practical workplace skills, as we saw in Chapter 2. As the continuous improvement movement has matured, that list has grown significantly, explains Jon Miller, a co-founder at Gemba Academy, and co-author of the book *Creating a Kaizen Culture*. Gemba Academy supports organizations and individuals pursuing continuous improvement through a combination of coaching, certification, and e-learning resources.

"We started the business based on the Lean background of our founders," says Miller, "so we emphasized the technical side of continuous improvement. But as we've helped other companies do this, it became abundantly clear that the leadership and human development side is hugely important and is often missing. That's understandable because this is primarily an engineering-based methodology, although respect for human development has always been acknowledged as a huge pillar of it. So, to make a long story short, we have moved heavily into developing content and learning materials for leadership development, management skills, and various human topics."

Many of the materials offered are in an e-learning format, which makes it practical to introduce them at exactly the time when they are needed. This gives employees the opportunity to use their new skills immediately, increasing retention and engagement in the materials.

However, while the online format offers easy access to materials, Miller believes it's best when people learn these skills as a group. "We're not telling people to go to their cubicles and watch videos," says Miller. "We're saying you should bring a team together and use these materials with a trainer or facilitator. So, the format might be:

push play, watch for five minutes, pause and discuss, and then take action and move on to the next. You want groups to experience that together, to discuss it, and to come to a common understanding as much as possible."

REMOVE SYSTEMIC BARRIERS

As we saw in the case study examples, the conventional hierarchical management approach is reinforced by a plethora of policies, procedures, metrics, and reporting structures. Many of these will conflict with efforts to transform the organization to a continuous improvement model.

Deming called for the immediate removal of programs that created self-serving interests within the organization. MBOs and other rating and ranking systems were a prime target, as they place pleasing the boss over efforts to improve the value delivered to customers. Furthermore, these systems often encourage behavior that places the numerical results of one group over the best interests of the company.

Commission-based sales compensation systems, which are based on the idea that internal competition breeds top performance, were another Deming target. The idea here is that nobody should be incentivized to hide information from others, avoid admitting mistakes, keep management in the dark about problems, or bring in a questionable deal to make quota at the end of the quarter.

Removal of these artifacts calls for new structures to replace them. If sales reps are no longer governed by their quota, how will they be governed? As we saw in Chapter 3, there needs to be a fundamental reinvention of the job descriptions for all of the people who are affected by these changes.

Changes like this can be a huge relief for many people who have felt victimized by the old system, but the change can also cause a great deal of stress. Many people have thrived under these "old school" systems, and the transition needs to be conducted compassionately using a carefully orchestrated change management process. People must clearly understand why the company is making changes, and this message may take some time to get through. Recall Lippert CEO Jason Lippert's comment that when managers left because they were uncomfortable with the new order, the problem was that he and his senior management team hadn't prepared them for that change.

Transitioning to a continuous improvement approach also requires changes in the physical layout of facilities. In manufacturing, lines are typically reconfigured to accommodate demand-based production. This could involve rearranging work areas into cells, moving operations to different facilities, or reshoring production closer to home.

If the company is an office-based business that aspires to following in the footsteps of Menlo Innovations, this could involve taking out the walls to private offices and removing cubicles. It also might mean transitioning, in whole or in part, to an "in person" environment, as many businesses have done as the pandemic has abated.

From Functional Silos to Value Streams

Another milestone, which is common with large Lean companies, is transitioning from a corporate structure organized around functional assets to one based on value streams. Value streams are customarily created around classes of product that share production methods, suppliers, and customer relationships. Consequently, the people within a value stream have numerous opportunities to share goals and support each other.

Transitioning to value streams often involves breaking up large functional groups. Companies following this approach typically adopt a matrix reporting structure where a value stream leader is responsible for maximizing the performance of that value stream. At O.C. Tanner, as VP Gary Peterson pointed out, each value stream operates like a business, and has the resources to maintain its own profit-and-loss metrics.

When optimizing productivity in a value stream, the numbers coming from traditional corporate accounting become less relevant, and companies need to gather the right numbers to support continuous improvement. Former Wiremold CFO Orry Fiume, as we saw in Chapter 4, had to manually collect data – financial and nonfinancial – to create his Plain Language P&L spreadsheets.

More recently, companies are finding ways to generate these numbers with standard ERP systems such as SAP. That capability, however, cannot be taken for granted – this is still nonstandard reporting, and the results can be inconsistent and misleading, as executive advisor Randy Kesterson warned.

It should also be noted that Plain Language P&L reports are fully GAAP compliant, and it is legal to abandon the traditional standard cost reports when the organization no longer depends on them.

RAISE THE BAR

Continuous improvement is a never-ending process of solving problems and meeting new challenges. There's an underlying idea here that every known problem presents an opportunity for improving the overall results of a value stream. Accordingly, the fact that a problem has been identified is good news. Note that Nate Furuta chose to title his book *Welcome Problems, Find Success.*

This willingness to embrace problems is illustrated by a story I was told by a VP of manufacturing in a medical devices company. In Lean fashion, the plant displayed many whiteboards and easels showing progress in solving various gaps that they were trying to close, with substandard numbers indicated in red.

"You sure have a lot of problems," a visitor once said to him.

"If we didn't have problems, there would be nothing for us to do," he answered.

As discussed in Chapter 2, Toyota and many companies that follow the Lean approach use the eight-step Problem-Solving Process, or the A3 method, to investigate and correct workplace problems. When a problem is defined, a numerical gap is established between the current and target conditions. There are two kinds of gaps – caused gaps, which occur from a special cause influence, and created gaps, which are put in place intentionally to raise the standard.

In other words, if there aren't problems, you create them by raising the bar. In *The Toyota Engagement Equation*, Toyota veteran Tracy Richardson, who co-authored the book with her husband, Ernie Richardson, explains that once a process had stabilized and expectations were being met consistently, it was expected that the target might be revised to a higher standard.

"For example, if your scrap rate was 1.5 percent and you had met that standard for a period of time, there would be an evaluation to consider 1 percent as the new standard," wrote Richardson. "This raising of the bar would give you a 0.5 percent gap to solve. And remember, having a gap to solve was considered a good thing."[4] A gap being a "good thing" means that there is opportunity for people to undertake challenging work to make things better.

Having goals adjusted upwards every time you feel you've arrived might strike some people as almost cruel – somewhat like dangling a carrot in front of a donkey. Not so, according to Richardson, who during her years at Toyota took enormous pride in meeting challenges that she never knew she was capable of. "This is exactly what Taiichi Ohno was referring to when he said, 'Having no problem is the biggest problem of all,'" she wrote.

It's not hard, however, to imagine yearning for that comfortable feeling of getting through a day of work without having to face any challenges. As we've seen, attachment to this secure feeling is what creates inertia in traditionally managed companies – people figure out how to make their numbers consistently, and then they coast.

That state of comfort could perhaps be described as delusional – environments change all the time, processes deteriorate if they aren't constantly reviewed, and there can never be an end to the pursuit of aspirational goals. A hospital can pursue zero wait times, a manufacturer can pursue zero defects, and a software company can pursue zero bugs, but those destinations will never be fully realized. There's always room for improvement, and that's good news for employee engagement, and for leaders committed to creating an environment in which everybody continues to learn.

SHARE AND LEARN

One of the most rewarding aspects of transitioning to a continuous improvement model is the opportunity to share experiences and accomplishments with others. As mentioned, hosting tours is a frequent practice for continuous improvement companies. This follows the tradition of Toyota, which shares its methods with suppliers in order to improve collaboration and deepen relationships with them.

While community building is vitally important, perhaps even more important is that frontline employees get the opportunity to share the expertise they've gained from taking an active role in improving their processes. One company that encourages this is Wyoming, Rhode

Island–based Vibco, which manufactures mechanical vibrators used for transporting and pouring concrete. The company has maintained its competitive edge against cheaper overseas imports by delivering on customer orders within a rapid time frame, which it was able to accomplish using Lean methodology.

Karl Wadensten, Vibco's CEO, says his employees get enormous satisfaction from conversations with executives from large corporations and professors from universities such as Harvard and Yale. "How often do people in the workplace get asked about their work processes by an eminent professor at Harvard?" Wadensten says.

It's not just recognition though – the dialogue also helps bring fresh ideas into the plant. "When we do tours, we let people talk to anybody they want, and we don't listen in on their conversations," says Wadensten. "So there are some amazing interactions, and our people learn a lot as well. Sometimes a visitor inspires somebody to make a change on the spot. I've had people come into the office area if the tour hasn't left yet and say, 'Come with me. Let me show you what I did. You inspired me to change this just by the questions you asked.' That just blows me away."

The point is that plant workers at Vibco, unlike workers in plants that ascribe to the top-down approach, are valued as experts in their work processes, and being questioned by business professors and senior executives reinforces that and gives them more confidence in their knowledge.

"We've had over 10,000 visitors in the past 15 years," says Wadensten. "That includes small companies to Fortune 100, universities like Harvard and Yale, and hospitals like Mayo Clinic and Mass General. It's just crazy how many people we've connected with by doing that."

Lean companies often share their expertise with nonprofit or government organizations, sometimes loaning them an expert for several months at a time. Again, this provides phenomenal learning opportunities for the employees who participate.

Conferences are also an important outlet for companies to share both their accomplishments and their challenges, either through presentations or tours. The continuous improvement community is special in that it places a high value on transparency and a willingness to admit mistakes. This means that employees with little presentation experience can stand up at a podium without feeling they have to hide behind a facade.

The driving force here is that the continuous improvement community is made up of true believers. The leaders you have met in this book are committed to using business as a means for creating a better world and believe that there is something at stake that is larger than themselves. This is exactly the kind of leadership that the world needs today.

REFLECTING ON THE FUTURE

Chapter 1 opened with the widely lauded 2019 Business Roundtable statement that corporations have a "fundamental commitment" not just to shareholders, but to customers, employees, suppliers, and communities. As we noted, little has changed.

If you've read this far, this should be no surprise. In a nutshell, stakeholder capitalism makes no sense under the conventional hierarchical management model by which these corporations operate. Seen through traditional lens of finance, any deference to non-shareholders – environmental stewardship, decent wages, hiring people with disabilities, higher-quality standards, avoiding layoffs – comes with a price tag attached. These benefits don't flow naturally from the conventional system, so they must be superimposed.

Continuous improvement provides the framework for these benefits to be natural outcomes of a well-run business. When companies monitor and pursue productivity in a value stream, as we've seen in the examples, they can create conditions where cost, quality, and speed aren't mutually exclusive, but improve together.

If a food company improves its carbon footprint by diverting waste from landfill, that costs money. But if it improves its processes to prevent that waste from occurring in the first place, that increases output and lowers costs. If a company invests in enforcing safety regulations, that's an expense. But if it invests in establishing a company-wide safety culture, this leads to higher productivity and lower turnover. If a company retains employees instead of laying them off, that helps them grab market share from competitors when the economy picks up.

Businesses need not be shackled by the false equivalencies that are entrenched in traditional management practices. They don't have to treat employees badly to ensure profitability. They don't have to sacrifice safety for quality, quality for cost, or profitability for saving the planet.

When productivity is pursued by an engaged workforce, all these gains go hand in hand.

Companies have access to the methods, the mentors, the role models, and a vibrant continuous improvement community to transform themselves according to this new vision. As Taiichi Ohno might have reflected on the world today, there is no shortage of problems for people to solve. It's time to turn those problems into opportunities.

Notes

Preface

1. Gallup Employee Engagement Indicators, 2023, https://www.gallup.com/394373/indicator-employee-engagement.aspx

Chapter 1

1. Business Roundtable. Statement on the Purpose of a Corporation. August 19, 2019. Available from: https://purpose.businessroundtable.org/
2. Lucian A. Bebchuk, Roberto Tallarita. The Illusory Promise of Stakeholder Governance. Cornell Law Review. February 2021, pp. 93–176.
3. Bureau of Labor Statistics, Productivity Page. Available from https://www.bls.gov/productivity/home.htm
4. J. Assa, J. I. H. Kvangraven. Imputing Away the Ladder: Implications of Changes in GDP Measurement for Convergence Debates and the Political Economy of Development. New Political Economy. 2021;26(6):985–1014. https://doi.org/10.1080/13563467.2020.1865899
5. Ibid., p. 6.
6. David Pilling, The Growth Delusion, Wealth, Poverty, and the Well-Being of Nations. New York: Tim Duggan Books, 2018, p. 69.
7. Rana Foroohar. Makers and Takers: The Rise of Finance and the Fall of Business. New York: Crown Business, 2016, p. 16.
8. Mordecai Kurz. On the Formation of Capital and Wealth: IT, Monopoly Power, and Rising Inequality. Stanford Institute for Economic Policy Research Working Paper 17-016, 2017.

9. J. De Loecker, J. Eeckhout, G. Unger. The Rise of Market Power and the Macro-economic Implications. Quarterly Journal of Economics. 2020;135(2):561–644.

10. Joseph Stiglitz. People, Power, and Profits: Progressive Capitalism for an Age of Discontent. New York: Norton, 2019, p. 52.

11. Jay Shambaugh, Ryan Nunn. Why Wages Aren't Growing in America. Harvard Business Review. October 24, 2017.

12. Nick Hanauer, Eric Beinhocker. Capitalism Redefined. Democracy: A Journal of Ideas; Winter 2014(31). Available from: https://democracyjournal.org/magazine/31/capitalism-redefined/

13. If Japan Can, Why Can't We? NBC Special Report, June 10, 1980.

14. Ibid.

15. Ibid.

16. The Productivity Slowdown: Causes and Policy Responses. Congressional Budget Office, June 1, 1981, p. 1.

17. Alfred Sloan Jr. My Years at General Motors. New York: Doubleday & Company, 1964, p. 150.

18. Kiyoshi "Nate" Furuta. Welcome Problems, Find Success: Creating Toyota Cultures Around the World. Boca Raton, FL: Routledge, 2022, p. 88.

19. Ibid.

20. Ibid., p. 103.

21. Ibid., p. 89.

22. Ibid., p. 46.

23. Ibid.

24. John R. Graham, Campbell R. Harvey, Shiva Rajgopal. The Economic Implications of Corporate Financial Reporting. NBER Working Paper No. 10550, June 2004, JEL No. G35, G32, G34, p. 2.

25. Rana Foroohar, op cit, p. 16.

26. Charlotte Cowles. We Aren't Asking for the Moon: Millennials' Real Fears about Money. New York Times, July 11, 2022. Available from: https://www.nytimes.com/interactive/2022/07/11/style/economic-anxiety-millennials.html

Chapter 2

1. Kiichiro Toyoda (1945), quoted in Kazuo Sato, *The Anatomy of Japanese Business*, New York: Routledge, 2010, p. 135.

2. Taiichi Ohno. Toyota Production System: Beyond Large-Scale Production. New York: Productivity Press, 1988, p. 3.

3. W. Edwards Deming. The New Economics for Industry, Government, Education. Cambridge, MA: Massachusetts Institute of Technology Center for Advanced Engineering Study, 1994, pp. 57–8.

4. Ibid., p. 132.

5. Ibid.
6. Masaaki Imai. Kaizen: The Key to Japan's Competitive Success. New York: McGraw-Hill, 1991, p. 74.
7. W. Edwards Deming, op cit, p. 49.
8. Ibid., p. xv.

Chapter 3

1. George Lakoff and Mark Johnson, Metaphors We Live By. Chicago: University of Chicago Press, 1980, p. 3.
2. Debra Smith and Chad Smith. Demand Driven Performance Using Smart Metrics. New York: McGraw-Hill Education, 2014, p. 185.
3. W. Edwards Deming, The New Economics, 2nd ed. Cambridge, MA: Massachusetts Institute of Technology Center for Advanced Engineering Study, 1994, p. 50.
4. Ibid., p. 60.
5. Ibid., p. 50.
6. Ibid.
7. Ibid., p. 30.
8. Ibid., pp. 97–8.

Chapter 4

1. C. Jackson Grayson Jr., Carla O'Dell. American Business: A Two-Minute Warning. New York: Free Press, 1988, pp. 209–10.
2. H. Thomas Johnson. Relevance Regained: From Top-Down Control to Bottom-Up Empowerment. New York: Free Press, 1992, p. 16.
3. Jean E. Cunningham, Orest J. Fiume. Real Numbers: Management Accounting in a Lean Organization. Cambridge, MA: Lean Enterprise Institute, 2019, loc. 1562.
4. Ibid., loc 1565.
5. Kiyoshi "Nate" Furuta. Welcome Problems, Find Success: Creating Toyota Cultures Around the World. Boca Raton, FL: Taylor & Francis Group, 2022, p. 89.

Chapter 5

1. W. Edwards Deming, Out of Crisis. Cambridge, MA: MIT Press, 2000, p. 134.
2. Peter Drucker, Concept of the Corporation. New York: Routledge, 1993, p. 183.

Chapter 6

1. Daniel Pink. Drive: The Surprising Truth About What Motivates Us. New York: Riverhead Books, 2011, loc 1118.
2. Edward L. Deci. Why We Do What We Do: Understanding Self-Motivation. New York: Penguin Books, 1995, p. 60.
3. Joel Goh, Jeffrey Pfeffer, Stefanos A. Zenios. The Relationship Between Workplace Stressors and Mortality and Health Costs in the United States. Management Science 2015;62(2):608–28.

Chapter 7

1. Tripp Mickle, Cade Metz, Yiwen Lu. G.M.'s Cruise Moved Fast in the Driverless Race. It Got Ugly. New York Times, November 3, 2023.
2. Johannes Deichmann, Eike Ebel, Kersten Heineke, Ruth Heuss, Martin Kellner, Fabian Steiner. Autonomous Driving's Future: Convenient and Connected. McKinsey and Company Automotive & Assembly Report, January 6, 2023. Available from: https://www.mckinsey.com/industries/automotive-and-assembly/our-insights/autonomous-drivings-future-convenient-and-connected
3. Robert Solow. We'd Better Watch Out. New York Times Book Review, July 12, 1987, p. 36.
4. Michael Bloch, Sven Blumberg, Jürgen Laartz. Delivering large-scale IT projects on time, on budget, and on value, McKinsey digital, October 1, 2012. Available from: https://www.mckinsey.com/capabilities/mckinsey-digital/our-insights/delivering-large-scale-it-projects-on-time-on-budget-and-on-value
5. Gary Marcus. What if Generative AI Turned Out to be a Dud? Substack, August 13, 2023. Available from: https://garymarcus.substack.com/p/what-if-generative-ai-turned-out

Chapter 8

1. Vaclav Smil. How the World Really Works. New York: Viking, 2022, pp. 189–90.

Chapter 9

1. John Toussaint et al., The Better Care Plan: A Blueprint for Improving America's Healthcare System, Health Affairs Scholar. July 2023;1(1):1. Available from: https://doi.org/10.1093/haschl/qxad007

2. Ibid., p. 1.
3. Ibid., p. 2.
4. John Toussaint, Leonard Berry. The promise of Lean in health care. Mayo Clinical Proceedings. 2013;88(1):74–82. doi: 10.1016/j.mayocp.2012.07.025
5. George C. Halvorson. KP Inside: 101 letters to the people of Kaiser Permanente. May 16, 2008, pp. 62–63.
6. Niklas Modig, Par Ahlstrom, This Is Lean: Resolving the Efficiency Paradox. Stockholm: Rheologica Publishing, 2013.

Chapter 10

1. Mauricio L. Miller. The Alternative: Most of What You Believe about Poverty Is Wrong, Oakland, CA: Updated and Abridged – 2023, Self-published, p. 18.
2. Ibid., p. 19.
3. Ibid., p. 95.

Chapter 11

1. Hillary Wool, Brad Loftus, Miguel Carrasco, Ruth Ebeling, Ashley Dartnell, Gretchen May, Kaitlin Roh, Lucia Vairo Marchione. Your Workforce Includes People with Disabilities. Does Your People Strategy?, Boston Consulting Group, May 10, 2023. Available from: https://www.bcg.com/publications/2023/devising-people-strategy-for-employees-with-disabilities-in-the-workplace
2. Companies Leading in Disability Inclusion Have Outperformed Peers, Accenture Research Finds. Accenture Press Release, October 29, 2018. Available from: https://newsroom.accenture.com/news/2018/companies-leading-in-disability-inclusion-have-outperformed-peers-accenture-research-finds

Chapter 12

1. Richard Sheridan, Joy Inc., How We Built a Workplace People Love. New York: Portfolio/Penguin, 2013, p. 14.
2. Ibid., p. 15.
3. Mihaly Csikszentmihalyi. Flow: The Psychology of Optimal Experience. New York: Harper Perennial Modern Classics, 1991, p. 72.
4. Ibid., p. 74.
5. Ibid., p. 154.

6. ABC Nightline: IDEO Shopping Cart. Available from: https://www.youtube .com/watch?v=rVMZmqtJvvA
7. Richard Sheridan. Chief Joy Officer: How Great Leaders Elevate Human Energy and Eliminate Fear. New York: Portfolio/Penguin, 2018, p. 28.
8. Ibid., p. 30.
9. Ibid.

Chapter 13

1. H. Bauchner, P. B. Fontanarosa. Waste in the US health care system. JAMA. 2019;322(15):1463–64. doi: 10.1001/jama.2019.15353
2. Kiyoshi "Nate" Furuta. Welcome Problems, Find Success: Creating Toyota Cultures Around the World. Boca Raton, FL: Routledge, 2022, p. 88.
3. Peter M. Senge. The Fifth Discipline: The Art and Practice of the Learning Organization. New York: Crown Business, 2006, p. 100.
4. Tracey Richardson, Ernie Richardson. The Toyota Engagement Equation: How to Understand and Implement Continuous Improvement Thinking in Any Organization. New York: McGraw-Hill Education, 2017, p. 107.

About the Author

J acob Stoller is a journalist, speaker, facilitator, and Shingo Prize–winning author of *The Lean CEO*. He has published hundreds of articles on technology and business management, and is known for demystifying complex topics for general business audiences. Jacob has delivered keynote speeches and workshops in Canada, Europe, and the US, and has created training materials and strategic documents for clients such as Microsoft, Dell Computer Corporation, Staples, Pitney Bowes, International Data Corporation (IDC), CMA Canada, and the Conference Board of Canada.

Index

Page numbers followed by *f* refer to figures.